Successful Evolution of Software Systems

For a listing of recent titles in the *Artech House Computing Library,* turn to the back of this book.

Successful Evolution of Software Systems

Hongji Yang
Martin Ward

Artech House
Boston • London
www.artechhouse.com

Library of Congress Cataloging-in-Publication Data
Yang, Hongji.
  Successful evolution of software systems / Hongji Yang, Martin Ward.
    p. cm.—(Artech House computing library)
  Includes bibliographical references and index.
  ISBN 1-58053-349-3 (alk. paper)
  1. Software reengineering.   2. Software maintenance.
  I. Ward, Martin, Dr.   II. Title.   III. Series.
  QA76.758 .Y365   2003
  005.1—dc21   2002038277

British Library Cataloguing in Publication Data
Yang, Hongji
  Successful evolution of software systems.—(Artech House computing library)
  1. Software reengineering
  I. Title   II. Ward, Martin
  005.1

ISBN 1-58053-349-3

Cover design by Yekaterina Ratner

© 2003 ARTECH HOUSE, INC.
685 Canton Street
Norwood, MA 02062

All rights reserved. Printed and bound in the United States of America. No part of this book may be reproduced or utilized in any form or by any means, electronic or mechanical, including photocopying, recording, or by any information storage and retrieval system without permission in writing from the publisher.
  All terms mentioned in this book that are known to be trademarks or service marks have been appropriately capitalized. Artech House cannot attest to the accuracy of this information. Use of a term in this book should not be regarded as affecting the validity of any trademark or service mark.

International Standard Book Number: 1-58053-349-3
Library of Congress Catalog Card Number: 2002038277

10 9 8 7 6 5 4 3 2 1

To Xiaodong Zhang and Tianxiu Yang

Hongji Yang

To Kate, Rebecca, and Tom

Martin Ward

Contents

	Preface	*xiii*
	Acknowledgments	*xv*
1	**Constant Software Changes**	1
	1.1 Legacy systems	1
	1.2 Business changes	2
	1.3 Software evolution	3
	References	4
2	**Software Engineering and Evolution**	5
	2.1 Computer system evolution	5
	2.2 Software engineering	8
	2.3 Software quality	11
	2.4 Software everywhere	12
	2.5 Software maintenance	14
	2.6 Evolving software	19
	References	19
3	**Software Reengineering for Evolution**	23
	3.1 Introduction	23
	3.2 Software reengineering cycle	24

3.3	Taxonomy of software reengineering	26
3.4	Reverse engineering	29
3.5	Current state of formal methods in reengineering	31
3.6	Classification of formal methods	33
	3.6.1 Model-based approach	33
	3.6.2 Logic-based approach	34
	3.6.3 Algebraic approach	38
	3.6.4 Process algebra approach	38
	3.6.5 Net-based approach	40
3.7	Criteria and results	42
3.8	Analysis and summary	45
References		47

4 WSL and Transformation Theory — 53

4.1	Introduction	53
4.2	Background	55
4.3	Syntax and semantics of the kernel language	57
	4.3.1 Syntax	57
	4.3.2 The specification statement	59
	4.3.3 States and state transformations	60
	4.3.4 Refinement of state transformations	60
	4.3.5 Recursion	61
	4.3.6 Weakest preconditions	61
	4.3.7 Weakest preconditions of statements	62
4.4	Proving the correctness of a refinement	64
	4.4.1 Expressing a statement as a specification	66
	4.4.2 Some basic transformations	66
	4.4.3 Proof rules for implementations	68
4.5	Algorithm derivation	70
4.6	Extending the kernel language	71
4.7	Example transformations	73
	4.7.1 Notation	73
	4.7.2 Examples of transformations	75

| | | 4.7.3 | Loops and exits. . . . . | 75 |
| | | 4.7.4 | Action systems . . . . | 75 |

4.8 Why invent WSL? 76
References. 80

5 The FermaT Evolution Workbench 83

5.1 Introduction 83
5.2 Previous transformation tools 84
5.3 Analyzing assembler code. 88
5.4 The FermaT workbench 89
    5.4.1 The function catalog 90
    5.4.2 The function call graph. 90
    5.4.3 The text editor 91
    5.4.4 The program flowchart 91
    5.4.5 The data catalog. 95
    5.4.6 Analysis tools. 95
5.5 Results 100
References. 101

6 An Integrated Evolution Framework 103

6.1 Characteristics of legacy systems 103
    6.1.1 Typical problems. 103
    6.1.2 Structure and data dependency. 104
6.2 The expanded evolution approach 106
    6.2.1 Extending WSL 106
    6.2.2 Architecture of extended WSL (EWSL). 108
    6.2.3 Working flow of EWSL 109
6.3 EWSL 110
    6.3.1 ITL. 110
    6.3.2 Timed guarded command language (TGCL). 112
    6.3.3 Object-oriented TAM 113

	6.3.4	Common structural language (CSL).	114
	6.3.5	Common object-oriented language (COOL)	115
6.4	Summary		116
References			116

7 Process for Evolution . . . 119

7.1	A process for evolution.	119
7.2	Implementing the process.	119
7.3	Translating into EWSL	123
7.4	Restructuring.	123
7.5	Abstracting	124
	7.5.1 Abstraction and abstraction patterns	125
	7.5.2 Definitions	127
	7.5.3 Healthiness obligation	129
	7.5.4 Relations between abstractions	130
	7.5.5 Elementary abstraction rules	131
	7.5.6 Further abstraction rules	132
7.6	Understanding with the support of the domain knowledge-based analysis (DKBA) tool	132
	7.6.1 Knowledge representation	134
	7.6.2 Uncertainty reasoning and nonmonotonic reasoning.	135
	7.6.3 Program space partitioning	146
	7.6.4 Programming style and program partitioning.	147
	7.6.5 The DKBA tool.	149
7.7	Reusing components	149
	7.7.1 Definition of component.	151
	7.7.2 Mining components.	152
7.8	Retargeting	154
7.9	Measuring software evolution.	155
	7.9.1 Software metrics for reverse engineering.	156
	7.9.2 Adaptation and development	157
	7.9.3 Five categories of measures.	158
	7.9.4 The metric tool in RA	169
References.		169

8 Case Studies in Evolution **175**

8.1 First case study: Book index generator 177
    8.1.1 Goals *178*
    8.1.2 WSL transformations *178*
    8.1.3 Abstracting a specification *184*
    8.1.4 Reimplementation *188*
    8.1.5 Conclusion *190*
8.2 Second case study: Topological sorting algorithm 190
    8.2.1 Toplogical sorting *191*
    8.2.2 Knuth's topological sorting algorithm *193*
    8.2.3 Restructuring *195*
    8.2.4 Abstraction to a specification *198*
    8.2.5 Changing the data representation— adding abstract variables *200*
    8.2.6 The abstract program *202*
    8.2.7 Remarks *204*
8.3 Third case study: Assembler reengineering 204
    8.3.1 IBM 370 assembler *204*
    8.3.2 The sample program *207*
    8.3.3 The assembler source *208*
    8.3.4 Automatic program transformation *210*
    8.3.5 Abstracting a specification *213*
    8.3.6 Comments *218*
8.4 Fourth case study: A mass migration exercise 218
    8.4.1 The assembler problem *219*
    8.4.2 Decompilers *220*
    8.4.3 Our approach *220*
    8.4.4 The assembler modules *221*
    8.4.5 Experimental method *223*
    8.4.6 Results *224*
    8.4.7 Contributing factors *227*
8.5 Fifth case study: Migrating a telecommunications system 228
    8.5.1 Assembler-to-WSL translation *228*

	8.5.2 WSL restructuring.	*229*
	8.5.3 WSL-to-C translation	*229*
8.6	Sixth case study: Mine drainage system.	229
	8.6.1 Extracting the specification	*231*
	8.6.2 Comments	*235*
8.7	Summary	235
References.		237

9 Concluding Remarks 239

9.1	Is software evolution a bridge too far?.	239
9.2	Formal or not formal?	240
9.3	Coping with new development paradigms	240
9.4	Questions answered	242

Appendix A WSL Transformations 243

Appendix B Abstraction rules. 261

About the Authors 271

Index 273

Preface

No one will doubt today that information systems (IS) are business-critical for almost all institutions. Due to the fast changing nature of business in modern society and the ever rapid growth of information technology (IT), an IS that has just been developed will soon become a legacy system. Therefore people are struggling to cope with the task of synchronizing ISs with the pace of business change. Evolving information (software) systems is claimed to be a far more economical solution than developing new systems from scratch.

Are IT engineers fighting a losing battle in updating ISs? Is evolving software systems feasible? If so, what are the techniques and tools? At this crucial moment, software evolution should come out of the research laboratories to become an everyday off-the-shelf technique for IT engineers.

Described in understandable terms, written in a clear format, demonstrated with detailed examples, and supported by an industrial strength tool, this book aims to make the principles and techniques of software evolution easy to follow for managers, IT engineers, and other practitioners, so that they will have confidence in dealing with IS evolution. In addition, researchers can use this book to conduct successful research projects: In particular they can build on the results from the FermaT workbench for other software evolution and program transformation research.

Who should read this book

We have written the book for industrial practitioners who are involved in business system evolution and for academics who study methodologies of software system evolution or who are interested in the practical applications of formal methods.

Book structure

The book is comprised of nine chapters and two appendixes, Appendix A, which details wide spectrum language (WSL) transformations, and Appendix B, which outlines the abstraction rules.

Chapter 1 suggests that constant software changes are a normal part of business life in the twenty-first century. Chapter 2 introduces relevant background information for the book to develop its arguments, including the software lifecycle, recent technology advances, and software maintenance and evolution. Chapter 3 describes related studies in reverse engineering and reengineering techniques for software evolution, in particular, approaches to formal software development and redevelopment. Chapter 4 introduces the foundation on which our evolution framework is built (i.e., the techniques of program transformations with WSL). Chapter 5 describes a program-transformation-based evolution workbench (FermaT); the environment in which the workbench operates, including the tools in the workbench; and a detailed demonstration of the evolution process. Chapter 6 introduces, through extending the approach described in Chapters 4 and 5, an integrated framework for evolving a software system. Chapter 7 describes a practical software evolution process. Chapter 8 describes the results of several experiments involving real program examples with industrial systems and summarizes these case studies. Finally, Chapter 9 summarizes the book.

FermaT download Web sites

The FermaT tool used in the book can be downloaded from the following URLs:

- http://www.dur.ac.uk/~dcs6mpw/fermat.html
- http://www.cse.dmu.ac.uk/~mward/fermat.html

Acknowledgments

We would like to thank our colleagues at the Software Technology Research Laboratory at De Montfort University, Professor H. Zedan, Dr. A. Cau, Dr. X. Liu, Dr. Y. Li, and Dr. S. Zhou, for their contribution to the research work into software reengineering and evolution in recent years.

We would also like to thank Professor K. H. Bennett and Dr. T. Bull in the Centre for Software Maintenance at Durham University for their contribution to the Reverse Engineering via Formal Methods (REFORM) project, which has made it possible for the authors of this book to work together since 1989.

CHAPTER 1

Contents

1.1 Legacy systems

1.2 Business changes

1.3 Software evolution

References

Constant Software Changes

1.1 Legacy systems

The term *legacy system* is currently a well-accepted and well-defined one within the software community, which was not the case a number of years ago. This implies that many people have already been convinced that new software becomes legacy software quickly and that this causes many problems in business and daily life.

The work described in this book was motivated by the increasing industrial demand to carry out software evolution more efficiently, because software maintenance has become the most costly stage of the software life cycle [1].

The purpose of the book is to establish the feasibility of using techniques such as program transformation and program abstraction to evolve legacy systems into more reliable and flexible systems, to ease the evolution process and, thus, to prolong the productive life of a software system.

In the original "waterfall" software life-cycle model, the following main stages are described as taking place in sequence:

- Requirements analysis;
- Design;
- Implementation;
- Maintenance.

Requirements analysis establishes what the system should do and under what circumstances it is to be done; design establishes how it is to be done; implementation builds a software system to meet the design; and maintenance tries to keep the system performing its function effectively and efficiently.

Many years have passed, but the waterfall model, documented in 1970 by Royce [2] is still the most widely accepted software life-cycle model. However, the maintenance stage has to be expanded to represent much broader activities: not only maintaining the originally designed functions but also adding new functions, coping with a changing environment, and keeping up with radically changing and expanding requirements.

The word "maintenance" suggests fixing parts that are broken and replacing parts that wear out. Software is not subject to wear in the sense that mechanical systems are, so it can never wear out; therefore maintenance would appear to mean simply fixing faults in the original implementation. This ignores the problems of rapidly changing environments and requirements: An aircraft engineer would not consider upgrading a Cessna light aircraft to a supersonic jet airliner to be a "maintenance task"(!). Yet there are many software systems that have had to undergo similarly dramatic enhancements.

These considerations suggest that the word "maintenance" should be replaced by "reengineering" or "evolution."

In practice, most software has been heavily modified. This is the so-called legacy problem, that many people are facing.

1.2 Business changes

The success of many businesses is critically dependent on all the software they develop, in terms of providing services and managing the company. This is true not just for companies whose business is developing software, but also for many other companies; for example, the merger of two U.K. building societies fell through when it was discovered that they could not effectively merge their software systems.

Businesses need to be increasingly more flexible and responsive to the marketplace, developing and marketing new products and services in a timely manner. To do this, the supporting ISs need to be just as flexible and capable of rapid modification and enhancement. Handling software properly can be financially vital to the sucess of the company. As a result, in software development, the goals of reliability and flexibility are becoming significantly more important.

1.3 Software evolution

Twenty years ago, software needed to be corrected occasionally and a new release issued perhaps once a year. We could use the term *maintenance* to imply to that we were working to enable our software to continue to do what it used to do. Ten years ago, software needed a major release with new functionality twice a year, and we used the term *reengineering* to imply that we were adding new user-required functions to the software. Today, software needs to be changed on an ongoing basis with major enhancements required on a short timescale (days or weeks rather than months or years) in order to meet new business opportunities and reduce the "time to market" for new products and services. In this case, the term *evolution* better describes a situation in which maintenance and reengineering are needed so often.

Reengineering is still the basic technique for evolving software systems but rapid reengineering is a necessity and future reengineering must be anticipated every time reengineering is carried out.

The main steps for reengineering are to determine what the existing software does (i.e., understanding the existing software) to decide what to modify in the software and how to actually carry out the modifications.

Understanding software means to identify and extract the actual, current design of the software. The current design will typically be very different from the original design. Therefore, it is meaningless and unnecessary to attempt to extract the original design. Documentation of the original design may be available, but it is rarely kept up-to-date with changes to the software and therefore may no longer describe the current design of the system.

However, there may be an opportunity to extract the current design from the current version of the code, as the current design is reflected in the current code. This suggests that a major understanding of existing software will be needed, along with ways to cope with complexity, to generate alternate views, to recover lost information, to detect side effects, and to synthesise higher abstractions.

Deciding what to modify in the software involves knowing what to delete and what to add to the software according to the business needs. Carrying out the modifications to the software involves employing the best suitable techniques available to ensure that the modified software has a better quality.

This book attempts to answer questions on evolving software for reliability and flexibility by discussing the following issues:

- If we start with old, heavily modified software, including software code that was not developed using a formal or informal method [though most organizations have been using some kind of informal methods in their development process (e.g., use cases and requirement definition cards)] how viable is it to extract a high-level representation (a design or specification) from the software?

- If it is possible under certain restrictions, what are these restrictions? What exactly does the user need to supply?

- What is the framework and method for extracting a design from the existing software?

- What is the framework for changing or modifying the software to meet current business needs and to achieve higher quality?

- Are there any tools that support this approach?

- What are the metrics to measure the resultant code that has been reengineered by our method?

To summarize, this book combines formal methods, transformational programming, abstraction and crossing levels of abstraction techniques for evolving existing software systems. The book discusses an integrated framework from theory to practice and uses a commercial workbench to illustrate the approach with its application to real case studies.

References

[1] Yang, H., and K. H. Bennett, "Acquiring Entity-Relationship Attribute Diagrams from Code and Data Through Program Transformation," *IEEE International Conference on Software Maintenance (ISCM '95)*, Nice, France, October 1995.

[2] Royce, W. W., "Managing the Development of Large Software Systems," *IEEE WESCON*, August 1970.

CHAPTER 2

Contents

2.1 Computer system evolution
2.2 Software engineering
2.3 Software quality
2.4 Software everywhere
2.5 Software maintenance
2.6 Evolving software
    References

Software Engineering and Evolution

2.1 Computer system evolution

An up-to-date computer system has three main elements or subsystems: the hardware system, the software system, and the communication system. These three elements have been developed in a closely coupled way from the beginning of the modern computing era. Although the technological revolution of computing is just a few decades old, a number of significant subrevolutions have taken place. In terms of software systems, computer system evolution can be divided into the following periods:

1. From the late 1940s to the mid 1960s, hardware could only provide limited computing power; communication was not a part of computing; and software systems were mostly batch-oriented and custom-designed for a specifc application. Often implemented by a single person, programming was seen as a craft, and systems had a relatively limited distribution [1].

2. From the mid 1960s to the late 1970s, hardware development made significant progress; communication was still not a major part of computing, but software systems also underwent significant developments including the development of multiprogramming

5

and multiuser systems, real-time systems, and the first generation of database management systems. More importantly, people started to use "production software," and software began to be developed for widespread distribution in a multidisciplinary market. This software was extended by the addition of new program statements to meet new needs. The software products had to be corrected when faults were detected, modified as user requirements changed, or adapted to new hardware (activities collectively called *software maintenance*). People then realized that software was facing a crisis: The effort spent on software maintenance began to absorb resources at an alarming rate, and the customized nature of programs made them very difficult to maintain.

3. From the mid 1970s to the late 1980s, hardware made further significant progress in terms of chip integration and processing speed. Commmunication became an important part of computing, and this provided a platform for the development of distributed systems; software developers were faced with heavy demands on software for global and local area networks and high-bandwidth digital communications. The personal computer (PC) has created software companies with sales running into millions of copies.

4. From the beginning of the 1990s to the present, hardware and communication systems have continued to develop, and software development has not shown any sign of slowing. The ever rapid growth of software development has been aided by object-oriented technologies, expert systems and artificial intelligence software, and artificial neural network software. Meanwhile, the emergence of the World Wide Web (WWW) has presented information sharing in a manner more convenient than could have previously been imagined. At the same time there has been an explosion in software production.

The rapid increase in software production has precipitated many problems, and at present the software crisis continues to intensify. The software crisis alludes to a set of problems encountered in the development of computer software. The problems are not limited to software that does not function properly according to required criteria. Rather, the software crisis encompasses problems associated with how we develop software, how we maintain the growing volume of existing software, and how we can keep pace with the growing demand for more software.

Problems associated with the software crisis have been caused by the character of software itself. F. P. Brooks [2] notes the following properties of large software systems:

- *Complexity:* This is an essential property of all large pieces of software, essential in that it cannot be abstracted away from. This leads to several problems: Communication difficulties often occur among a large team of developers, which can lead to product flaws, cost overruns, and schedule delays; it may be difficult or impossible to visualize all the states of the system, which makes it impossible to understand the system completely; it is difficult to get an overview of the system, so maintaining conceptual integrity becomes increasingly difficult; it is hard to ensure that all loose ends are accounted for; and the learning curve is too steep for new personnel.

- *Conformity:* Many systems are constrained by the need to conform to complex human institutions and systems (e.g., the tax regulations of a state).

- *Change:* As it is used any successful system will be subject to change to enhance its capabilities, or even apply it beyond the original domain, as well as to enable it to survive beyond the normal life of the machine it runs on and to be ported to other machines and environments.

- *Invisibility:* For complex software systems there is no geometric representation, as is available to the designers and builders of complex mechanical or electronic machines or large buildings. There are several distinct but interacting graphs of links between parts of the system to be considered (e.g., control flow, data flow, dependency, and time sequence). One way to simplify these, in an attempt to control the complexity, is to cut links until the graphs become hierarchical structures [3]. However, even an accurate model or abstraction of the system may become unreliable as the system is enhanced and modified over a period of time.

Further observations from a review of the state of the practice in requirements modeling include the following [4]:

- Requirements were invented, not elicited (i.e., in many projects, there was a potential market but no customer). Also, the requirements were actually preferences that were prioritized so that the low-priority requirements could be abandoned if the schedule slipped.

- Most specification is incremental (i.e., customers are rarely able to provide a complete specification at any stage of the project).

- Most development is maintenance. System evolution is so common that a development from scratch is the exception.

- There is a gulf between developer and user (i.e., few developers had adequate knowledge of the users' work, which leads to major misunderstandings about the system's purpose).

- User interface requirements continually change.

Recognizing problems and their causes is the first step toward finding solutions. Then the solutions themselves must provide practical assistance to the software developer, improve software quality, and allow the "software world" to keep pace with the business world.

There is no single best approach to a solution for the software crisis. However, by combining comprehensive methods for all phases of software development, better tools for automating these methods, more powerful building blocks for software implementations, better techniques for software quality assurance, and an overriding philosophy for coordination, control, and management, a discipline for software development (i.e., the discipline of software engineering) can be achieved.

2.2 Software engineering

Use of the term *software engineering* can be traced back at least as far as a 1968 NATO conference held in Garmisch, West Germany and the follow-up conference held near Rome, Italy, in 1969. The following definition is from Naur [5]:

> Software engineering is the establishment and use of sound engineering principles in order to economically develop software that is reliable and works efficiently on real machines.

This was partly prompted by the problems encountered in developing the operating system OS360 for the IBM-360 computer.

Software engineering has three elements: (1) methods, which provide the techniques for building software including the design of data structures, program architecture, and algorithmic procedure, coding, testing, and maintenance; (2) tools, which provide automated or semiautomated support

2.2 Software engineering

for methods; and (3) processes, the glue that holds the methods and tools together and enables rational and timely development of computer software (i.e., they define the sequence in which methods would be applied, the deliverables, the controls that help assure quality and coordinate change, and the milestones that enable software managers to assess progress.

Different ways of combining the above three elements of software engineering yield different software engineering models. There have been many models for software engineering. The choice of the right model is based on the nature of the project and application, the methods and tools to be used, and the controls and deliverables that are required. Three typical examples discussed here [1] are "the classic life cycle," "prototyping," and "fourth-generation techniques."

The classic life-cycle model is also called the waterfall model, because there is no iteration in the process from the beginning to the end of a project. It demands a strictly systematic sequential approach to carrying out the following activities: software requirements analysis, design, coding, testing, and maintenance.

The prototyping model enables the developer to create a prototype of the software to be built to allow problems and requirements to be seen quickly [6]. Prototyping begins with requirements gathering, where developers and customers meet and define the overall objects for the software, identify whatever requirements are known, and outline areas where further definition is mandatory. A quick design then occurs. The quick design focuses on a representation of those aspects of the software visible to the user. The quick design leads to the construction of a prototype. The prototype is evaluated by the customer or user and is used to refine requirements for the software to be developed. A process of iteration occurs as the prototype is "tuned" to satisfy the need of the customer, while at the same time enabling the developer to understand better what needs to be done.

The fourth-generation technique (4GT) model encompasses a broad array of software tools that have one thing in common: each enables the software developer to specify some characteristic of the software at a high level [7]. The tool then automatically generates source code based on the developer's specification. The 4GT paradigm for software engineering focuses on the ability to specify software to a machine at a level that is close to natural language or in a notation that imparts significant function, but it tends to be used in a single, well-defined application domain. Also the 4GT approach reuses certain elements, such as existing packages and databases rather than reinventing them.

The classic life cycle is the oldest and the most widely used paradigm for software engineering. It provides a template into which methods for analysis, design, coding, testing, and maintenance can be placed. It has weaknesses as well (e.g., real projects rarely follow the sequential flow that the model proposes, and iteration always occurs and creates problems in the application of the paradigm); thus, it is often difficult in the beginning for the customer to state all requirements explicitly, and there is a significant time lapse between the completion of the design phase and final delivery of the finished product. During this time it is likely that significant changes to the requirements will have occurred. Prototyping is an effective paradigm for software engineering. The key is to define the rules of the game at the beginning; that is, the customer and developer must both agree that the prototype is built to serve as a mechanism for defining requirements. The problem with this paradigm is that the customer sees what appears to be a working version of the software, unaware that in the rush to get it working overall software quality or long-term maintainability have not been considered (i.e., often the prototype will become the final product that is put into operation). Though it has been claimed that the 4GTs are likely to become an increasingly important part of software development, because of the dramatic reductions in software development time and greatly improved productivity for people who build software, current 4GT tools are not much easier to use than programming languages because the source code produced by such tools is "inefficient," and the maintainability of large software systems developed using 4GT is open to question. Existing problems include (1) poorly defined languages (incomplete or inconsistent), (2) inefficient implementations, (3) mixing of levels (breaking out to the lower-level language), (4) shortage of trained personnel [exacerbated by (1)], and (5) a lack of support from 4GL developers. As a result of these problems, some large companies have seriously considered throwing away all their 4GL code and instead attempting to maintain their multimillion lines of machine-generated COBOL.

A generic view of software engineering can be obtained by examining the process of software development [1]. The process contains three generic phases, regardless of the software engineering model chosen: the definition, development, and maintenance phases, are encountered in all software development. The definition phase focuses on *what* (i.e., the software developer attempts to identify what information is to be processed, what function and performance are desired, what interfaces are to be established, what design constraints exist, and what validation criteria are required to define a successful system). Three specific subprocesses occur in this phase: (1) system analysis, defining the role of each element in a computer-based system, ultimately allocating the role software will play; (2) software project planning, allocating resources, estimates costs, defining work tasks and schedules, setting quality plans, and identifying risks; and (3) requirements analysis, defining in more detail the information domain and software function before work can begin.

The development phase focuses on *how* (i.e., the software developer attempts to describe how the software architecture and associated data structures are to be designed, how procedural details are to be implemented, how the design will be translated into a programming language, and how testing will be performed). Three specific steps also occur in this phase: (1) software design, translating the requirements for the software into a set of representations that describe data structure, architecture, and algorithmic procedure; (2) coding, performing the translation from design representations into an artificial language that results in instructions executable by the computer; and (3) software testing, uncovering defects in function, in logic, and in implementation.

The maintenance phase focuses on change that is associated with error correction, adaptations required as the software's environment evolves, and modifications due to enhancements brought about by changing customer requirements. The maintenance phase reapplies the steps of the definition and development phases but does so in the context of existing software.

2.3 Software quality

Software engineering works toward a single goal: producing high-quality software. It is therefore useful to clarify the term quality and its factors.

Software quality is defined as conformance to explicitly stated functional and performance requirements, explicitly documented development standards, and implicit characteristics that are expected of all professionally developed software [1]. Software quality factors [8] include the following:

- *Correctness* (the extent to which a program satisfies its specification and fulfills the customer's mission objectives);
- *Reliability* (the extent to which a program can be expected to perform its intended function with the required precision);
- *Flexibility* (the effort required to modify an operational program);
- *Efficiency* (the amount of computing resources and code required by a program to perform its function);

- *Integrity* (the extent to which access to software or data by unauthorised persons can be controlled);

- *Usability* (the effort required to learn, operate, prepare input, and interpret the output of a program);

- *Maintainability* (the effort required to locate and fix an error or implement some other change in a program);

- *Testability* (the effort required to test a program to ensure that it performs its intended function);

- *Portability* (the effort required to transfer the program from one hardware and/or software system environment to another);

- *Reusability* (the extent to which a program (or part of a program) can be reused in other applications);

- *Interoperability* (the effort required to couple one system to another).

Software quality assurance is an activity that should be applied at each step in the software engineering process. Software quality assurance encompasses procedures for the effective application of methods and tools, formal technical reviews, testing strategies and techniques, procedures for change control, procedures for assuring compliance to standards, and measurement and reporting mechanisms.

Software reliability and flexibility are two important software quality factors, especially, when software is undergoing constant change. *Reliability* can be interpreted as the capacity of the software to maintain the level of performance of the system when used under specified conditions. Producing reliable software is a crucial objective in terms of software engineering. Unreliable software may cause large financial losses to its users or even injury and death. Flexibility is closely related to reliability in the situation in which software needs to be changed constantly—because high flexibility in the software will enable the next change to be carried out more easily while maintaining reliability.

2.4 Software everywhere

Nowadays, software may be found everywhere. However, more and more software is still being developed. An important consideration in

2.4 Software everywhere

the development of a software system is the entire development environment. In its most general sense, the development environment includes the technical methods, the management procedures, the computing equipment, the mode of computer use, the automated tools to support development, the software development staff, and the physical work space. An ideal development environment should enhance the productivity of the system developers and provide a set of tools (both manual and automated) that simplifies the process of software production. The environment should contain facilities both for the individual member of a development group and for the overall management of the project [9].

Today, software engineering has become a well-defined, constantly evolving discipline. Software production is very different now than it was in 1968 when the concept of software engineering was first introduced. The state of the art of software production at that time can be seen by examining the problems being discussed at the two NATO conferences on software engineering in 1968 and 1969. For example, some of the following issues were raised [10, 11]:

- Problems of scale;
- The order in which to do things;
- Strategies and techniques to use;
- How to specify software systems;
- Project planning and control;
- The proliferation of unreliable software

Although some of these are still problems today, progress has been made, especially in the following areas:

- *Modeling:* requirements modeling and systems modeling;
- *Formalization:* specification and verification;
- *Computer science:* languages, software concepts such as modularity, and abstract data types;
- *Method and design paradigms:* structured programming and object-oriented design, for example;
- *Support:* databases, tools, and software development environments;

- *Human factors:* user participation, project management, and human-computer interfaces;
- *Metrics:* quality, reliability, and costing.

Despite such advances, there are still many unsolved problems in the following areas:

- *Formal methods:* further development of specification and verification and their scaling up to cope with large real-life problems, particularly with tool support;
- *Metrics:* improved methods for assessing and predicting cost and software quality and reliability, maintainability, and other quality attributes;
- *Reuse:* potentially a major way of effecting the desperately needed increases in productivity, if software practice is going to have any chance of coping with the demand for software products;
- *Reengineering:* improved and new methods to reduce cost and to increase reliability and flexibility;
- *Management:* more reliable, more effective techniques for managing all aspects of the life cycle;
- *Tool support:* increased provision of automated software tools to support all activities of software engineering, both on an individual basis and as an integrated support environment;
- *Applied technologies:* application of other techniques (e.g., AI) to the general enhancement of software engineering.

The above issues are all related to the subject of this book, software evolution. Therefore, they merit further analysis. Section 2.5 begins this analysis with a discussion of software maintenance.

2.5 Software maintenance

In the early days of computing (1950s and early 1960s), software maintenance comprised a very small part of the software life cycle. In the late 1960s and the 1970s, as more and more software was produced, people began to realize that old software does not simply die. At that point software

2.5 Software maintenance

maintenance started to be recognized as a major activity. By the late 1970s, industry was suffering major problems with the applications backlog, and software maintenance was taking more effort than initial development in some sectors. In the 1980s, it was becoming evident that old architectures were severely constraining new design [12].

All of these factors increased demand for significant change to software. Such changes included fixing errors, adding enhancements, and making optimizations. Besides the problems whose solutions required the changes in the first place, the implementation of the changes themselves created additional problems.

One of Lehman's five laws of the evolution of a software system directly addresses the modification of software. It states that "a program that is used in a real world environment must change or become less and less useful in that environment" [13]. Accordingly, mechanisms must be developed for evaluating, controlling, and making changes.

Software maintenance is defined as the modification of a software product after delivery to correct faults, to improve performance or other attributes, or to adapt the product to a changed environment [14]. Software maintenance is required to meet the needs of the four principal change types described in Section 2.4. Thus, maintenance activities can be divided into these corresponding categories [15].

The first category is called corrective maintenance. There may be a *fault* in the software, so that its behavior does not conform to its specification. This fault may contradict the specification, or it may demonstrate that the specification is incomplete (or possibly inconsistent), so that the user's assumed specification is not sustained. Corrective maintenance involves removing these faults.

Even if a software system is fault-free, the environment in which it operates will often be subject to change (e.g., the upgrade of computer hardware or moving a system from a mainframe to a PC). Modifications performed as a result of changes to the external environment are categorized as adaptive maintenance (e.g., the manufacturer may introduce new versions of the operating system or remove support for existing facilities, and the software may be ported to a new environment or to different hardware).

The third category of maintenance is called perfective maintenance. This is undertaken as a consequence of a change in user requirements of the software. For example, a payroll suite may need to be altered to reflect new taxation laws; a real-time power station control system may need upgrading to meet new safety standards.

Finally, preventive maintenance may be undertaken on a system in order to anticipate future problems and make subsequent maintenance easier [16, 17]. For example, one part of a large suite may have been found to require sustained corrective maintenance over a period of time. It could be sensible to reimplement this part, using modern software engineering technology, in the expectation that subsequent maintenance efforts will be substantially reduced.

The large cost associated with software maintenance is the result of the fact that software has proved difficult to maintain. Early systems tended to be unstructured and ad hoc. This makes it hard to understand their underlying logic. System documentation is often incomplete, or out-of-date. With current methods it is often difficult to retest or verify a system after a change has been made. Successful software will inevitably evolve, but the process of evolution will lead to degraded structure and increasing complexity [13, 18, 19].

Now it is well established that software maintenance is the most costly stage of the software lifecycle for most projects. In the 1970s, 30% to 40% of the budget was used on software maintenance, with 40% to 60% in the 1980s. Today the budget for software maintenance is up to 70% to 80%.

Software maintenance has its own life cycle and its own features. Over the years, several software task models have been proposed; the model by Bennett is used here. Software maintenance can occur due to changing user needs, to errors that must be fixed, and to a changing environment. Although these types are different at the detailed level, at a high level they can be described by an iterative three-stage process:

1. *Request Control:* The information about the request is collected; the change is analyzed using impact analysis to assess costs and benefits; and a priority is assigned to each request.

2. *Change Control:* The next request is taken from the top of the priority list; the problem is reproduced (if there is one); the code (and design and the specifications if available) are analyzed; the changes are designed and documented and tests produced; the code modifications are written; and quality assurance is implemented.

3. *Release Control:* The new release is determined; the release is built; confidence testing is undertaken; the release is distributed; and acceptance testing by the customer takes place.

Currently, these three steps are almost always undertaken in terms of source code. Design information and even adequate documentation often do not exist. Thus software maintenance is thought of predominantly as

2.5 Software maintenance

a source code activity. Understanding the functions and behavior of a system from the code is hence a vital part of the maintenance programmer's task [20]. Approaches to program comprehension will be described in Chapters 3 to 7.

Most of the effort for software maintenance research has focused upon the methods, techniques, and tools that support the maintenance process. When maintenance activities are carried out, an essential characteristic of all software—maintainability—must be considered. Maintainability is a key goal that guides the steps of a software maintenance method, as well as a software engineering method. Software maintainability is the ease with which software can be understood, corrected, adapted, and enhanced [1].

The maintainability of software is affected by many factors. It is difficult to quantify software maintainability (no adequate, widely accepted, quantitative definition exists). However, many efforts have been made to tackle this problem from different angles. The three developed by Kopetz, Gilb, and Sneed are described in the following paragraphs.

Kopetz [21] defined a number of factors related to the development environment: the availability of qualified software staff, an understandable system structure, ease of system handling, the use of standardized programming languages, the use of standardized operating systems, the standardized structure of documentation, the availability of test cases, built-in debugging facilities, and the availability of a proper computer to conduct maintenance.

Gilb [22] provides maintainability metrics by measuring the effort expended during maintenance in the following categories:

- Problem recognition time;
- Administrative time;
- Maintenance tools collection time;
- Problem analysis time;
- Change specification time;
- Active correction time;
- Local testing time;
- Global testing time;
- Maintenance review time;
- Total recovery time.

Sneed [23] measures maintainability in terms of the original development expenditure. The smaller the expenditure on maintaining the system—relative to the expenditure on development—the greater the maintainability. The factors affecting this expenditure include the following:

- *Modularity:* an operating measure of the extent to which a system can be broken down into small independent building blocks;

- *Flexibility:* an operating measure of a software system's independence from any specific application;

- *Portability:* an operating measure of a software system's independence from its technical environment;

- *Complexity:* an operating measure of a software system's aggregation and distribution of components/complexes [24].

Attributes of software can be divided into two types, internal and external. Internal attributes are a property of the software itself (e.g., complexity, size, data structure, coupling, cohesion, quality, and reliability. External attributes are a property of the environment (e.g., availability of debugging tools, skill and training, repository and management).

Possibly the most important factor that affects maintainability is planning for maintainability. If software is viewed as a system element that will inevitably undergo change, the chances that maintainable software will be produced are likely to increase substantially [1]. However, maintainability is also dependent on the process as well as the software itself [2]. A major problem with maintenance is implementing those changes that were not even conceived of when the software was first designed—and this cannot be planned for. On the other hand, some changes (such as the fact that 2000 would eventually arrive) can certainly be anticipated, and there is no excuse for being taken by surprise!

Nevertheless, because maintainability is an essential characteristic of software, at each stage of the software engineering process, maintainability must be considered. For example, during the requirements stage, areas of future enhancement and potential revision should be noted, software portability issues discussed, and system interfaces that might impact software maintenance considered; during the design stage, data design, architecture design, and procedural design should be evaluated for ease of modification, modularity, and functional independence; during the coding stage, style and internal documentation (two factors that have an influence on maintainability) should be stressed.

Also, maintenance activities should be carried out in a careful way, because modification of software is dangerous in the sense that errors and other undesirable behaviors—or side effects [1] may occur as the result of software modification. Software maintenance side effects include coding side effects, data side effects and documentation side effects. Coding side effects are introduced when changes to one part of a system have an unintended effect on another, apparently unrelated, part of the system. Data side effects occur when data changes in the software design may no longer fit the data and when modifications are made to software information structures. Documentation side effects occur when changes to source code are not reflected in design documentation or user-oriented manuals.

2.6 Evolving software

It is safe to say that from the day that a large software system goes into service, functional, performance, operator, and environmental requirements will be subject to change. Moreover, the delivered software system will contain some latent defects that were not detected during testing. These factors cause software systems inevitably to evolve in scale, environment and functionality, especially those successful enough to survive a long period [25, 26]. To summarize: Due to the rapid development of computer hardware and software, the demands and costs of software changes are increasing continuously. Software changes now comprise a major portion of software life-cycle costs. Because changes to software are needed so constantly, the term software maintenance, is no longer expressive enough to describe such changes. Software evolution is now becoming the essential technique to control software life-cycle costs.

References

[1] Pressman, R. S., *Software Engineering—A Practitioner's Approach*, New York: McGraw-Hill, 1987.

[2] Brooks, F. P., "No Silver Bullet," *IEEE Computer*, Vol. 20, No. 4, April 1987, pp. 10–19.

[3] Parnas, D. L., "Designing Software," *IEEE Trans. on Software Engineering*, Vol. 5, No. 2, March 1979.

[4] Lubers, M., C. Potts, and C. Richter, "A Review of the State of the Practice in Requirements Modeling," *Proc. International Requirements Engineering Symposium*, Los Alamitos, California, 1993.

[5] "Report on the NATO Software Engineering Conference, Garmisch, 1968" in *Software Engineering Concepts and Techniques*, P. Naur and B. R. Randell (eds.), Petrocelli/Charter, 1976.

[6] Carey, J. M., "Prototyping: Alternative Systems Development Methodology," *Information and Software Technology*, Vol. 32, No. 2, 1990.

[7] Fisher, A. S., *CASE: Using Software Development Tools*, New York: John Wiley and Sons, 1988.

[8] McCall, J., P. Richards, and G. Walters, "Factors in Software Quality," presented at *NTIS*, November 1977.

[9] Wasserman, A. I., "Software Engineering Environments," *Advances in Computers*, Vol. 22, 1983.

[10] Ramamoorthy, C. V., et al., "Software Engineering: Problems and Perspectives," *IEEE Computer*, October 1984.

[11] Ratcliff, B., *Software Engineering Principles and Methods*, Oxford, England: Blackwell Scientific Publications, 1987.

[12] Bennett, K. H., "An Overview of Maintenance and Reverse Engineering," in *The REDO Compendium*, Chichester, England: John Wiley and Sons, 1993.

[13] Lehman, M. M., "Programs, Life Cycles, and Laws of Software Evolution," *Proc. IEEE*, Vol. 19, No. 9, 1980, pp. 1060–1076.

[14] ANSI standard 729, *IEEE Standard Glossary of Software Engineering Terminology*, 1983.

[15] Swanson, E. B., "The Dimension of Maintenance," in *Second International Conference on Software Engineering*, Los Alamitos, California: IEEE Computer Society, 1976.

[16] Bennett, K. H., "The Software Maintenance of Large Software Systems: Management Method and Tools," Durham University, Technical Report, 1989.

[17] Yang, H., "Is Year 2000 Problem a Paper Tiger or a Real Tiger," presented at the *IEEE International Computer Software and Application Conference (CompSac'97)*, Washington, D.C., August 1987.

[18] Bennett, K. H., J. Denier, and J. Estublier, "Environments for Software Maintenance," Durham University, Technical Report, 1989.

[19] *Standard FIPS PUB 106*, "Guidelines on Software Maintenance," U.S. Department of Commerce/National Bureau of Standards, June 1984.

[20] Robson, D. J., et al., "Approaches to Program Comprehension," *Journal of Systems Software*, Vol. 14, February 1991, pp. 79–84.

[21] Kopetz, H., *Software Reliability*, Berlin: Springer-Verlag, 1979.

[22] Gilb, T., "A Comment on the Definition of Reliability," *ACM Software Engineering Notes*, Vol. 4, No. 3, July 1979.

[23] Sneed, H. M., *Software Engineering Management*, Chichester, England: Ellis Horwood Limited, 1989.

[24] Ejiogu, L. O., *Software Engineering with Formal Metrics*, London: McGraw-Hill, 1991.

[25] Arthur, L. J., *Software Evolution: The Software Maintenance Challenge*, New York: John Wiley and Sons, 1988.

[26] Behfoorooz, A., and F. J. Hudson, *Software Engineering Fundamentals*, Oxford: Oxford University Press, 1996.

CHAPTER 3

Software Reengineering for Evolution

Contents

3.1 Introduction

3.2 Software reengineering cycle

3.3 Taxonomy of software reengineering

3.4 Reverse engineering

3.5 Current state of formal methods in reengineering

3.6 Classification of formal methods

3.7 Criteria and results

3.8 Analysis and summary

References

3.1 Introduction

Software evolution is the process of conducting continuous software reengineering. Reengineering implies a single change cycle, but evolution can go on forever. In other words, to a large extent, software evolution is repeated software reengineering. Therefore, this book discusses many technical details of reengineering.

Any computing system, including hardware and software systems, will inevitably grow in scale and functionality. Because of this complexity, the likelihood of subtle errors is much greater. Moreover, some of these errors may cause catastrophic loss of money, time, or even human life. Large systems are so complex that it is impossible for a single individual to build and maintain all aspects of the system's design. A major goal of software engineering is to enable developers to construct systems that operate reliably despite this complexity [1–4]. One way of achieving this goal is using formal methods, mathematically-based languages, techniques, and tools for specifying and verifying software systems. Using formal methods does not guarantee correctness, but they can greatly increase our understanding of a system by revealing inconsistencies, ambiguities, and incompleteness that might otherwise go undetected [5].

As a combination of reverse engineering and forward engineering, software reengineering technology is a practical solution for the problem of evolving existing computing systems. Dynamic change management of software systems has been largely performed by using ad hoc techniques that are normally rather expensive and in some cases, impossible (if the designer has not documented the system and has left the company). There are at least two advantages of using formal methods as the foundation of software reengineering. First, formal methods can help software engineers to acquire a rigorous and precise description of the system being reengineered, therefore greatly increasing the quality of the new system. Second, automation is one of the key goals of reengineering. By applying formal methods, it may be possible to automate more of the process of reengineering.

These two advantages will naturally bring flexibility and reliability to the reengineered software, because future reengineering can still enjoy automated tool support, and reliability is enhanced by the rigor and precision provided by formal methods.

This chapter investigates the current situation of software reengineering and the application of formal methods to this area. It proposes some basic criteria for formal methods applied in the software reengineering domain. Real-time systems with parallelism are among the range of the application areas of software reengineering. Based on these criteria, an investigation and assessment is made of existing popular formal methods, especially those potentially suitable for software reengineering. Section 3.8 summarizes the results of the analysis and discussions.

It is worth noting that this book, besides illustrating many useful features of formal methods, emphasizes the applications of formal techniques in the practice of software reengineering and the ways in which formal techniques and nonformal techniques work together.

3.2 Software reengineering cycle

To understand better the process of software reengineering, we first examine the reengineering cycle chart (Figure 3.1) introduced by Bachman [6], which features both forward and reverse engineering. Reverse engineering begins at the bottom left of Figure 3.1 with the definition of existing applications and raises the applications to successively higher levels of abstraction. At the top of Figure 3.1, the design objects created by the reverse engineering steps are enhanced and validated to become the revised design objects that may be used in the forward engineering process. At the bottom

3.2 Software reengineering cycle

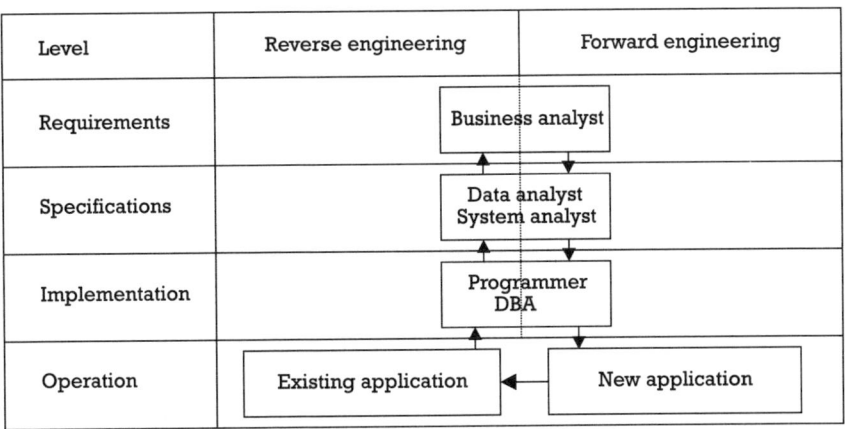

Figure 3.1 Bachman's reengineering cycle.

of Figure 3.1, a new application system becomes an existing application system at the moment that it goes into production.

To generalize this model, many software systems typically undergo the following stages:

Specification → Design → Implementation → Design → Specification

This represents a process whereby before implementing a program, a specification was written first. Then, a design was derived from the given specification, and the program was implemented and operated for a period of time. When the program needed to be changed, a design or specification (which may be different from the original one) was obtained through reverse engineering (the design or specification can be used for such purposes as maintenance and reengineering).

A specification states what a program does; a design states both what a program does and how it does it, and the program itself implements how to do the job. Therefore the above process can be represented as follows:

what? → what & how? → how? → what & how? → what?

A specification, a design, and an implementation of a program usually entail different levels of abstraction. To move from one stage (e.g., the specification stage) to another stage (e.g., the design stage) involves a process of crossing levels of abstraction. Usually a specification is more abstract than its implementation; therefore, the above process can again be represented as follows:

abstract → less abstract → concrete → more abstract → abstract

This suggests that the abstraction level of software is an important feature when both forward and reverse engineering are carried out and therefore that abstraction is significant for both reverse and forward engineering.

3.3 Taxonomy of software reengineering

In this section, the following key terms provide a clear scope and taxonomy of the domain of software reengineering [1–3, 7]:

- *Forward engineering* is the traditional process of moving from high-level abstractions and logical, implementation-independent designs to the physical implementation of a system.

- *Reverse engineering* is the process of analyzing a subject system to (1) identify the system's components and their interrelationships and (2) create representations of the system in another form or higher level of abstraction.

- *Redocumentation* is the creation or revision of a semantically equivalent representation within the same relative abstraction level. The resulting forms of representation are usually considered alternate views (for example, data flow, data structures, and control flow) intended for a human audience. Redocumentation is the simplest and oldest form of reverse engineering and can be considered to be an unintrusive, weak form of restructuring.

- *Design recovery* or *reverse design* is a subset of reverse engineering in which domain knowledge, external information, and deduction or fuzzy reasoning are added to the observations of the subject system to identify meaningful higher-level abstractions beyond those obtained directly by examining the system itself. Design recovery recreates design abstractions from a combination of code, existing design documentation (if available), personal experience, and general knowledge about problem and application domains.

- *Program understanding* or *program comprehension* is a term related to reverse engineering. Program understanding implies always that understanding begins with the source code while reverse engineering can start at a binary and executable form of the system or at high-level descriptions of the design. The science of program understanding includes the cognitive science of human mental

3.3 Taxonomy of software reengineering

processes in program understanding. Program understanding can be achieved in an ad hoc manner, and no external representation has to arise. While reverse engineering is the systematic approach to developing an external representation of the subject system, program understanding is comparable with design recovery because both of them start at source code level.

- *Restructuring* is the transformation from one representation form to another at the same relative abstraction level, while preserving the subject system's external behavior (i.e., functionality and semantics).

- *Reengineering* is the examination and alteration of a subject system to reconstitute it in a new form and the subsequent implementation of the new form. The process of reengineering computing systems involves three main steps: reverse engineering, functional restructuring, and forward engineering.

- *Reverse specification* is a kind of reverse engineering where a specification is abstracted from the source code or design description. Specification in this context means an abstract description of what the software does. In forward engineering, the specification tells us what the software has to do. However, this information is not included in the source code. Only in rare cases, it can be recovered from comments in the source code and from the people involved in the original forward engineering process.

- *Recode* involves changing the implementation characteristic of the source code. Language translation and control flow restructuring are source-code-level changes. Other possible changes include conforming to coding standards, improving source code readability, and renaming program items.

- *Redesign* involves changing the design characteristics. Possible changes include restructuring a design architecture, altering a system's data model as incorporated in data structures or in a database, and improving an algorithm.

- *Respecify* involves changing the requirement characteristics. This type of change can refer to changing only the form of existing requirements (i.e., taking informal requirements expressed in English and generating a formal specification expressed in a formal language, such as Z). This type of change can also refer to changing system requirements, such as the addition of new requirements, or the deletion or alteration of existing requirements.

Figure 3.2 presents a general model of reverse engineering, and Figure 3.3 presents a general model of reengineering, in terms of the above definitions.

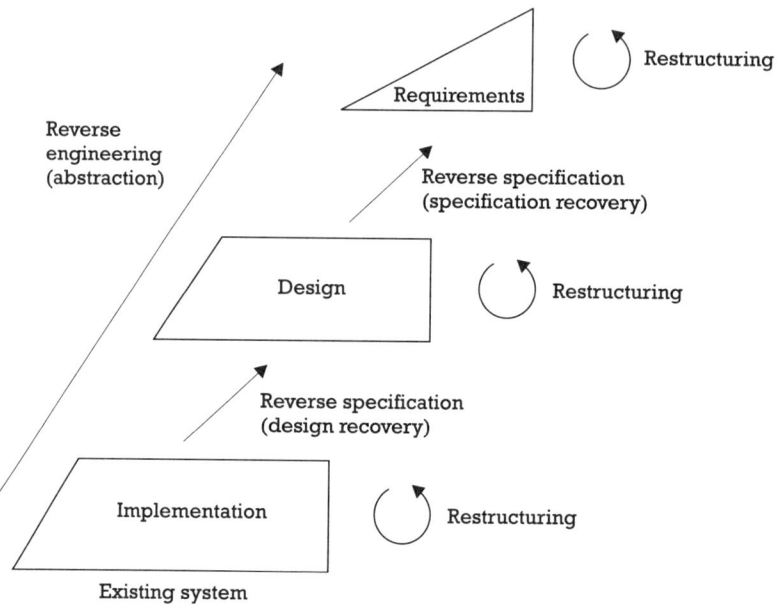

Figure 3.2 General model for reverse engineering.

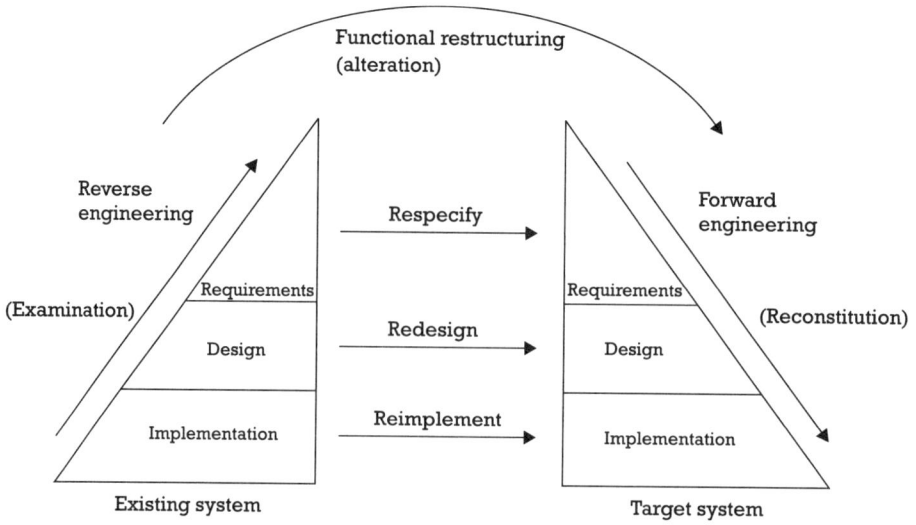

Figure 3.3 General model for software reengineering.

3.4 Reverse engineering

Reverse engineering involves the identification or recovery of program requirements and/or design specifications that can aid in understanding and modifying the program. The main objective is to discover the underlying features of a software system including requirements, specification, design, and implementation. In other words, it is to recover and record high-level information about the system including the following:

- The system structure in terms of its components and their interrelationships expressed by the interfaces;
- Its functionality in terms of what operations are performed on what components;
- The dynamic behavior of the system, or how input is transformed to output;
- Its rationale (the design process that decides between a number of alternatives at each design step);
- Its construction, modules, documentation, and test suites.

There are several purposes for undertaking reverse engineering listed in [8]. They can be separated into the quality issues (e.g., to simplify complex software, to improve the quality of software that contains errors, and to remove side effects from software), management issues (e.g., to enforce a programming standard and to enable better software maintenance management techniques), and technical issues (e.g., to allow major changes in a software to be implemented, to discover and record the design of the system, and to discover and represent the underlying business model implicit in the software).

It is seen that reverse engineering is an activity that neither changes the subject system, nor creates a new system based on the reversed engineered subject system. It is the process of examining and understanding the object system and of recording the results of that examination and understanding. On the other hand, reverse engineering is a key to the rest of the process of reengineering, because it enables us to take an existing software system that is being reengineered (e.g., in terms of its source code) and to recover an abstract representation that can be used for subsequent reengineering or even reimplementation.

Because the techniques and methods of reverse engineering are still immature, the six following precautions must be considered when reverse engineering is carried out:

1. The code may be specific, and not generic, so that few advantages are gained when the system is reengineered.
2. The code may have errors, and it is not clear if it is useful to reverse engineer error-filled code.
3. Reverse engineering itself may introduce errors, and revalidation will be essential in the project plan.
4. Reverse engineering can be very expensive, and the returns are not always clear. Thus, a cost benefit analysis will be needed.
5. There are no standards or standard methods for reverse engineering.
6. There are no well-established measures for reengineering.

One typical reverse engineering objective is to extract the program design or specification from the program code. There are two reasons for this. The first is that in order to achieve major productivity gains, software alteration must be undertaken at a higher abstraction level than code (i.e., at the design level or specification level). This is true for the following six reasons [8]:

1. The representation of a system at higher levels of abstraction is more compact than at lower levels, so the system is easier to understand as a whole.
2. The objects that represent the system at high levels of abstraction (e.g., modules, requirements, and specifications) are structures that encourage highly maintainable systems. Furthermore, they are closer to the application domain, and many changes are expressed in terms of the application domain.
3. The documentation for systems maintained in this way can be clearly specified.
4. Modification can be better controlled leading to less structural degradation.
5. Modern software engineering techniques become available to the software engineer, leading to high quality in the reengineering phase.

6. The high abstraction level objects are appropriate vehicles in which to express the testing plan.

The second reason is that this need is often encountered in software reengineering projects. First, the documentation and relevant reference materials are not complete, and the personnel with relevant knowledge may have already forgotten about it or left. Second, there might be some documentation available, but the software may not be implemented consistently with the documentation. Third, the original documentation and reference materials may not have been written in a modern specification language and thus will be unusable in a modern software reengineering environment; they may not even be machine-readable.

This means that the extraction of the program design or the specification of an old program code is a vital step especially when the program is the only available documentation or is the only source on which to rely. The purpose of this kind of reverse engineering is (1) to reimplement the system or (2) to help understand the existing software. We cannot simply reimplement the software directly, because of the considerable investment in the existing software, which means that it is not cost-effective to throw it away and rewrite it with the latest development techniques. The significance of reverse engineering can be seen in many early reverse engineering projects; see, for example [9–13].

3.5 Current state of formal methods in reengineering

The debate about the use and relevance of formal methods in the development of computing systems has always attracted considerable attention and continues to do so. One school of thought (the protagonists) claims that formal techniques offer a complete solution to the problems of system development. Another school claims that formal methods have little, or no, use in the development process (at least due to the cost involved). There is a third viewpoint, which we share, that states that formal methods are both *oversold* and *underused*.

Whatever school of thought one ascribes to, it is important to realize that as the complexity of building computing systems is continually growing, a disciplined, systematic, and rigorous methodology is essential for attaining a reasonable level of dependability and trust in these systems. The need for such a methodology increases as fatal accidents are attributable to software errors.

In response to this, intense research activity has developed, resulting in the production of formal development techniques and their associated verification tools that have been successfully applied in forward-engineering such systems. For example, assertional methods, temporal logic, process algebra, and automata have all been used with some degree of success.

In the area of reverse engineering, formal methods have also been put forward as a means to achieve the following:

1. Formally specifying and verifying existing systems, particularly those already operating in safety-critical applications;
2. Introducing new functionalities;
3. Taking advantage of the improvement in systems design techniques.

We attempt to review a large class of formal methods that have been suggested for reengineering computing systems [14–18]. We shall also discuss some of their benefits and limitations. However, first it is necessary to lay some terminological groundwork and to consider current practices.

The term *formal methods* is used to refer to methods with a sound basis in mathematics. These should be distinguished from *structured methods*, which are well-defined but do not have a sound mathematical basis to describe system functionalities [19]. Formal methods allow system functionalities to be precisely specified, while structured methods permit the precise specification of systems structure. However, recently, there have been substantial research activities to do the following:

- Integrate formal and structured methods (i.e., integrating the formal specification language Z [20, 21] with the structured method known as SSADM);
- Extend some formal methods allowing the treatment of nonfunctional requirements such as timing and probability [22–27].

We take the view that a formal method should consist of some essential components: a semantic model, a specification language (notation), a verification system and refinement calculus, development guidelines, and supporting tools:

1. The *semantic model* is a sound mathematical or logical structure within which all terms, formulae, and rules used have a precise meaning. The semantic model should reflect the underlying computational model of the intended application.

2. The *specification language* is a set of notations that are used to describe the intended behavior of the system. This language must have proper semantics within the semantic model.

3. *Verification system and refinement calculi* are sound rules that allow for the verification of properties and the refinement of specifications.

4. *Development guidelines* are steps showing the use of the method.

5. *Supporting tools* include tools such as a proof assistant, a syntax and type checker, an animator, and a prototyper.

Formal methods can be applied in two different ways:

1. To produce specifications that are then the basis for a conventional system development. In this case, specifications are used as a precise documentation medium that has the advantages of manipulability, abstraction, and conciseness. Consistency checks and automatic generation of prototypes could be performed at this stage with the aid of the associated supporting tools.

2. To produce formal specifications, as above, to use as a basis against which the correctness of the system is verified or as a basis to derive the verified system through correctness preserving refinement rules. This will give the developed system a degree of certainty and trustworthiness.

3.6 Classification of formal methods

Formal methods can be classified into the following five types: model-based, logic-based, algebraic, process algebra and net-based (graphical) methods. Sections 3.6.1 to 3.6.5 briefly discuss each of these approaches.

3.6.1 Model-based approach

General A system is modeled by explicitly defining the states and operations that transform the system from one state to another. In this approach, there is no explicit representation of concurrency. Nonfunctional requirements (such as the temporal requirement) can be expressed in some cases.

Examples

- *Z [20]:* With the first version proposed in 1979, the Z notation is based on a predicate calculus and Zermelo Fraenkel set theory. A Z specification is written in terms of schemas, each of which contains a signature part that declares the items of interest and a predicate part that places a logical constraint on them.

- *Vienna development method (VDM) [28–30]:* VDM is a formal method for rigorous computing system development. It is similar to Z in most aspects, although it is not as popular as Z. VDM supports model composition and decomposition, which greatly facilitates both forward and reverse engineering.

- *B-method [31–33]:* The B-method uses the abstract machine notation to support the description of the target systems. The most eminent success of the B-method is that it already has a strong and quite mature tool, the B Toolkit, to support and automate the development of application systems. The B-method is complete in the sense that it provides abstract machine specifications and their proofs, refinements and their proofs, and compositions and their proofs. The development method of B matches typical top-down forward engineering methods. A complete development may be performed and recorded. Changes may be accommodated using the replay tools. Refinement, implementation, and composition steps have precise notions of correctness and a mechanical generation of proof obligations. By using the animator, tests may be performed. The final implementation step may be mechanized for common languages (e.g., C and Ada) and for some specification constructs.

    In the B-method, no guidance is provided regarding (1) design decisions or their recording, (2) testing or inspection methodology, and (3) presentation of specifications. The B toolkit is still evolving and as yet is not very mature, and the B-method has no timing features. New features will have to be added if B is to be used for real-time systems.

3.6.2 Logic-based approach

General   In this approach logic is used to describe the system's desired properties, including the low-level specification, temporal, and probabilistic behaviors. The validity of these properties is achieved using the associated axiom system of the logic. In some cases, a subset of the logic can be executed (e.g., the Tempura system) [25]. The executable specification can then be used for simulation and rapid prototyping purposes.

The logic can be augmented with some concrete programming constructs to obtain what is known as wide-spectrum formalism. The development of systems in this case is achieved by a set of correctness-preserving refinement steps. Examples of these forms are TAM [27], the refinement calculus [34], and FermaT [35–37].

Examples

- *Interval temporal logic (ITL) [22, 23, 25, 26, 38, 39]:* This kind of logic is based on intervals of time, thought of as representing finite chunks of system behavior. An interval may be divided into two contiguous subintervals, thus leading to the chop operator.

- *Duration calculus [40, 41]:* This was introduced as a logic to specify and reason about requirements for real-time systems. It is an extension of ITL where one can reason about integrated constraints over time-dependent and Boolean valued states without explicit mention of absolute time. Several rather large-scale case studies have shown that duration calculus provides a high level of abstraction for both expressing and reasoning about specifications.

- *Hoare logic [42–44]:* Hoare logic has a long history; it may be viewed as an extension of first-order predicate calculus [45] that includes inference rules for reasoning about programming language constructs.

    Hoare logic provides a means of demonstrating that a program is consistent with its specification. Hoare logic is not capable of specifying a system at high levels; however, it has distinct advantages in the low-level specifications. These two features make Hoare logic a suitable means in the first stage of reverse engineering (i.e., from a source code program to an abstraction at a very low level). Some research has been done in this area, such as the development of the reverse engineering tool AutoSpec [46, 47]. There are no real-time features in Hoare logic, but real-time Hoare logic has been proposed [48].

- *Weakest precondition [45, 49]:* WP-calculus was first proposed by E. W. Dijkstra in 1976. A precondition describes the initial state of a program, and a postcondition describes the final state. By using the semantics of predicate logic and other suitable formal logics, WP-calculus has been proven to be a suitable formalism for the reverse engineering of source code, especially at the low abstraction levels.

- *WSL:* WSL is based on the weakest proconditions but also uses a denotational semantic model approach [50]. Specifications and programs at every abstraction level can be expressed in the same language (hence the name "wide-spectrum language"). The lowest level transformations are proven correct either by using the weakest preconditions or the semantic model. More complex transformations are developed by composing existing transformations [51]. There has also been some work on extending WSL to deal with shared memory and concurrent processes [52, 53].

- *Modal logic [54, 55]:* Modal logic is the study of context-dependent properties such as necessity and possibility. In modal logic, the meaning of expressions depends on an implicit context, abstracted away from the object language. Temporal logic can be regarded as an instance of modal logic where the collection of contexts models a collection of moments in time. Modal logic is equipped with modal operators through which elements from different contexts can be combined. Two of the most popular modal operators are the necessity operator $\Box$ (always) and the possibility operator $\Diamond$ (sometimes). There are several approaches to the semantics of modal logic, such as "neighborhood" semantics. So far, modal logic has not been applied to the software reverse engineering area.

- *Temporal logic [56]:* Temporal logic has its origins in philosophy, where it was used to analyze the structure or topology of time. Philosophers found it useful to introduce special temporal operators, such as $\Box$ (henceforth) and $\Diamond$ (eventually), for the analysis of temporal connectives in languages. Various types of semantics can be given to the temporal operators depending on whether time is linear, parallel, or branching and whether time is discrete or continuous [57]. In recent years, temporal logic has been found to be very valuable in real-time applications.

    The various temporal logics can be used to reason about qualitative temporal properties. Safety properties that can be specified include mutual exclusion and absence of deadlock. Liveness properties include termination and responsiveness. Fairness properties include scheduling a given process infinitely often or requiring that a continuously enabled transition will ultimately fire.

3.6 Classification of formal methods

In real-time temporal logics, it is possible to express quantitative properties, such as periodicity, real-time response (deadline), and delays. Early approaches to real-time temporal logics were reported in [58, 59]. Since then, real-time logics have been explored in greater detail.

- *Temporal agent model (TAM) [27, 60, 61]:* TAM aims to be a realistic software development method for real-time systems. It has striven to support a computational model that is amenable both to analysis by run-time execution environment software and to efficient implementation. In doing so, TAM has not shared any of the simplifying assumptions that other techniques promote (e.g., the maximum parallelism hypothesis and the instantaneous communication assumption).

  Concurrency and communication are also provided to describe multitasking systems. However, as yet, there has been no attempt to apply TAM to reverse engineering or reengineering.

- *Real-time temporal logic (RTTL) [62, 63]:* RTTL uses a distinguished temporal domain, the extended state machine (ESM) state variables, and the set of ESM transitions to form temporal formulae. These are then proven using an axiomatization of the system's ESM trajectories.

  No special development method is proposed in RTTL or required by RTTL. If applied to the reverse engineering area, RTTL has the flexibility to fit different methodologies.

- *Real-time logic (RTL) [64]:* RTL has four basic concepts: actions, which may be composite or primitive; state predicates, which provide assertions regarding the physical system state; events, which are markers on the (sparse) time line; and timing constraints, which provide assertions about the timing of events.

  RTL has been used with some success in industrial applications, and it is also being used in a major IBM project called ORE, which is integrating RTL with a real-time programming language. There is a feeling of confidence with RTL due to its pragmatic nature.

- *Timed probabilistic computation tree logic [24]:* TPCTL deals with real-time constraints and reliability. Formulas of TPCTL are interpreted over a discrete time extension of Milner's calculus of communication systems called TPCCS. Probabilities are introduced by allowing two types of transitions, one labeled with actions and the other labeled with probabilities.

TPCTL is one of the few logics that can express both hard and soft real-time deadlines, and it is possible to represent levels of criticality in TPCTL.

3.6.3 Algebraic approach

General In this approach, an implicit definition of operations is given by relating the behavior of different operations without defining the meanings of the actual states. Similar to the model-based approach, there is no explicit representation of concurrency.

Examples

- *OBJ [65, 66]:* OBJ is a wide spectrum first-order functional language that is rigorously based on equational logic. This semantics basis supports a declarative, specificational style, facilitates program verification, and allows OBJ to be used as a theorem prover.

- *Larch [67]:* The Larch family of algebraic specification languages was developed at MIT and Xerox PARC to support the productive use of formal specifications in programming. One of its goals is to support a variety of different programming languages, including imperative languages, while localizing programming language dependencies as much as possible. Each Larch language is composed of two components: the interface language, which is specific to the particular programming language under consideration, and the shared language, which is common to all programming languages.

3.6.4 Process algebra approach

General In this approach, an explicit representation of concurrent processes is allowed. System behavior is represented by constraints on all allowable observable communications between processes.

Examples

- *Communicating sequential processes (CSP) [68, 69]:* The CSP formal specification notation for concurrent systems was first introduced in [69]. Since this original proposal did not include a proof method, a complete version of CSP was proposed in [68].

- *Calculus of communicating systems (CCS) [70, 71]:* CCS was proposed by Milner in 1989. It is a formalism similar to CSP. CCS is

3.6 Classification of formal methods

also suitable for distributed and concurrent systems. At present, several variations of CCS have been developed, forming a CCS family. The CCS family includes CCS, CCS+, CCS*, SCCS, TCCS, and TPCCS [72].

Two underlying concepts of CCS are agents and actions. A CCS model consists of a set of communicating processes (agents in CCS terminology). CCS adopts operational semantics.

CCS is not a real-time formalism, but some extensions of CCS with real-time features have been developed, such as TCCS, SCCS, and TPCCS.

- *Algebra of communicating processes (ACP) [73, 74]*: ACP was proposed by J. A. Bergstra in 1984. To date, a number of varieties of ACP have been proposed, including real-time ACP (ACP_ρ) and discrete time ACP. ACP is also an action-based process algebra, which may be viewed as a modification of CCS. However, ACP is an executable formalism.

- *Language of temporal ordering specification (LOTOS) [75, 76]*: LOTOS was developed to define implementation-independent formal standards of OSI services and protocols. LOTOS has two very clearly separated parts. The first part provides a behavioral model derived from process algebra, principally from CCS but also from CSP. The second part of LOTOS allows specifiers to describe abstract data types and values and is based on the abstract data type language ACT ONE.

    LOTOS has a formally defined syntax, static semantics, and dynamic semantics. The static semantics are defined by an attributed grammar [75] and the dynamic semantics are described operationally in terms of inference rules.

    Since LOTOS has an operational semantics, it is possible to implement these semantics in an interpreter. LOTOS has a number of support tools, which, although not mature or narrow-aspected, do have some successful points [77].

    LOTOS does not support real-time specifications. Although a timed LOTOS has been proposed, it has not proven to be a suitable formalism for real-time systems. Also, LOTOS has weak data specification mechanisms and cannot express time explicitly.

- *Timed CSP (TCSP) [78]*: TCSP is an extension of Hoare's CSP, with a dense temporal model providing a global clock. A delay operator is included along with some extended parallel operators. There is an assumption of a minimum delay between any two dependent action occurrences, but no minimum delay on any two independent actions. The semantics of TCSP is given by timed traces, and a specification relation *sat* is provided for verifying predicates over traces.

Processes in TCSP are built from sequences of communication actions. The semantic model of TCSP is based on observation and refusal timed traces. There exist no tools for the manipulation of specifications written in TCSP.

- *Timed probabilistic calculus of communicating systems (TPCCS) [24]:* TPCCS is essentially an extension of Milner's CCS with discrete time and probabilities. To increase the descriptive power, a logic named TPCTL is proposed to describe the logic of and relations between TPCCS processes. Therefore TPCCS, together with TPCTL, forms a framework for specification and verification of real-time properties and reliability in distributed systems. TPCCS, as a process algebra, is used for modeling the operational behavior of distributed real-time systems; and TPCTL, as a logic, is used for expressing properties of the systems. A verification method for automatically proving that a system described in TPCCS satisfies properties formulated in TPCTL, is also well defined [24].

    TPCCS has very formally defined syntax and semantics, which brings convenience to the automation of specification and verification. However, the calculation of probabilities is not mentioned in TPCCS and TPCTL. A tool named the timing and probability workbench (TPWB) has been developed. TPWB partially supports automatic verification of TPCCS.

3.6.5 Net-based approach

General Graphical notations are popular notations for specifying systems as they are easier to comprehend and, hence, more accessible to non-specialists. This approach uses graphical languages with formal semantics, which brings particular advantages in system development and reengineering.

Examples

- *Petri net [79, 80]:* Petri net theory is one of the first formalisms to deal with concurrency, nondeterminism, and causal connections between events. According to [81], it was the first unified theory, with levels

3.6 Classification of formal methods

of abstraction, in which to describe and analyze all aspects of a computer in the context of its environment.

Petri nets provide a graphic representation with formal semantics of system behavior. A large number of varieties of Petri net theory have been proposed. Generally, Petri nets can be classified into ordinary (classic) Petri nets and timed Petri nets.

- *Timed Petri net [82–87]:* Petri net theory was the first concurrent formalism to deal with realtime. Two basic timed versions of Petri nets have been introduced: timed Petri nets [88] and time Petri nets [87]. Both have been used in recent work [82–85, 87]. There are two questions that arise when time is introduced to net theory: (1) the location of the time delays (at places or transitions) and (2) the type of delay (fixed delays, intervals, or stochastic delays).

  Timed Petri nets are derived from classical Petri nets by associating a finite firing duration (a delay) with each transition of the net. The transition is disabled during the delay period, but is fired immediately after becoming enabled. These nets are used mainly in performance evaluation.

  Time Petri nets (TPNs) are more general than timed Petri nets. Both a lower and an upper bound are associated with each transition in a TPN.

- *Statecharts [89, 90]:* Statecharts provides an abstraction mechanism based on a finite state machine. It represents an improved version of the structured methods. A graphic tool called "Statemate" [91] exists to implement the formalism. Methods similar to that of statecharts may be found in [92].

  In statecharts, conventional finite state machines are extended by AND/OR decompositions of states, interlevel transitions, and an implicit intercomposition broadcast communication. Statecharts denote the composition of state machines into supermachines that may execute concurrently. The state machines contain transitions that are marked by enabling and output events. It is assumed that events are instantaneous, and a global discrete clock is used to trigger sets of concurrent events. Statecharts are hierarchical and may be composed of complex charts.

  Statecharts support the typical structural top-down system development methods. They do not fit in with the procedures of reverse engineering, which involve the abstraction of specifications from source code. Real time is incorporated in statecharts by the incorporation of an implicit clock, allowing transitions to be triggered by timeouts relative to this clock, and by requiring that if a transition can be taken, then it must be taken immediately.

3.7 Criteria and results

This section summarizes a wide spectrum of existing formal methods from the point of view of software reengineering. Generally speaking, some of them already have advantages in certain aspects. However, all of them have certain flaws or weaknesses in some aspects as described in Section 3.6.

Tables 3.1 to 3.6 list our findings according to the following criteria:

- *Temporal model:* This is the model of time used by the formal methods. A sparse model has discrete instances of time, and there is a minimum granularity. A dense model is not discrete: Between any two instances in time there are an infinite number of other instances.

- *Automated tools:* This criterion refers to whether the formal method has relevant automated tools to support its development, such as tools for checking syntax, verifying semantics, and autoexecution.

- *Reliability:* This criterion refers to the reliability of the formalism.

- *Proof system:* This refers to whether there is any proof system and what type of proof system exists.

- *Industrial strength:* This criterion refers to the potential of the formal method for large-scale industrial applications.

- *Methods of verification:* This criterion refers to the existing methods of verification of the formal method. Normally, there are two different methods of verification: model checking and theorem proving.

- *Concurrency:* This criterion refers to the explicit representation and reasoning of concurrency.

- *Communication:* This criterion refers to the explicit representation and reasoning of communication.

- *Reverse engineering:* This criterion refers to whether the formal method has been applied in any reverse engineering domain.

The above five categories represented in Tables 3.1 to 3.5 correspond to subsections of Section 3.6. We believe we should use a sixth category in order to better summarize those so-called combined approaches (see Table 3.6).

3.7 Criteria and results

Table 3.1 Model-State-Based Formalisms

Criteria	Z	VDM	B
Temporal model	None	None	None
Automated tools	A few	None	Good
Reliability	Good	Good	Good
Proof system	Semiaxiomatic	Semiaxiomatic	Axiomatic
Industrial strength	Great	Some	Great
Methods of verification	Model-checking	Model-checking	Both
Concurrency	None	None	None
Communication	None	None	None
Reverse engineering	No	No	No

Table 3.2(a) Logic-Based Formalisms

Criteria	HL	WP-Calculation	WSL	TL	ML
Temporal model	None	None	None	Dense/sparse	None
Automated tools	Some	Some	Good	Some or few	Few
Reliability	Good	Good	Great	Good	Good
Proof system	Axiomatic	Axiomatic	Axiomatic	Axiomatic	Axiomatic
Industrial strength	Some	Some	Great	Great	Great
Methods of verification	Theorem proving	Theorem proving	Both	Both	Both
Concurrency	None	None	None	Norm exist	None
Communication	None	None	None	Norm exist	None
Reverse engineering	Yes	Yes	Yes	No	No

Table 3.2(b) Logic-Based Formalisms

Criteria	ITL	DC	TAM	RTTL	RTL
Temporal model	Sparse	Dense	Sparse	Sparse	Sparse
Automated tools	Few	None	None	Few	None
Reliability	Good	Good	Good	Good	Good
Proof system	Axiomatic	Axiomatic	Axiomatic	Axiomatic	Axiomatic
Industrial strength	Great	Some	Great	Some	Some
Methods of veriification	Theorem proving	Theorem proving	Theorem proving	Theorem proving	Theorem proving
Concurrency	Parallel composition	None	Exist	Interleaved	Interleaved
Communication	Synchronous/ asynchronous	None	Exist	Synchronous	None
Reverse engineering	No	No	No	No	No

Table 3.3 Algebraic Formalisms

Criteria	OBJ	Larch
Temporal model	None	None
Automated tools	Few	Some
Reliability	Good	Good
Proof system	Axiomatic	Axiomatic
Industrial strength	Some	Great
Methods of verification	Theorem proving	Theorem proving
Concurrency	Interleaved	Interleaved
Communication	Synchronous	Synchronous
Reverse engineering	No	No

Table 3.4 Process Algebra Formalisms

Criteria	CSP	CCS	ACP	LOTOS	TCSP
Temporal model	None	None	None	None	Dense
Automated tools	Some	None	Good	Some	None
Reliability	Good	Good	Good	Good	Good
Proof system	Axiomatic	Bisimulation	Bisimulation	Bisimulation	Axiomatic
Industrial strength	Some	Some	Some	Great	Some
Methods of verification	Both	Both	Both	Model-checking	Both
Concurrency	Interleaved	Interleaved	Interleaved	Interleaved	Both
Communication	Synchronous/ asynchronous	Synchronous	Synchronous	Synchronous	Synchronous
Reverse engineering	No	No	No	No	No

Table 3.5 Graphic-Based Formalisms

Criteria	Petri Nets	Timed Petri Nets	Statecharts
Temporal model	None	Dense/sparse	Sparse
Automated tools	Some	None	None
Reliability	Good	Good	Good
Proof system	Reachability	Reachability	Axiomatic
Industrial strength	Some	Some	Some
Methods of verification	Model-checking	Model-checking	Model-checking
Concurrency	Interleaved	Interleaved	Exist
Communication	Synchronous	Synchronous	Synchronous
Reverse engineering	Yes	No	No

Table 3.6 Combined Formalisms

Criteria	TPCCS + TPCTL	Petri Nets + Predicate
Temporal model	Sparse	Sparse/dense
Automated tools	None	None
Reliability	Good	Good
Proof system	Axiomatic	Axiomatic
Industrial strength	Some	Unknown
Methods of verification	Theorem proving	Model-checking
Concurrency	Interleaved	Interleaved
Communication	Synchronous	Synchronous
Reverse engineering	No	No

Through reading Tables 3.1 to 3.6, we can draw the following conclusions regarding the current situation of formal methods for reengineering:

- Some formalisms are rather good in certain aspects of software development while others are good in other aspects. For example, ITL has a strong ability for representing and reasoning about most features of real-time systems. TPCCS and TPCTL are good at dealing with systems with reliability and probability features. Z is capable for large-scale industrial applications. B has a comprehensive automated toolkit. DC has advantages for its ability to deal with dense temporal models. Various process algebras are excellent for their abilities to represent and reason concurrency and communication. Finally, the most important features of net-based formalisms are their graphical representations: They are concise, easy to understand, and very clear.

- Only a very few formalisms have been applied as the theoretical foundation of reverse engineering, and of these, WSL/FermaT is clearly the best suited for reverse engineering sequential systems. For reengineering communicating processes, the best approach would be to combine WSL with an ITL-based logic with real-time features. Unlike all the other formal methods, WSL/FermaT was designed from the beginning for reverse engineering as well as forward engineering.

3.8 Analysis and summary

Reengineering generally consists of three stages—reverse engineering, funtional restructuring, and forward engineering. Because most existing formal approaches were developed for forward engineering, whether or not a formal approach has been used for reverse engineering is specially used as a criterion.

Graphical notations are also popular notations for reverse engineering (understanding) existing systems. Petri nets are useful for building a graphical model for reengineering.

Another factor that should be taken into consideration when reengineering computing systems is the recent rapid development of object-oriented technology. We believe that an approach that integrates formal methods, particular system domain features, and object-oriented techniques can contribute to improve reengineering in the following ways:

- *Existing software* can be easily understood and reengineered with the help of a successfully extracted semantics-oriented specification. An approach with a full consideration of the features of the system being reengineered will be more effective and efficient.

- *Object-oriented techniques,* which have been recognized as the best way currently available for structuring software systems, can help reengineering in grouping together data and operations performed on them, thereby encapsulating the whole system behind a clean interface, and organizing the resulting entities in a hierarchy based on specialization in functionalities.

- *Formal methods* can provide a solid theoretical foundation for the correctness and unambiguity of the approach and give more potential for automation of the approach. As a result, a practical software reengineering tool becomes feasible.

The following chapters introduce our approach to software evolution with the following features: (1) the ability to deal with sequential systems for both reverse engineering and forward engineering, (2) the ability to deal with parallel systems with communicating processes for both reverse

Key: FE—Forward engineering
FR—Functionality restructuring
RE—Reverse engineering

Figure 3.4 Evolutionary life of software.

engineering and forward engineering, and (3) the ability to deal with object-oriented systems. Finally, the evolutionary life of software is depicted in Figure 3.4.

References

[1] Arnold, R., *Software Reengineering,* Los Alamitos, CA: IEEE Computer Society Press, 1993.

[2] Arnold, R. S., and S. A. Bohner, "Impact Analysis—Towards a Framework for Comparison," in *Proceedings of the International Conference on Software Maintenance,* Lake Tahoe, Nevada: IEEE Computer Society Press, September 1993, pp. 292–301.

[3] Chikofsky, E., and J. Cross, "Reverse Engineering and Design Recovery: A Taxonomy," *IEEE Software,* Vol. 7, No. 1, January 1990, pp. 13–17.

[4] Karlsson, E. A., *Software Reuse—A Holistic Approach,* New York: John Wiley Ltd., 1995.

[5] Tilborg, A. M. V., and G. M. Koob, *Foundations of Real-Time Computing—Formal Specification and Methods,* Norwall, MA: Kluwer Academic Publishers, 1991.

[6] Bachman, R., *A CASE for Reverse Engineering,* Newton, MA: Cahner's, July 1988, reprinted from DATAMATION.

[7] Gallagher, K. B., and J. R. Lyle, "Using Program Slicing in Software Maintenance," *IEEE Trans. on Software Engineering,* August 1991.

[8] Bennett, K. H., "An Overview of Maintenance and Reverse Engineering," in *The REDO Compendium,* Chichester, U.K.: John Wiley and Sons, 1993.

[9] Antonini, P., et al., "Maintenance and Reverse Engineering: Low-Level Design Documents Production and Improvement," *Proc. Conference* in *Software Maintenance,* Austin, Texas, September 1987.

[10] Arango, G., et al., "TMM: Software Maintenance by Transformation," *IEEE Software,* May 1986.

[11] Bush, E., "Reverse Engineering: What and Why," *Software Maintenance Workshop,* Durham, U.K., 1990.

[12] Engberts, A., W. Kozaczynski, and J. Ning, "Concept Recognition–Based Program Transformation, *IEEE Conference on Software Maintenance, 1991,* Sorrento, Italy, 1991, pp. 73–82.

[13] Sneed, H. M., and G. Jandrasics, "Inverse Transformation of Software from Code to Specification," *IEEE Conference on Software Maintenance, 1988,* Phoenix, Arizona, 1988.

[14] Chen, Z., et al., "A Wide-Spectrum Language for Object-Based Development of Real-Time Systems," *Journal of Information Science*, 1999.

[15] Chen, Z., H. Zedan, and H. Yang, "Integrating Structured OO Approaches with Formal Techniques for the Development of Real-Time Systems," *Journal on Information and Software Technology*, 1999.

[16] Liu, X., H. Yang, and H. Zedan, "Formal Methods for the Reengineering of Computing Systems: A Comparison," *IEEE International Computer Software and Application Conference (COMPSAC'97)*, Washington, D.C., August 1997.

[17] Lu, C., et al., "Reverse Engineering," *Software Engineering and Knowledge Engineering Handbook* (accepted), 2002.

[18] Zedan, H., et al., "ATOM: An Object-Based Formal Method for Real-Time Systems," *Annals of Software Engineering*, 1999.

[19] Fraser, M. D., K. Kumer, and V. K. Vaishnavi, "Informal and Formal Requirements Specification Languages: Bridging the Gap," *IEEE Trans. on Software Engineering*, SE-17, No. 5, May 1991.

[20] Abrial, J. R., S. A. Schuman, and B. Meyer, *Specification Language Z*, Boston, MA: Computer Associates, Inc., 1979.

[21] Spivey, J. M., *Understanding Z*, Cambridge, England: Cambridge University Press, 1988.

[22] Cau, A., and H. Zedan, "Refining Interval Temporal Logic Specification," *Fourth AMAST Workshop on Real-Time Systems, Concurrent and Distributed Software (ARTS'97)*, Mallorca, Spain, May 1997.

[23] Cau, A., "Compositional Verification and Specification of Refinement for Reactive Systems in Dense Time Temporal Logic," Technical Report, January 1996.

[24] Hansson, H. A., "Time and Probability in Formal Design of Distributed Systems," *Real-Time Safety Critical Systems Series*, Vol. 2, 1994.

[25] Moszkowski, B., *Executing Temporal Logic Programs*, Cambridge, England: Cambridge University Press, 1986.

[26] Moszkowski, B., *A Temporal Logic for Multilevel Reasoning About Hardware*, IEEE Computer Society, February 1985.

[27] Scholefield, D., and H. Zedan, "TAM: A Formal Framework for the Development of Distributed Real-Time Systems," *Symposium on Formal Techniques in Real-Time and Fault-Tolerant Systems*, Nijmegen, the Netherlands, January 1992.

[28] Bjorner, D., and C. B. Jones, *Formal Specification and Software Development*, Englewood Cliffs, NJ: Prentice Hall, 1982.

[29] Jones, C. B., *Software Development: A Rigorous Approach*, Englewood Cliffs, NJ: Prentice Hall, 1980.

3.8 Analysis and summary

[30] Jones, C. B., *Systematic Software Development Using VDM,* Englewood Cliffs, NJ: Prentice Hall, 1986.

[31] Lano, K. C., and H. P. Haughton, "Formal Development in B," *Information and Software Technology,* Vol. 37, June 1995, pp. 303–316.

[32] Lano, K., *The B Language and Method: A Guide to Practical Formal Development,* Berlin: Springer-Verlag, 1996.

[33] Wordsworth, J., *Software Engineering with B,* Reading, MA: Addison-Wesley, 1996.

[34] Scholefield, D., *A Refinement Calculus for Real-Time Systems,* Ph.D. thesis, 1992.

[35] Ward, M., "Reverse Engineering Through Formal Transformation Knuths 'Polynomial Addition' Algorithm," *Comput. J.,* Vol. 37, No. 9, 1994, pp. 795–813 (http://www.dur.ac.uk/~dcs0mpw/martin/papers/poly-t.ps.gz).

[36] Ward, M., "Program Analysis by Formal Transformation," *Comput. J.,* Vol. 39, No. 7, 1996 (http://www.dur.ac.uk/~dcs0mpw/martin/papers/topsort-t.ps.gz).

[37] Ward, M., and K. H. Bennett, "A Practical Program Transformation System for Reverse Engineering," presented at the *Working Conference on Reverse Engineering,* Baltimore, MD, May 21–23, 1993 (http://www.dur.ac.uk/~dcs0mpw/martin/papers/icse.ps.gz).

[38] Cau, A., et al., "Using ITL and Tempura for Large Scale Specification and Simulation," *Proceedings of the Fourth EUROMICRO Workshop on Parallel and Distributed Processing,* Braga, Portugal: IEEE, 1996, pp. 493–500.

[39] Narayana, K. T., and A. A. Aaby, "Specification of Real-Time Temporal Interval Logic," *Proc. of Real-Time Systems Symposium,* IEEE Computer Society, December 1988, pp. 86–95.

[40] Chaochen, Z., C. A. R. Hoare, and A. P. Ravn, "A Calculus of Durations," *Information Processing Letters,* Vol. 40, May 1991, pp. 269–276.

[41] Chaochen, A., A. P. Ravn, and M. R. Hansen, "An Extended Duration Calculus for Hybrid Systems," R. L. Grossman et al. (eds.).

[42] Hoare, C. A. R., "An Axiomatic Basis for Computer Programming," *Comm. ACM,* 1969.

[43] Hoare, C. A. R., "Notes on Data Structuring," in *Structured Programming,* London: Academic Press, Inc., 1972.

[44] Hoare, C. A. R., "Proof of a Structured Program: The Sieve of Eratosthenes," *Computer,* Vol. 14, No. 4, 1972.

[45] Dijkstra, E. W., and C. S. Scholten, *Predicate Calculus and Program Semantics,* Berlin: Springer-Verlag, 1990.

[46] Cheng, B. H. C., and G. C. Gannod, "Abstraction of Formal Specifications from Program Code," *Proceedings for the Third International Conference on Tools for Artificial Intelligence,* 1991, pp. 125–128.

[47] Gannod, C., and B. H. C. Cheng, "Strongest Postcondition Semantics as a Basis for Reverse Engineering," *Proc. of IEEE Working Conference on Reverse Engineering*, Toronto, Ontario, July 1995, pp. 188–197.

[48] Hooman, J., *Specification and Compositional Verification of Real-Time Systems*, Ph.D. thesis, Eindhoven, the Netherlands, 1991.

[49] Dijkstra, E. W., *A Discipline of Programming*, Englewood Cliffs, NJ: Prentice Hall, 1976.

[50] Ward, M., *Proving Program Refinements and Transformations*, Oxford University, Ph.D. thesis, 1989.

[51] Ward, M., "Recursion Removal/Introduction by Formal Transformation: An Aid to Program Development and Program Comprehension," *Comput. J.*, Vol. 42, No. 8, 1999, pp. 650–673.

[52] Younger, E. J., and M. Ward, "Understanding Concurrent Programs Using Program Transformations," presented at the *Proc. of the 1993 2nd Workshop on Program Comprehension*, Capri, Italy, July 8–9, 1993 (http://www.dur.ac.uk/~dcs0mpw/martin/papers/cap.ps.gz).

[53] Younger, E. J., and M. Ward, "Inverse Engineering: A Simple Real-Time Program," *J. Software Maintenance: Research and Practice*, Vol. 6, 1993, pp. 197–234 (http://www.dur.ac.uk/~dcs0mpw/martin/papers/eddy-t.ps.gz).

[54] Chllas, B. F., *Modal Logic: An Introduction*, Cambridge, U.K.: Cambridge University Press, 1980.

[55] Mehmet, A., and M. Wanli, "An Overview of Temporal Logic Programming," First International Conference, *ICTL'94, Lecture Notes in AI*, Vol. 827, Berlin: Springer-Verlag, 1994, pp. 445–481.

[56] Rescher, N., and A. Urqhart, "Temporal Logic," *Library of Exact Philosophy*, Berlin: Springer-Verlag, 1971.

[57] Manna, Z., and A. Pnueli, *The Temporal Logic of Reactive and Concurrent Systems*, Berlin: Springer-Verlag, 1996.

[58] Benveniste, A., and P. K. Harter, "Proving Real-Time Properties of Programs with Temporal Logics," *Proceedings of ACM SIGOPAS Eighth Annual ACM Symposium on Operating Systems Principles*, December 1981, pp. 1–11.

[59] Ostroff, J. S., and W. M. Wonham, "A Temporal Logic Approach to Real-Time Control," *Proc. of the 24th IEEE Conference on Decision and Control*, Florida, December 1985, pp. 656–657.

[60] Scholefield, D., and H. Zedan, "TAM: A Temporal Agent Model for Distributed Real-Time Systems," FTRTFT 1992, Nijmegen, the Netherlands, LNCS 571, Berlin: Springer-Verlag, 1992, pp. 411–428.

[61] Scholefield, D., H. Zedan, and J. He, "A Specification-Oriented Semantics for the Refinement of Real-Time Systems," *Theoretical Computer Science*, Vol. 30, August 1994.

[62] Ostroff, J. S., "Temporal Logic for Real-Time Systems," *Advanced Software Development Series*, Sommerset, England, 1989.

[63] Ostroff, J. S., "Deciding Properties of Timed Transition Models," *IEEE Trans. on Parallel and Distributed Systems*, Vol. 1, April 1990, pp. 170–183.

[64] Jahanian, F., and A. Mok, "Safety Analysis of Timing Properties in Real-Time Systems," *IEEE Trans. on Software Engineering*, Vol. 12, September 1986.

[65] Goguen, J. A., and J. J. Tardo, "An Introduction to OBJ: A Language for Writing and Testing Formal Algebraic Program Specifications," *Software Specification Techniques*, Reading, MA: Addison-Wesley, 1986.

[66] Goguen, J., and J. Tardo, "An Introduction to OBJ: A Language for Writing and Testing Software Specifications," Marvin Zelkowitz (ed), *Specification of Reliable Software*, 1979, reprinted by Addison Wesley in 1985, *Specification Techniques*, pp. 391–420.

[67] Guttag. J., and J. Horning, *Larch: Languages and Tools for Formal Specification*, Berlin: Springer-Verlag, 1993.

[68] Hoare, C. A. R., *Communicating Sequential Processes*, Englewood Cliffs, NJ: Prentice Hall, 1985.

[69] Hoare, C. A. R., "Communicating Sequential Processes," *Communication of ACM*, Vol. 21, August 1978, pp. 666–677.

[70] Milner, R., "A Calculus of Communicating Systems," presented at *LNCS 90*, 1980.

[71] Milner, R., *Communication and Concurrency (Prentice-Hall International Series in Computer Science)*, Englewood Cliffs, NJ: Prentice Hall, 1989.

[72] Fencott, C., *Formal Methods for Concurrency*, London: International Thomson Publishing Company, 1996.

[73] Baeten, J. C. M., and J. A. Bergstra, "Real-Time Process Algebra," *Formal Aspects of Computing*, Vol. 3, February 1991, pp. 142–188.

[74] Bergstra, J. A., and J. W. Klop, "Process Algebra for Synchronous Communication," *Information and Control*, Vol. 60, January 1984, pp. 109–137.

[75] ISO, "Information Systems Processing—Open Systems Interconnection—LOTOS," Technical Report, 1987.

[76] Logrippo, L., T. Melanchuck, and R. J. D. Wors, "The Algebraic Specification Language LOTOS: An Industrial Experience," *ACM SIGSOFT Software Engineering Notes*, Vol. 15, April 1990, pp. 59–66.

[77] Eijk, P. H. J. van, C. A. Vissers, and M. Diaz, *The Formal Description Technique LOTOS*, Amsterdam: Elsevier Science Publishers, 1989.

[78] Reed, G. M., and A. W. Roscoe, "Timed CSP: Theory and Practice," *REX Workshop—Real Time: Theory and Practice*, Berlin: Springer-Verlag, 1992.

[79] Peterson, J. L., *Petri Net Theory and the Modeling of Systems*, Englewood Cliffs, NJ: Prentice Hall, 1981.

[80] Reisig, W., *Petri Nets: An Introduction*, Berlin: Springer-Verlag, 1985.

[81] Milner, R., "Some Directions in Concurrency Theory (panel statement)," *Proc. of the International Conference on the Fifth-Generation Computer Systems*, 1988.

[82] Berhomieu, B., and M. Diaz, "Modeling and Verification of Time-Dependent Systems Using Timed Petri Nets," *IEEE Trans. on Software Engineering*, Vol. 17, March 1991, pp. 259–273.

[83] Billington, J., G. R. Wheeler, and M. C. Wilbur-Ham, "PROTEAN: A High-Level Petri Net Tool for the Specification and Verification of Communication Protocols," *IEEE Trans. on Software Engineering*, Vol. 14, March 1988, pp. 301–316.

[84] Etessami, F. S., and G. S. Hura, "Rule-Based Design Methodology for Solving Control Problems," *IEEE Trans. on Software Engineering*, Vol. 17, March 1991, pp. 274–282.

[85] Leveson, N. G., and J. L. Stolzy, "Safety Analysis Using Petri Nets," *IEEE Trans. on Software Engineering*, Vol. 13, March 1987, pp. 386–397.

[86] Merlin, P. M., and A. Segall, "Recoverability of Communication Protocols—Implications of a Theoretical Study," *IEEE Trans. on Communications*, September 1976.

[87] Razouk, R. R., and C. V. Phelps, "Performance Analysis of Timed Petri Nets," *Proc. of the 4th International Workshop on Protocol Verification and Testing*, June 1984.

[88] Ramchandani, C., "Analysis of Asynchronous Concurrent Systems by Timed Petri Nets," Technical Report, February 1974.

[89] Hooman, J., S. Ramesh, and W. P. de Roever, "A Compositional Semantics for Statecharts," *Theoretical Computer Science* 101(2): 289–335, July 1992.

[90] Hooman, J. and W. P. de Roever, "Design and Verification in Real-Time Distributed Computing: An Introduction to Compositional Methods," in *Proceedings of the Ninth International Symposium on Protocol Specification, Testing, and Verification*, Enschede, North Holland, 1989.

[91] Alur, R., C. Courcoubetis, and D. L. Dill, "Model Checking for Real-Time Systems," *Proceedings of the 5th Annual IEEE Symposium on Logic in Computer Science*, 1990.

[92] Gabrielian, A., and M. K. Franklin, "State-Based Specification of Complex Real-Time Systems," *Proceedings of the Ninth Real-Time Systems Symposium*, December 1988, pp. 2–11.

CHAPTER 4

WSL and Transformation Theory

Contents

4.1 Introduction

4.2 Background

4.3 Syntax and semantics of the kernel language

4.4 Proving the correctness of a refinement

4.5 Algorithm derivation

4.6 Extending the kernel language

4.7 Example transformations

4.8 Why invent WSL?

References

Chapter 3 gave an overview of a number of different formal methods and discussed their application to systems evolution. This chapter focuses on one of the most successful formal methods for reengineering sequential systems: the WSL program transformation theory and the supporting FermaT workbench.

4.1 Introduction

A computer program is traditionally thought of as a list of detailed instructions, intended to be executed on a machine in order to produce a particular result. For example, the program in Figure 4.1 is intended to set z to the value x^n for nonnegative integer values of n. It also sets n to zero. Another way to think of a computer program is as a description of a function which translates an input state to an output state. If we start the program in Figure 4.1 in a state where x has the value 2 and n has the value 3, then it will run for a while (passing through various intermediate states) and then terminate in a state where z has the value 8 and n has the value 0.

Another way of describing the same mathematical function is the program in Figure 4.2. In this case, there is only one intermediate state.

A specification is also a description of a function, but in this case it does not have to be an executable program. For example, a program that sets x to a value that when squared equals 4 might be described as

$$z := 1;$$
$$\textbf{while}\ n > 0\ \textbf{do}$$
$$z := z*x;$$
$$n := n - 1\ \textbf{od}$$

Figure 4.1 A simple program.

$$z := x^n; n := 0$$

Figure 4.2 Another program.

$$x := x'.(x'^2 = 4)$$

Informally this specification says "assign a new value x' to x so that the condition $x'^2 = 4$ is satisfied." (The prime on x' allows us to describe a relationship between the old value of x and the new value x', which is about to be assigned to x).

In this case, there are two possible cases for the final value of x: $+2$ and -2. The specification does not specify which value is required, so we can assume that an implementor of the specification is allowed to choose whichever value is most convenient. To capture this range of implementation choices, the function we are describing must map an initial state to a *set* of possible final states.

A possible implementation of our specification is the simple assignment $x := 2$. This is a refinement of the original specification because the set of possible final states for the implementation is a subset of the final states for the program.

If a program S_1 is a refined by another program S_2 then we write $S_1 \leq S_2$. If also $S_2 \leq S_1$ then we say that the two programs are equivalent and write $S_1 \approx S_2$. In this case, the functions described by the two programs are identical—even if the programs themselves may look completely different.

If our specifications are written in a formally defined mathematical language, then it is possible to prove that a given program is a correct implementation of a given specification. For most programs however we want to break down this proof into a number of steps with a number of intermediate stages between specification and program. The easiest way to do this is to include specifications as part of our programming language: Then all the intermediate stages can be written in the same language, and all the proof steps can be carried out in that language. If our language also includes low-level programming constructs then it is called a wide-spectrum language (WSL) because it covers the whole spectrum from abstract mathematical specifications to executable implementations.

A program transformation is an operation that can be applied to a program to generate another equivalent program (provided any given applicability conditions are satisfied). This uses a wide spectrum language called WSL for which a powerful set of transformations can be used for refining specifications into programs, reverse-engineering programs into specifications, and analyzing the properties of programs.

4.2 Background

The following requirements went into the development of the WSL language and transformation theory:

1. General specifications in any sufficiently precise notation should be included in the language. For sufficiently precise we will mean anything that can be expressed in terms of mathematical logic with suitable notations. This will allow a wide range of forms of specification, for example **Z** specifications [1] and **VDM** [2] both use the language of mathematical logic and set theory (in different notations) to define specifications.

2. Nondeterministic programs should be used. Since we do not want to have to specify everything about the program with which we are working (certainly not in the first versions) we need some way of specifying that some executions will not necessarily result in a particular outcome but one of an allowed range of outcomes. The implementor can then use this latitude to provide a more efficient implementation that still satisfies the specification.

3. A well-developed catalog of proven transformations that do not require the user to discharge complex proof obligations before they can be applied is also necessary. In particular, it should be possible to introduce, analyze, and reason about iterative and recursive constructs without requiring loop invariants.

4. Techniques are needed to bridge the abstraction gap between specifications and programs.

5. The language needs to be applicable to real programs—not just those in a "toy" programming language with few constructs. This is achieved by (programming) language independence and the extendibility of the notation via definitional transformations.

6. The language must be scalable to large programs: This implies a language that is expressive enough to allow automatic translation from existing programming languages, together with the ability to cope with unstructured programs and a high degree of complexity.

The FermaT transformation system that is built on the transformation theory has applications in the following areas:

- Improving the maintainability (in particular, flexibility and reliability, and hence extending the lifetime) of existing mission-critical software systems;

- Translating programs to modern programming languages (for example, from obsolete assembler languages to modern high-level languages);

- Developing and maintaining safety-critical applications;[1]

- Extracting reusable components from current systems, deriving their specifications, and storing the specification, implementation, and development strategy in a repository for subsequent reuse;

- Reverse engineering from existing systems to high-level specifications, followed by subsequent reengineering and evolutionary development.

The WSL language is built up in a series of stages or levels, starting with a very small and mathematically tractable kernel language.

Sections 4.3 and 4.4 develop the theory of how to prove the correctness of a program transformation. It is not necessary for the user to understand this theory in order to use program transformations in a reverse engineering or reengineering project. Program transformation users who are not interested in the theory are encouraged to skip to Section 4.5.

---

1   Such systems can be developed by transforming high-level specifications down to efficient low-level code with a very high degree of confidence that the code correctly implements every part of the specification. When enhancements or modifications are required, these can be carried out on the appropriate specification, followed by rerunning as much of the formal development as possible. Alternatively, the changes could be made at a lower level, with formal inverse engineering used to determine the impact on the formal specification.

4.3 Syntax and semantics of the kernel language

4.3.1 Syntax

Our kernel language consists of four primitive statements, two of which contain formulae of infinitary first-order logic, and three compound statements. Let **P** and **Q** be any formulae, and **x** and **y** be any nonempty lists of variables. The following are primitive statements:

1. *Assertion:* {**P**} is an assertion statement that acts as a partial **skip** statement. If the formula **P** is true then the statement terminates immediately without changing any variables, otherwise it aborts (we treat abnormal termination and nontermination as equivalent, so a program that aborts is equivalent to one that never terminates).

2. *Guard:* [**Q**] is a guard statement. It always terminates, and enforces **Q** to be true at this point in the program without changing the values of any variables. It has the effect of restricting previous nondeterminism to those cases that will cause **Q** to be true at this point. If this cannot be ensured then the set of possible final states is empty, and therefore all the final states will satisfy any desired condition (including **Q**).

3. *Add variables:* **add**(**x**) adds the variables in **x** to the state space (if they are not already present) and assigns arbitrary values to them.

4. *Remove variables:* **remove**(**y**) removes the variables in **y** from the state space (if they are present).

There is a rather pleasing duality between the assertion and guard statements, and the **add** and **remove** statements.

For any kernel language statements S_1 and S_2, the following are also kernel language statements:

1. *Sequence:* $(S_1; S_2)$ executes S_1 followed by S_2;

2. *Nondeterministic choice:* $(S_1 \sqcap S_2)$ chooses one of S_1 or S_2 for execution, the choice being made nondeterministically;

3. *Recursion:* $(\mu X.S_1)$ where X is a statement variable (taken from a suitable set of symbols). The statement S_1 may contain occurrences of X as one or more of its component statements. These represent recursive calls to the procedure whose body is S_1.

At first sight, this kernel language may seem to be missing some essential programming constructs such as assignment statements and **if** statements. However, the guard statement can be composed with a nondeterministic statement to get a deterministic result. For example, an assignment such as $x := 1$ is constructed by giving x an arbitrary value and then restricting its value to the one required: **add**($\langle x \rangle$); $[x = 1]$. For an assignment such as $x := x + 1$, where the new value of x depends on the old value, we need to record the required new value of x in a new variable, x' say, before copying it into x. So we can construct $x := x + 1$ as follows:

add($\langle x' \rangle$); $[x' = x + 1]$; **add**($\langle x \rangle$); $[x = x']$; **remove**(x')

An **if** statement such as **if** B **then** S_1 **else** S_2 **fi** is constructed from a nondeterministic choice with guards to make the choice deterministic:

([**B**]; S_1) ⊓ ([¬**B**]; S_2)

For Dijkstra's guarded commands [3] such as: **if** $B_1 \rightarrow S_1 \square B_2 \rightarrow S_2$ **fi** we need to ensure that the command will abort in the case where none of the guard conditions are true:

{$B_1 \vee B_2$}; ([B_1]; S_1) ⊓ ([B_2]; S_2)

Three fundamental statements can be defined immediately:

abort $=_{DF}$ {**false**}   **null** $=_{DF}$ [**false**]   **skip** $=_{DF}$ {**true**}

where **true** and **false** are universally true and universally false formulae. The **abort** statement never terminates when started in any initial state. **skip** is a statement that always terminates immediately in the same state in which it was started. **null** is a rather unusual statement: It always terminates but the set of final states is empty. This statement is a correct refinement of any specification whatsoever. Morgan [4] uses the term *miracle* for such statements. Clearly, any null statement and guard statements in general cannot be directly implemented: If a program terminates, then it must terminate in some state or other, and a program cannot in general force a condition to be true without changing the value of a variable.

Null statements are nonetheless a useful theoretical tool, but as it is only null-free statements that are implementable, it is important to be able to distinguish easily which statements are null-free. This is the motivation for the definition of our specification statement in Section 4.3.2.

The kernel language statements have been described as "the quarks of programming," mysterious objects that (in the case of the guard at least) are not implementable in isolation, but that in combination form the familiar atomic operations of assignment and **if** statements.

4.3 Syntax and semantics of the kernel language

4.3.2 The specification statement

A specification describes what a program should do while abstracting away the implementation details of how the result is to be achieved. In mathematical terms, a specification is a description of the relationship between input and output states of the program; however, it does not necessarily describe how this relationship is to be achieved. Suppose we have a list x of variables that are the outputs of the program and suppose that the formula **Q** describes the relationship between the new values x' that we wish to assign to x and the original values. This specification is described by the statement

$$x := x'.\mathbf{Q}$$

This statement assigns new values to the variables in x so that the formula **Q** is true where (within **Q**) x represents the old values and x' represents the new values. If there are no values x' that satisfy **Q** then the statement aborts. The formal definition of this specification statement is:

$$x := x'.\mathbf{Q} =_{\text{DF}} \{\exists x'.\mathbf{Q}\}; \mathbf{add}(x'); [\mathbf{Q}]; \mathbf{add}(x); [x = x']; \mathbf{remove}(x')$$

The initial assertion ensures that this statement is null-free.

As an example, we can specify a program to sort the array A using a single specification statement:

$$A := A'.(\mathbf{sorted}\ (A') \land \mathbf{permutation\_of}\ (A', A))$$

This says "assign a new value A' to A, which is a sorted array and a permutation, of the original value of A"; it precisely describes what we want our sorting program to do without saying how it is to be achieved. In other words, it is not biased toward a particular sorting algorithm. In [5] we take this specification as our starting point for the "derivation by formal transformation" of several efficient sorting algorithms, including insertion sort, quicksort, and a hybrid sort.

The simple assignment $v := e$, where v is a variable and e is an expression, is defined as the specification statement $\langle v \rangle := \langle v' \rangle.(v' = e)$. Morgan and others [4, 6–8] use a different specification statement, written

x: [Pre, Post]

where **x** is a sequence of variables and **Pre** and **Post** are formulae of finitary first-order logic. This statement is guaranteed to terminate for all initial states that satisfy **Pre** and will terminate in a state that satisfies **Post**, while only assigning to variables in the list **x**. In our notation an equivalent statement is {**Pre**}; **add**(**x**); [**Post**]. The disadvantage of this notation is that it is not necessarily null-free (the statement ⟨⟩: [**true**, **false**], for example, is equivalent to **null**). As a result, the user is responsible for ensuring that he or she never accidentally refines a specification into an (unimplementable) null statement.

4.3.3 States and state transformations

The functions that are defined by WSL programs are called state transformations. These functions map an initial state to a set of possible final states, with a special state, denoted $\bot$, to include the possibility that the program may never terminate. A state s other than $\bot$ is a partial function that gives the values of all the variables in the state space (the set of variables on which the program operates).

For example, the state transformation for the assignment $i := i + 1$ maps each initial state s to a singleton set $\{s'\}$ of final states, where s' gives the value $s(i) + 1$ to the variable i and for all other variables, $s'(x) = s(x)$.

Despite the large amount of research and development on stateless functional programming, the vast majority of programs in the world are written in imperative languages, so for a reverse engineering technology it is important (if not imperative) that we can cope easily with imperative programs.

4.3.4 Refinement of state transformations

When we say that one program is a refinement of another, we mean that any specification the program satisfies is guaranteed to be satisfied by the program's refinement. In other words, the refinement is at least as good at satisfying specifications as the original program. A specification of a program can be defined by giving a set of states (those initial states for which the program's behavior is to be specified) called the *defined set* and for each of these initial states, a set of allowed final states. A program satisfies the specification if, for each initial state in the defined set, the program is guaranteed to terminate in one of the allowed final states. A specification can therefore be given in the form of a state transformation f where $f(s)$ contains $\bot$ if s is not in the defined set of states, and for every other s, $f(s)$ is the set of allowed final states. Conversely, any state transformation also defines a specification.

We can therefore define *satisfaction of a specification* as a relation between state transformations. We can also define a refinement of a state transformation to be a state transformation that satisfies all the specifications satisfied by the first state transformation.

4.3 Syntax and semantics of the kernel language

With these definitions it turns out that refinement and satisfaction are identical concepts: A state transformation f_2 is a refinement of state transformation f_1 if and only if it satisfies f_1 (considered as a specification).

4.3.5 Recursion

A program containing calls to a procedure whose definition is not provided can be thought of as a function from state transformations to state transformations, because the incomplete program can be completed by filling in the body of the procedure. For a recursive procedure call, we fill in the procedure body with copies of itself, but this means that the result of the fill in is still incomplete because it will still contain recursive calls. However, the expanded program is nearer to completion in some sense that we will make precise. A recursive procedure can be considered as the limit formed by joining together the results of an infinite sequence of such filling-in operations.

Definition 4.1 *Recursion:* Suppose we have a function $\mathscr{F}$ that maps the set of state transformations $F_{\mathscr{H}}(V, V)$ to itself. We want to define a recursive state transformation from $\mathscr{F}$ as the limit of the sequence of state transformations $\mathscr{F}(\Omega)$, $\mathscr{F}(\mathscr{F}(\Omega))$, $\mathscr{F}(\mathscr{F}(\mathscr{F}(\Omega)))$, ... (where Ω is the state transformation for **abort**). With the definition of state transformation given above, this limit $(\mu.\mathscr{F})$ has a particularly simple and elegant definition:

$$(\mu.\mathscr{F}) =_{\text{DF}} \bigsqcup_{n<\omega} \mathscr{F}^n(\Omega) \quad \text{i.e., for each } s \in V_{\mathscr{H}}: \quad (\mu.\mathscr{F})(s) = \bigcap_{n<\omega} \mathscr{F}^n(\Omega)(s)$$

From this definition we see that $\mathscr{F}((\mu.\mathscr{F})) = (\mu.\mathscr{F})$. Accordingly, the state transformation $(\mu.\mathscr{F})$ is a fixed point for the function $\mathscr{F}$; it is, in fact, the least fixed point.

We say $\mathscr{F}^n(\Omega)$ is the *n*th truncation of $(\mu.\mathscr{F})$: as n increases the truncations get closer to $(\mu.\mathscr{F})$. The larger truncations provide more information about $(\mu.\mathscr{F})$—more initial states for which it terminates and a more restricted set of final states. The $\bigsqcup$ operation collects together all this information to form $(\mu.\mathscr{F})$.

4.3.6 Weakest preconditions

We define the weakest precondition, wp(f, e) of a state transformation f and a condition on the final state e to be the weakest condition on the initial state space such that if s satisfies this condition then all elements of $f(s)$ satisfy e. A condition on states is simply a set of states: the set of states that satisfies the condition. The special state $\perp$ is defined as not satisfying any condition. Thus, $\text{wp}(f, e)$ is simply the set of proper initial states s such that $f(s)$ is a subset of e.

The importance of weakest preconditions is shown by the fact that the refinement relation can be characterized using the weakest preconditions. State transformation f_1 is refined by f_2 if and only if for every final state condition e we have $\text{wp}(f_1, e) \subseteq \text{wp}(f_2, e)$.

This characterization of refinement still requires us to examine every possible final state condition in order to determine if one state transformation is a refinement of another. A theorem in [9] shows that it is only necessary to examine two special postconditions: the condition **true** and the condition $\mathbf{x} \neq \mathbf{x}'$, where $\mathbf{x}$ is a list of all the variables used in the program and $\mathbf{x}'$ is a list of variables not used anywhere in the program (and the length of the two lists is the same).

The fact that refinement can be defined directly from the weakest precondition will later prove to be vitally important.

4.3.7 Weakest preconditions of statements

We can also define a weakest precondition for kernel language statements as a formula of infinitary logic. Infinitary logics are an extension of first-order logic that allows conjunction and disjunction over infinite lists of formulae. See [10, 11] for a general introduction to infinitary logics. These were first used to define the semantics of programs by Engeler [12] and are used to express weakest preconditions by Back [13].

WP is a function that takes a statement (a syntactic object) and a formula from our infinitary logic $\mathscr{L}$ (another syntactic object) and returns another formula in $\mathscr{L}$.

Definition 4.2 For any kernel language statement $\mathbf{S}: V \to W$, and formula $\mathbf{R}$ whose free variables are all in W, we define $\mathbf{WP}(\mathbf{S}, \mathbf{R})$ as follows:

1. $\mathbf{WP}(\{\mathbf{P}\}, \mathbf{R}) =_{\text{DF}} \mathbf{P} \wedge \mathbf{R}$
2. $\mathbf{WP}([\mathbf{Q}], \mathbf{R}) =_{\text{DF}} \mathbf{Q} \Rightarrow \mathbf{R}$
3. $\mathbf{WP}(\mathbf{add}(\mathbf{x}), \mathbf{R}) =_{\text{DF}} \forall \mathbf{x}.\mathbf{R}$
4. $\mathbf{WP}(\mathbf{remove}(\mathbf{x}), \mathbf{R}) =_{\text{DF}} \mathbf{R}$
5. $\mathbf{WP}((\mathbf{S}_1; \mathbf{S}_2), \mathbf{R}) =_{\text{DF}} \mathbf{WP}(\mathbf{S}_1, \mathbf{WP}(\mathbf{S}_2, \mathbf{R}))$

4.3 Syntax and semantics of the kernel language

6. $\text{WP}((S_1 \sqcap S_2), R) =_{DF} \text{WP}(S_1, R) \wedge \text{WP}(S_2, R)$
7. $\text{WP}((\mu X.S), R) =_{DF} \bigvee_{n<\omega} \text{WP}((\mu X.S)^n, R)$

where $(\mu X.S)^0 = \textbf{abort}$ and $(\mu X.S)^{n+1} = S[(\mu X.S)^n/X]$, which is **S** with all occurrences of X replaced by $(\mu X.S)^n$.

For the fundamental statements we have

$\text{WP}(\textbf{abort}, R) = \textbf{false}$
$\text{WP}(\textbf{skip}, R) = R$
$\text{WP}(\textbf{null}, R) = \textbf{true}$

For the specification statement $\mathbf{x} := \mathbf{x}'.Q$ we have

$\text{WP}(\mathbf{x} := \mathbf{x}'.Q, R) \iff \exists \mathbf{x}' Q \wedge \forall \mathbf{x}'.(Q \Rightarrow R[\mathbf{x}'/\mathbf{x}])$

For Morgan's specification statement $\mathbf{x}: [\textbf{Pre}, \textbf{Post}]$ we have

$\text{WP}(\mathbf{x}: [\textbf{Pre}, \textbf{Post}], R) \iff \textbf{Pre} \Rightarrow \forall \mathbf{x}.(\textbf{Post} \Rightarrow R)$

The Hoare predicate (defining partial correctness): $\{\textbf{Pre}\}S\{\textbf{Post}\}$ is true if whenever **S** terminates after starting in an initial state that satisfies **Pre** then the final state will satisfy **Post**. We can express this in terms of WP as

$\textbf{Pre} \Rightarrow (\text{WP}(S, \textbf{true}) \Rightarrow \text{WP}(S, \textbf{Post}))$.

For the **if** statement discussed in Section 4.3.1:

$\text{WP}(\textbf{if } B \textbf{ then } S_1 \textbf{ else } S_2 \textbf{ fi}, R)$
$\iff (B \Rightarrow \text{WP}(S_1, R)) \wedge (\neg B \Rightarrow \text{WP}(S_2, R))$

Similarly, for the Dijkstra guarded command:

$\text{WP}(\textbf{if } B_1 \rightarrow S_1 \square B_2 \rightarrow S_2 \textbf{ fi}, R)$
$\iff (B_1 \vee B_2) \wedge (B_1 \Rightarrow \text{WP}(S_1, R)) \wedge (B_2 \Rightarrow \text{WP}(S_2, R))$

The weakest precondition captures the semantics of a program in the sense that, for any two programs $S_1: V \rightarrow W$ and $S_2: V \rightarrow W$, the statement S_2 is a correct refinement of S_1 if and only if the formula

$(\text{WP}(S_1, \mathbf{x} \neq \mathbf{x}') \Rightarrow \text{WP}(S_2, \mathbf{x} \neq \mathbf{x}')) \wedge (\text{WP}(S_1, \textbf{true}) \Rightarrow \text{WP}(S_2, \textbf{true}))$

is a theorem of first-order logic, where **x** is a list of all variables assigned to by either S_1 or S_2, and $\mathbf{x}'$ is a list of new variables. This means that proving a refinement or implementation or equivalence amounts to proving a theorem of first order logic. Back [13, 14] and Morgan [4, 7] both use weakest preconditions in this way, but Back has to extend the logic with a new predicate symbol to represent the postcondition, and Morgan has to use second-order logic with quantification over formulae.

4.4 Proving the correctness of a refinement

We can define refinement between statements as the refinements of their interpretations under some structure. This is called *semantic refinement*.

Definition 4.3 *Semantic refinement of statements:* If $\mathbf{S}, \mathbf{S}': V \rightarrow W$ have no free statement variables and $\text{int}_M(\mathbf{S}, V) \leqslant \text{int}_M(\mathbf{S}', V)$ for a structure M of $\mathscr{L}$ then we say that $\mathbf{S}$ is refined by $\mathbf{S}'$ under M and write $\mathbf{S} \leqslant_M \mathbf{S}'$. If Δ is a set of sentences in $\mathscr{L}$ (formulae with no free variables) and $\mathbf{S} \leqslant_M \mathbf{S}'$ is true for every structure M in which each sentence in Δ is true then we write $\Delta \vDash \mathbf{S} \leqslant \mathbf{S}'$. A structure in which every element of a set Δ of sentences is true is called a *model* for Δ.

It is also useful to be able to prove the correctness of a refinement of statements directly from their weakest preconditions, without first having to calculate the corresponding state transformations. From Chapter 3 we know that refinement can be characterized by two special weakest preconditions. This is the motivation for the proof-theoretic definition of statement refinement that uses the weakest precondition **WP**.

Definition 4.4 *Proof-theoretic refinement:* If $\mathbf{S}, \mathbf{S}': V \rightarrow W$ have no free statement variables and $\mathbf{x}$ is a sequence of all variables assigned to in either $\mathbf{S}$ or $\mathbf{S}'$, and the formulae $\mathbf{WP}(\mathbf{S}, \mathbf{x} \neq \mathbf{x}') \Rightarrow \mathbf{WP}(\mathbf{S}', \mathbf{x} \neq \mathbf{x}')$ and $\mathbf{WP}(\mathbf{S}, \mathbf{x} \neq \mathbf{x}') \Rightarrow \mathbf{WP}(\mathbf{S}', \mathbf{x} \neq \mathbf{x}')$ are provable from the set Δ of sentences, then we say that $\mathbf{S}$ is refined by $\mathbf{S}'$ and write: $\Delta \vdash \mathbf{S} \leqslant \mathbf{S}'$.

Theorem 4.1 shows that, for countable sets Δ, these two notions of refinement are equivalent.

Theorem 4.1 If $\mathbf{S}, \mathbf{S}': V \rightarrow W$ have no free statement variables and Δ is any countable set of sentences of $\mathscr{L}$, then

$$\Delta \vDash \mathbf{S} \leqslant \mathbf{S}' \iff \Delta \vdash \mathbf{S} \leqslant \mathbf{S}'$$

This theorem provides two different methods for proving a refinement. More importantly though, it proves the connection between the intuitive model of a program as something that starts in one state and terminates (if at all) in some other state, and the weakest preconditions $\mathbf{WP}(\mathbf{S}, \mathbf{x} \neq \mathbf{x}')$ and

4.4 Proving the correctness of a refinement

WP(S, true). For a nondeterministic program there may be several possible final states for each initial state. This idea is precisely captured by the state transformation model of programs and refinement. In the predicate transformer model of programs, which forms the foundation for [4] and others, the meaning of a program **S** is defined to be a function that maps a postcondition **R** to the weakest precondition **WP(S, R)**. This model certainly does not "correspond closely with the way that computers operate" [15] although it does have the advantage that weakest preconditions are generally easier to reason about than state transformations. Thus a theorem that proves the equivalence of the two models allows us to prove refinements using the weakest preconditions, while doing justice to the more intuitive model.

The theorem also illustrates the importance of using the infinitary logic $\mathscr{L}_{\omega_1 \omega}$ rather than a higher-order logic, or indeed a larger infinitary logic. Back and von Wright [16] describe an implementation of the refinement calculus, based on (finitary) higher-order logic using the refinement rule $\forall \mathbf{R}.\mathbf{WP}(\mathbf{S}_1, \mathbf{R}) \Rightarrow \mathbf{WP}(\mathbf{S}_2, \mathbf{R})$ where the quantification is over all predicates (boolean state functions). However, the completeness theorem fails for all higher-order logics. Karp [10] proved that the completeness theorem holds for $\mathscr{L}_{\omega_1 \omega}$ and fails for all infinitary logics larger than $\mathscr{L}_{\omega_1 \omega}$. Finitary logic is not sufficient because it is difficult to determine a finite formula giving the weakest precondition for an arbitrary recursive or iterative statement. Using $\mathscr{L}_{\omega_1 \omega}$ (the smallest infinitary logic) we simply form the infinite disjunction of the weakest preconditions of all finite truncations of the recursion or iteration. We avoid the need for quantification over formulae because, with our proof-theoretic refinement method, the two postconditions $\mathbf{x} \neq \mathbf{x}'$ and **true** are sufficient. Thus we can be confident that the proof method is both consistent and complete, considering the following:

1. If the weakest precondition formula can be proved, for statement $\mathbf{S}_1$ and $\mathbf{S}_2$, then $\mathbf{S}_2$ is certainly a refinement of $\mathbf{S}_1$.

2. If $\mathbf{S}_1$ is refined by $\mathbf{S}_2$ then there certainly exists a proof the corresponding **WP** formula.

Basing our transformation theory on any other logic would not provide the two different proof methods we require.

Definition 4.5 *Statement equivalence:* If $\Delta \vdash \mathbf{S} \leq \mathbf{S}'$ and $\Delta \vdash \mathbf{S}' \leq \mathbf{S}$, then we say that statements **S** and **S**′ are equivalent and write: $\Delta \vdash \mathbf{S} \approx \mathbf{S}'$. Similarly, if $\Delta \vDash \mathbf{S} \leq \mathbf{S}'$ and $\Delta \vdash \mathbf{S}' \leq \mathbf{S}$, then we write $\Delta \vdash \mathbf{S} \approx \mathbf{S}'$. From Theorem 4.1 we have $\Delta \vDash \mathbf{S} \approx \mathbf{S}'$ iff $\Delta \vdash \mathbf{S} \approx \mathbf{S}'$.

4.4.1 Expressing a statement as a specification

The formulae **WP**(**S**, **x** ≠ **x**′) and **WP**(**S**, **true**) tell us everything we need to know about **S** in order to determine whether a given statement is equivalent to it. In fact, as the next theorem shows, if we also know **WP**(**S**, **false**) (which is always **false** for null-free programs) then we can construct a specification statement equivalent to **S**.

Theorem 4.2 *The representation theorem:* Let $\mathbf{S}: V \to V$, be any kernel language statement and let **x** be a list of all the variables assigned to by **S**. Then for any countable set Δ of sentences:

$$\Delta \vdash \mathbf{S} \approx [\neg \mathbf{WP}(\mathbf{S}, \mathbf{false})]; \mathbf{x} := \mathbf{x}'.(\neg \mathbf{WP}(\mathbf{S}, \mathbf{x} \neq \mathbf{x}') \wedge \mathbf{WP}(\mathbf{S}, \mathbf{true}))$$

Although this would seem to solve all reverse engineering problems at a stroke, and therefore be a great aid to software maintenance and re-engineering, the theorem has fairly limited value for practical programs, especially those that contain loops or recursion. This is partly because there are many different possible representations of the specification of a program, only some of which are useful for software maintenance. In particular the maintainer wants a short, high-level, abstract version of the program, rather than a mechanical translation into an equivalent specification (see [17] for a discussion on defining different levels of abstraction). In practice, a number of techniques are needed including a combination of automatic processes and human guidance to form a practical program analysis system. An example of such a system is the FermaT system [18–20], which uses transformations developed from the theoretical foundations presented here.

The theorem is of considerable theoretical value however in showing the power of the specification statement: In particular it tells us that the specification statement is certainly sufficiently expressive for writing the specification of any computer program whatsoever. Second, we will use the theorem in Chapter 3 to add a join construct to the language and derive its weakest precondition. This means that we can use join to write programs and specifications, without needing to extend the kernel language. Third, we use it in Chapter 3 to add arbitrary (countable) join and choice operators to the language, again without needing to extend the kernel language.

4.4.2 Some basic transformations

This section proves some fundamental transformations of recursive programs. The general induction rule shows how the truncations of a recursion capture

4.4 Proving the correctness of a refinement

the semantics of the full recursion—each truncation contains some information about the recursion, and the set of all truncations is sufficient for proving refinement and equivalence. This induction rule proves to be an essential tool in the development of a transformation catalog. We will use it almost immediately in the proof of a fold/unfold transformation (Lemma 4.4).

Lemma 4.1 The induction rule for recursion: If Δ is any countable set of sentences and the statements $\mathbf{S}, \mathbf{S}': V \to V$ have the same initial and final state spaces, then

1. $\Delta \vdash (\mu X.\mathbf{S})^k \leq (\mu X.\mathbf{S})$ for every $k < \omega$;
2. If $\Delta \vdash (\mu X.\mathbf{S})^n \leq \mathbf{S}'$ for all $n < \omega$ then $\Delta \vdash (\mu X.\mathbf{S}) \leq \mathbf{S}'$.

An important property for any notion of refinement is the replacement property: If any component of a statement is replaced by any refinement then the resulting statement is a refinement of the original one. This is easily proved by induction on the structure of statements. The induction steps use Lemma 4.2.

Lemma 4.2 *Replacement:* if $\Delta \vdash \mathbf{S}_1 \leq \mathbf{S}'_1$ and $\Delta \vdash \mathbf{S}_2 \leq \mathbf{S}'_2$, then

1. $\Delta \vdash (\mathbf{S}_1; \mathbf{S}_2) \leq (\mathbf{S}'_1; \mathbf{S}'_2)$;
2. $\Delta \vdash (\mathbf{S}_1 \sqcap \mathbf{S}_2) \leq (\mathbf{S}'_1 \sqcap \mathbf{S}'_2)$;
3. $\Delta \vdash (\mu X.\mathbf{S}_1) \leq (\mu X.\mathbf{S}'_1)$.

Proof: Cases (1) and (2) follow by considering the corresponding weakest preconditions. For case (3) use the induction hypothesis to show that for all $n < \omega$: $(\mu X.\mathbf{S}_1)^n \leq (\mu X.\mathbf{S}'_1)^n$ [since $(\mu X.\mathbf{S}_1)^n$ has a lower depth of recursion nesting than $(\mu X.\mathbf{S}_1)$] and then apply the induction rule for recursion.

We can use these lemmas to prove a much more useful induction rule that is not limited to a single recursive procedure but can be used on statements containing one or more recursive components. For any statement $\mathbf{S}$, define $\mathbf{S}^n$ to be $\mathbf{S}$ with each recursive statement replaced by its nth truncation.

Lemma 4.3 The general induction rule for recursion: If $\mathbf{S}$ is any statement with bounded nondeterminacy, and $\mathbf{S}'$ is another statement such that $\Delta \vdash \mathbf{S}^n \leq \mathbf{S}'$ for all $n < \omega$, then $\Delta \vdash \mathbf{S} \leq \mathbf{S}'$.

Lemma 4.4 uses the general induction rule to prove a transformation for folding (and unfolding) a recursive procedure by replacing all occurrences of the call by copies of the procedure. In [21] we generalize this transformation to a "partial unfolding" where selected recursive calls may be conditionally unfolded or replaced by a copy of the procedure body.

Lemma 4.4 *Fold/unfold:* For any $\mathbf{S}: V \to V$:

$$\Delta \vdash (\mu X . \mathbf{S}) \approx \mathbf{S}[(\mu X . \mathbf{S})/X]$$

4.4.3 Proof rules for implementations

This subsection develops two general proof rules. The first is for proving the correctness of a potential implementation $\mathbf{S}$, of a specification expressed in the form $\{\mathbf{P}\}; x := x'.\mathbf{Q}$. The second is for proving that a given recursive procedure statement is a correct implementation of a given statement. This latter rule is very important in the process of transforming a specification, probably expressed using recursion, into a recursive procedure that implements that specification. In [21–24] techniques are presented for transforming recursive procedures into various iterative forms. This theorem is also useful in deriving iterative implementations of specifications, since very often the most convenient derivation is via a recursive formulation.

Implementation of specifications The first proof rule is based on a proof rule in Back [13], we have extended this to include recursion and guard statements. This proof rule provides a means of proving that a statement $\mathbf{S}$ is a correct implementation of a specification $\{\mathbf{P}\}; x := x'.\mathbf{Q}$. Any $\mathbf{Z}$ specification, for example, can be cast into this form.

Theorem 4.3 Let Δ be a countable set of sentences of $\mathscr{L}$. Let V be a finite nonempty set of variables and $\mathbf{S}: V \to W$ a statement. Let $\mathbf{y}$ be a list of all the variables in $V - \tilde{\mathbf{x}}$ that are assigned to somewhere in $\mathbf{S}$. Let $\mathbf{x}_0, \mathbf{y}_0$ be lists of distinct variables not in $\mathbf{S}$ or V with $\ell(\mathbf{x}_0) = \ell(\mathbf{x})$ and $\ell(\mathbf{y}_0) = \ell(\mathbf{y})$.

If $\Delta \vdash (\mathbf{P} \wedge \mathbf{x} = \mathbf{x}_0 \wedge \mathbf{y} = \mathbf{y}_0) \Rightarrow \mathbf{WP}(\mathbf{S}, \mathbf{Q}[\mathbf{x}_0/\mathbf{x}, \mathbf{x}/\mathbf{x}'] \wedge \mathbf{y} = \mathbf{y}_0)$
then $\Delta \vdash \{\mathbf{P}\}; \mathbf{x} := \mathbf{x}'.\mathbf{Q} \leqslant \mathbf{S}$

The premise states that if $\mathbf{x}_0$ and $\mathbf{y}_0$ contain the initial values of $\mathbf{x}$ and $\mathbf{y}$ then $\mathbf{S}$ preserves the value of $\mathbf{y}$ and sets $\mathbf{x}$ to a value $\mathbf{x}'$ such that the relationship between the initial value of $\mathbf{x}$ and $\mathbf{x}'$ satisfies $\mathbf{Q}$.

4.4 Proving the correctness of a refinement

This theorem is really only useful for simple implementations of a single specification statement. More complex specifications will be implemented as recursive or iterative procedures; in either case we can use the following theorem to develop a recursive implementation as the first stage. This can be transformed into an iterative program (if required) using the techniques on recursion removal in [21–24].

Recursive implementation of general statements   This section proves an important theorem on the recursive implementation of statements. We use it to develop a method for transforming a general specification into an equivalent recursive statement. These transformations can be used to implement recursive specifications as recursive procedures, to introduce recursion into an abstract program to get a more concrete program (i.e., closer to a programming language implementation), and to transform a given recursive procedure into a different form. The theorem is used in the algorithm derivations of [5, 21, 25].

Suppose we have a statement $\mathbf{S}'$ that we wish to transform into the recursive procedure $(\mu X.\mathbf{S})$. We claim that this is possible whenever the following are true.

1. The statement $\mathbf{S}'$ is refined by $\mathbf{S}[\mathbf{S}'/X]$ (which denotes $\mathbf{S}$ with all occurrences of X replaced by $\mathbf{S}'$). In other words, if we replace recursive calls in $\mathbf{S}$ by copies of $\mathbf{S}'$ then we get a refinement of $\mathbf{S}'$.

2. We can find an expression t (called the *variant function*) whose value is reduced before each occurrence of $\mathbf{S}'$ in $\mathbf{S}[\mathbf{S}'/X]$.

The expression t need not be integer-valued: Any set Γ that has a well-founded order $\preccurlyeq$ is suitable. To prove that the value of t is reduced it is sufficient to prove that if $t \preccurlyeq t_0$ initially, then the assertion $\{t \prec t_0\}$ can be inserted before each occurrence of $\mathbf{S}'$ in $\mathbf{S}[\mathbf{S}'/X]$. The theorem combines these two requirements into a single condition.

Theorem 4.4   If $\preccurlyeq$ is a well-founded partial order on some set Γ, and t is an expression giving values in Γ, and t_0 is a variable that does not occur in $\mathbf{S}$, then if

$$\forall t_0.((\mathbf{P} \wedge t \preccurlyeq t_0) \Rightarrow \mathbf{S}' \leqslant \mathbf{S}[\{\mathbf{P} \wedge t \prec t_0\}; \mathbf{S}'/X]) \tag{4.1}$$

then $\mathbf{P} \Rightarrow (\mathbf{S}' \leqslant (\mu X.\mathbf{S}))$.

4.5 Algorithm derivation

It is frequently possible to derive a suitable procedure body **S** from the statement **S**′ by applying transformations to **S**′, (e.g., splitting it into cases) until we get a statement of the form **S**[**S**′/X], which is still defined in terms of **S**′. If we can find a suitable variant function for **S**[**S**′/X] then we can apply the theorem and refine **S**[**S**′/X] to ($\mu X.$**S**), which is no longer defined in terms of **S**′.

As an example we will consider the familiar factorial function. Let **S**′ be the statement $r := n!$. We can transform this (by appealing to the definition of factorial) to show that

$$\mathbf{S}' \approx \mathbf{if}\ n = 0\ \mathbf{then}\ r := 1\ \mathbf{else}\ r := n.(n-1)!\ \mathbf{fi}$$

Separate the assignment:

$\mathbf{S}' \approx \mathbf{if}\ n = 0$
  $\mathbf{then}\ r := 1$
  $\mathbf{else}\ n := n - 1;\ r := n!;\ n := n + 1;\ r := n.r\ \mathbf{fi}$

So we have

$$\mathbf{S}' \approx \mathbf{if}\ n = 0\ \mathbf{then}\ r := 1\ \mathbf{else}\ n := n - 1;\ \mathbf{S}';\ n := n + 1;\ r := n.r\ \mathbf{fi}$$

The positive integer n is decreased before the copy of **S**′, so if we set **t** to be n, Γ to be $\mathbb{N}$ and $\preccurlyeq$ to be $\leq$ (the usual order on natural numbers), and **P** to be **true** then we can prove that for all $n \leq t_0$, **S**′ is refined by

$$\mathbf{if}\ n = 0\ \mathbf{then}\ r := 1\ \mathbf{else}\ n := n - 1; \{n < t_0\}; \mathbf{S}'; n := n + 1; r := n.r\ \mathbf{fi}$$

So we can apply Theorem 4.4 to prove that **S**′ is refined by

$$(\mu X.\ \mathbf{if}\ n = 0\ \mathbf{then}\ r := 1\ \mathbf{else}\ n := n - 1; X; n := n + 1; r := n.r\ \mathbf{fi})$$

and we have derived a recursive implementation of factorial.

This theorem is a fundamental result toward the aim of a system for transforming specifications into programs since it bridges the gap between a recursively defined specification and a recursive procedure that implements it. It is of use even when the final program is iterative rather than recursive since many algorithms may be more easily and clearly specified as recursive functions—even if they may be more efficiently implemented as iterative procedures. This theorem may be used by the programmer to transform the recursively defined specification into a recursive procedure or function that can then be transformed into an iterative procedure. The theorem may also be used in reverse to prove that a given specification is a valid abstraction of a given program; this is used for reverse engineering in Chapter 8.

4.6 Extending the kernel language

The kernel language we have developed is particularly elegant and tractable but is too primitive to form a useful WSL for the transformational development of programs. For this purpose we need to extend the language by defining new constructs in terms of the existing ones using definitional transformations. A series of new language levels is built up, with the language at each level being defined in terms of the previous level; the kernel language is the level zero language which forms the foundation for all the others. Each new language level automatically inherits the transformations proved at the previous level; these form the basis of a new transformation catalog. Transformations of each new language construct are proved by appealing to the definitional transformation of the construct and carrying out the actual manipulation in the previous level language. This technique has proved extremely powerful and has led to the development of a practical transformation system (FermaT) that implements a large number of transformations. Over the last 16 years, the WSL language and transformation theory have been developed in parallel—we have only added a new construct to the language after we have developed a sufficiently complete set of transformations for dealing with that construct. We believe that this is one of the reasons for the success of our language, as witnessed by the practical utility of the program transformation tool.

The first level language consists of the following constructs:

1. *Sequential composition:* The sequencing operator is associative so we can eliminate the brackets:

    $\mathbf{S}_1; \mathbf{S}_2; \mathbf{S}_3; \ldots; \mathbf{S}_n =_{\mathrm{DF}} (\ldots((\mathbf{S}_1; \mathbf{S}_2); \mathbf{S}_3); \ldots; \mathbf{S}_n)$

2. *Deterministic choice:* We can use guards to turn a nondeterministic choice into a deterministic choice:

    if B then $\mathbf{S}_1$ **else** $\mathbf{S}_2$ **fi** $=_{\mathrm{DF}} (([\mathbf{B}]; \mathbf{S}_1) \sqcap ([\neg \mathbf{B}]; \mathbf{S}_2))$

3. *Specification statement:*

    $\mathbf{x} := \mathbf{x}'.\mathbf{Q} =_{\mathrm{DF}} \{\exists \mathbf{x}'.\mathbf{Q}\}; \mathbf{add}(\mathbf{x}'); [\mathbf{Q}]; \mathbf{add}(\mathbf{x}); [\mathbf{x} = \mathbf{x}']; \mathbf{remove}(\mathbf{x}')$

4. *Simple assignment:* If $\mathbf{Q}$ is of the form $\mathbf{x}' = \mathbf{t}$ where $\mathbf{t}$ is a list of terms that do not contain $\mathbf{x}'$ then we abbreviate the assignment as follows:

$\mathbf{x} := \mathbf{t} =_{DF} \mathbf{x} := \mathbf{x}'.(\mathbf{x}' = \mathbf{t})$
If x contains a single variable, we write $x := t$ for $\langle x \rangle := \langle t \rangle$;

5. *Nondeterministic choice:* The "guarded command" of Dijkstra [3]:

    if $\mathbf{B}_1 \rightarrow \mathbf{S}_1$ $=_{DF}$ $(\{\mathbf{B}_1 \vee \mathbf{B}_2 \vee \ldots \vee \mathbf{B}_n\};$
    $\square\ \mathbf{B}_2 \rightarrow \mathbf{S}_2$ $\quad (\ldots((([\mathbf{B}_1]; \mathbf{S}_1) \sqcap$
    $\vdots \qquad\qquad\qquad ([\mathbf{B}_2]; \mathbf{S}_2)) \sqcap$
    $\square\ \mathbf{B}_n \rightarrow \mathbf{S}_n\ \mathbf{fi} \quad \ldots))$

6. *Deterministic iteration:* We define a **while** loop using a new recursive procedure X that does not occur free in **P**:

    while $\mathbf{B}$ **do** $\mathbf{S}$ **od** $=_{DF}$ $(\mu X.(([\mathbf{B}]; \mathbf{S}) \sqcap [\neg \mathbf{B}]))$

7. *Nondeterministic iteration:*

    do $\mathbf{B}_1 \rightarrow \mathbf{S}_1$ $\quad =_{DF}$ **while** $(\mathbf{B}_1 \vee \mathbf{B}_2 \vee \ldots \vee \mathbf{B}_n)$ **do**
    $\square\ \mathbf{B}_2 \rightarrow \mathbf{S}_2$ $\qquad\qquad$ **if** $\mathbf{B}_1 \rightarrow \mathbf{S}_1$
    $\quad \ldots \qquad\qquad\qquad\qquad \square\ \mathbf{B}_2 \rightarrow \mathbf{S}_2$
    $\square\ \mathbf{B}_n \rightarrow \mathbf{S}_n\ \mathbf{od}$ $\qquad\qquad \ldots$
    $\qquad\qquad\qquad\qquad\qquad \square\ \mathbf{B}_n \rightarrow \mathbf{S}_n\ \mathbf{fi}\ \mathbf{od}$

8. *Initialized local variables:*

    begin $\mathbf{x} := \mathbf{t}:\ \mathbf{S}$ **end** $=_{DF}$ $(\mathbf{add}(\mathbf{x}); ([\mathbf{x} = \mathbf{t}]; (\mathbf{S}; \mathbf{remove}(\mathbf{x}))))$

9. *Counted iteration:* Here, the loop body **S** must not change i, b, f, or s:

    for $i := b$ **to** f **step** s **do** $\mathbf{S}$ **od** $=_{DF}$ **begin** $i := b$:
    $\qquad\qquad\qquad\qquad\qquad\qquad$ **while** $i \leq f$ **do**
    $\qquad\qquad\qquad\qquad\qquad\qquad \mathbf{S}; i := i + s$ **od end**

10. *Block with procedure calls:*

    begin S where proc $X \equiv \mathbf{S}'$. **end** $=_{DF}$ $\mathbf{S}[(\mu X.\mathbf{S}')/X]$

One aim for the design of the first-level language is that it should be easy to determine which statements are potentially null. A guard statement such as $[x = 1]$ is one example: If the preceding statements do not allow 1 as a possible value for x at this point then the statement is null. The guard [**false**] is another example that is always null. If a state transformation is nonnull for every initial state then it is called *null-free*. We claim that all first-level language statements without explicit guard statements are null-free. (This is why we do not include Morgan's specification statement **x**:[**Pre**, **Post**] in the first-level language, because it cannot be guaranteed to be null-free. For example the specification $\langle\rangle$: [**true**, **false**] is equivalent to [**false**], which is everywhere null).

A null-free statement will satisfy Dijkstra's "law of the excluded miracle" [3]:

$$\mathbf{WP(S, false)} \iff \mathbf{false}$$

The level-two language introduces multi-**exit** loops and action systems (cf. [26, 27]). Level three adds local variables and parameters to procedures, functions, and expressions with side effects.

4.7 Example transformations

This section introduces some basic program transformations that are useful in their own right and that also form the building blocks for more powerful transformations.

4.7.1 Notation

- *Sequences:* $s = \langle a_1, a_2, \ldots, a_n \rangle$ is a sequence, the ith element a_i is denoted $s[i]$, $s[i..j]$ is the subsequence $\langle s[i], s[i+1], \ldots, s[j] \rangle$, where $s[i..j] = \langle\rangle$ (the empty sequence) if $i > j$. The length of sequence s is denoted $\ell(s)$, so $s[\ell(s)]$ is the last element of s. We use $s[i..]$ as an abbreviation for $s[i..\ell(s)]$.

- *Sequence concatenation:* $s \mathbin{+\mkern-5mu+} t = \langle s[1], \ldots, s[\ell(s)], t[1], \ldots, t[\ell(t)] \rangle$.

- *Subsequences:* The assignment $s[i..j] := t[k..l]$ where $j - i = l - k$ assigns s the value $\langle s[1], \ldots, s[i-1], t[k], \ldots, t[l], s[j+1], \ldots, s[\ell(s)] \rangle$.

- *Stacks:* Sequences are also used to implement stacks; for this purpose we have the following notation: For a sequence s and variable x: $x \xleftarrow{\text{pop}} s$ means $x := s[1]; s := s[2..]$. For a sequence s and expression e: $s \xleftarrow{\text{push}} e$ means $s := \langle e \rangle \mathbin{+\mkern-5mu+} s$.

- *Map:* The map operator $*$ returns the sequence obtained by applying a given function to each element of a given sequence: $(f * \langle a_1, a_2, \ldots, a_n \rangle) = \langle f(a_1), f(a_2), \ldots, f(a_n) \rangle$.

- *Reduce:* The reduce operator $/$ applies an associative binary operator or function to a list and returns the resulting value: $(\oplus/\langle a_1, a_2, \ldots, a_n\rangle) = a_1 \oplus a_2 \oplus \ldots \oplus a_n$. So, for example, if s is a list of integers then $+/s$ is the sum of all the integers in the list, if q is a list of lists then $+/(\ell * q) = \ell(+\!\!+\!/q)$ is the total length of all the lists in q.

- *Projection:* The projection functions $\pi_1, \pi_2, \ldots$ are defined as $\pi_1(\langle x, y\rangle) = x$, $\pi_2(\langle x, y\rangle) = y$, and more generally, for any sequence s: $\pi_i(s) = s[i]$.

The operation of splitting a sequence into a sequence of nonempty sections at the points where a predicate fails is generally useful so we will define the following notation.

Suppose we have a sequence p that we want to split into sections at those points i where the predicate $B(p[i], p[i+1])$ is false. In other words, we want to define a new sequence of nonempty sequences q such that the concatenation of the sequences in q is equal to p (i.e. $+\!\!+\!/q = p$) and B is true within each section and false on the boundary from one section to the next.

Define the function $\text{index}_q : \mathbb{N} \times \mathbb{N} \to \mathbb{N}$ by $\text{index}_q(j, k) = +/(\ell * q[1..j-1]) + k$. This function maps the position of an element in the q structure (the kth component of the jth subsequence) into the corresponding position in the p structure. For all $j \in 1..\ell(q)$ and $k \in 1..\ell(q[j])$ we have $p = +\!\!+\!/q \Rightarrow p[\text{index}_q(j,k)] = q[j][k]$. On this domain, index_q is 1-1, so it has a well-defined inverse. This inverse index_q^{-1} maps an index i of p to a pair $\langle j, k\rangle$ such that $p[i] = q[j][k]$. Thus the function $\text{section}_q = \pi_1 \cdot \text{index}_q^{-1}$ will give the section in q in which an element of p occurs.

With this notation, we can define a split function $\text{split}(p, B) = q$, which splits p into nonempty sections with the section breaks occurring between those pairs of elements of p where B is false. The formal definition uses section_q to find the section breaks.

Definition 4.6 $\text{split}(p, B) = q$ where

$(+\!\!+\!/q) = p \wedge \langle\rangle \notin \text{set}\,(q)$

$\wedge\ \forall i \in 1..\ell(p) - 1.((B(p[i], p[i+1]) \Rightarrow \text{section}_q(i+1) = \text{section}_q(i))$

$\wedge\ (\neg B(p[i], p[i+1]) \Rightarrow \text{section}_q(i+1) = \text{section}_q(i) + 1))$

The **split** function will be used in the reengineering case study in Chapter 9.

4.7.2 Examples of transformations

This section describes a few of the transformations we will use later.

Expand IF statement The **if** statement

if B then S_1 else S_2 fi; S

can be expanded over the following statement to give

if B then S_1; S else S_2; S fi

4.7.3 Loops and exits

Statements of the form **do S od**, where **S** is a statement, are infinite or unbounded loops that can only be terminated by the execution of a statement of the form **exit**(n) (where n is an integer, not a variable or expression) that causes the program to exit the n enclosing loops. To simplify the language we disallow exits that leave a block or a loop other than an unbounded loop. This type of structure is described in [28] and more recently in [29];

A simple transformation is the following: If **S** is a proper sequence, then

$\Delta \vdash$ **do if B then exit fi; S od** $\approx$ **while $\neg$B do S od**

A proper sequence is any statement within which each **exit**(n) occurs nested within at least n loops. Such a statement cannot therefore terminate any enclosing **do** ... **od** loop; the next statement to be executed will always be the next statement in the sequence.

If S_1 is a proper sequence, then the loop

do S_1; S_2 od

can be inverted to

S_1; do S_2; S_1 od

This transformation can be used in the forward direction in order to move the **exit** statements closer to the top of the loop (preparatory to converting to a **while** loop perhaps). It can also be used in the reverse direction to merge the two copies of statement S_1 into a single copy and so reduce the size of the program.

4.7.4 Action systems

An action is a parameterless procedure acting on global variables (cf. [26, 27]). It is written in the form $A \equiv$ **S** where A is a statement variable (the name of the action) and **S** is a statement (the action body). A set of (mutually recursive) actions is called an action system. An occurrence of a statement **call** X within the action body refers to a call of another action. The action bodies may include calls to the special action Z, which does not have a body. Instead, a **call** Z causes immediate termination of the whole action system even if there are unfinished recursive calls.

A *regular* action system is one in which execution of any action body always leads to an action call (which may be a **call** Z). Within such a system, no action call ever returns and the system can only terminate by calling Z. Such an action system is equivalent to a collection of labels and **goto** statements; in fact, any program that is implemented using labels and **goto**s can be translated into a regular action system.

4.8 Why invent WSL?

For restructuring purposes it is useful to work within a language that has the following features:

- Simple, regular, and formally defined semantics;
- Simple, clear, and unambiguous syntax;
- A wide range of transformations with simple, mechanically-checkable correctness conditions.

No existing programming language that is widely in use today meets any of these criteria.

For reverse engineering it is extremely useful to work within a single WSL within which both low-level programs and high-level abstract specifications are easily represented.

For migration between programming languages it is important that the transformation system language should not be biased toward a particular source or target language.

These are the considerations that led to the development of the WSL language. The language has been developed gradually over the last 16 years, in parallel with the development of the transformation theory. This parallel development has ensured that WSL is ideally suited for program transformation work: The design of the language ensures that developing and proving the correctness of transformations is straightforward and, most importantly, the correctness conditions for the transformations are easy to check mechanically. This last point was important for the success of our transformation system.

We believe that the formal foundations of our language and transformation theory were essential to the success of the project. The practice of implementing any reasonable-looking transformation without a formal proof of correctness is very dangerous; the author has discovered errors in transformations published in reputable journals [27], but the errors were only uncovered after having attempted (and failed) to prove that the transformations were correct. Since our tool works by applying a vast number of transformations in sequence, any unreliability in the transformations will have serious repercussions on the reliability of the tool. In practice, the work on proving the correctness of known transformations has been a major driving force in the discovery of new transformations.

As a result, it turns out that, unlike any existing programming language, WSL is not Turing-equivalent, for the following two reasons.

1. WSL includes constructs, such as guard and join, that are not implementable. For example, the guard $[x > 0]$ is guaranteed to terminate, does not change the value of any variable, and guarantees that $x > 0$ on termination. Guards and joins are very useful for writing specifications, and therefore equally important for reverse engineering (see below).

2. Even if one were to exclude the miracles introduced by guard and join, WSL is still more powerful than a Turing machine, since it is based on infinitary first-order logic. It is possible to write a WSL program that solves the halting problem for Turing machines—but it is not possible to write a Turing machine that solves the halting problem for Turing machines.

To prove the second point, note the following:

1. There exists a Turing machine **will_term**(x, n) that can determine if the given (encoding of a) Turing machine x will terminate in n or fewer steps. (The machine simulates x for n steps—the details can be found in any text on computation theory.)

2. This Turing machine can be translated into a WSL program **T** that takes x and n as input variables and sets output variable r to 0 or 1 as appropriate.

3. From **T** one can construct the formula **WP**$(\mathbf{T}, r = 1)$, with free variables x and n, which is true if the value of x encodes a Turing machine which will terminate in n or fewer steps.

4. Then the WSL procedure

   proc Will_Term (x) =
      if $\exists n \in \mathbb{N}.\mathbf{WP}(\mathbf{T}, r = 1)$ **then** $r := 1$
      else $r := 0$ **fi**.

   will set r to 1 if the given x encodes a Turing machine that will terminate in any number of steps. (Note $\mathbb{N}$ denotes the set of all positive integers). This completes the proof.

General formulae, unrestricted set operations, references to infinite objects (e.g., the set $\mathbb{N}$ above), and so on, are not allowed in executable programming languages but are essential for a useable specification language. Therefore, they are equally important for a language that is to form the basis for a reverse engineering system.

For a usable program transformation system it is essential that the base language satisfies the replacement property. Informally, the property states that replacing any component of a program by a semantically equivalent component will result in a semantically equivalent program. This property is foundational to how our tool works: Select a component, apply a transformation, select another component. However, the authors are aware of no commercial programming language that satisfies this property.

For example, in C the statement **x = x*2 + 1** is equivalent to **x = x*2; x = x + 1**. But the statement **if (y == 0) x = x*2 + 1** is not equivalent to **if (y == 0) x = x*2; x = x + 1**.

In JOVIAL, among many other restrictions, there is a limit to the level of nesting of **FOR** loops. Therefore any transformation for replacing a **GOTO** construct with an equivalent **FOR** loop will fail in certain positions[2]. Particular implementations of other languages will almost certainly have similar limitations and restrictions which make it extremely difficult, if not impossible, to discover valid semantics-preserving transformations in that language—let alone prove their correctness.

An obvious disadvantage of working in a separate language to the source language of the legacy system is that translators to and from WSL will have to

---

2. We recall encountering a similar problem with BASIC on a Compukit UK101 microprocessor system many years ago!

4.8 Why invent WSL?

be written. Fortunately, for the old fashioned languages typical of legacy systems, this is not much more difficult than writing a parser for the language, which in turn is a simple application of well-developed compiler technology for which there is a wide variety of tool support available. In addition, there are three important advantages to our approach:

1. Using a collection of translators for different languages, it becomes possible to migrate from one language to another via WSL. We are currently working on an assembler to COBOL II migration; the aim is to produce high-level COBOL II, not something that looks as though it was written by an assembler programmer!

2. The translator can be very simple-minded and not have to worry about introducing such problems as redundancies, dead code, and unstructured code. Once we are within the formal language and transformation system, such redundancies and infelicities can be eliminated automatically by applying a series of general-purpose restructuring, simplification, and data-flow analysis transformations.

3. Our 16 year's work on transformation theory can be reapplied to a new language simply by writing a translator for that language. It would be impossible to reuse the development work for a COBOL transformation system in the development of a JOVIAL transformation system. Even a different version of COBOL could invalidate many transformations and involve a lot of rework.

Based on our results, translation to a formal language is the best way to set about any serious reverse engineering or migration work.

Our work has been criticized by some practitioners for its emphasis on the use of formal methods and formally specified languages. This is odd because the programming language and its support libraries form the basic building materials for software engineering. However, no serious engineer would expect to build with components whose properties are not precisely, formally, concisely specified (e.g., this beam is specified to be able to take this much load under these operating conditions). No serious engineer would tolerate standard components that differ in an undefined way in their properties and behavior from supplier to supplier. A serious engineer does not think twice about screwing a nut from one supplier onto a bolt from another supplier—she or he expects them to fit as a matter of course! A serious engineer expects to have to master a certain amount of mathematics in order to do his or her job properly including differential equations, integration, fluid dynamics, and stress modelling. This is far more than the elementary set theory and logic required to understand WSL.

With regard to the undefined behavior of many commercial languages in the presence of syntactic or semantic errors (including out-of-bounds subscripts and the infamous buffer overflow problem) Hoare [30] said:

> In any respectable branch of engineering, failure to observe such elementary precautions would have long been against the law.

This was way back in 1960.

D. L. Parnas at the International Conference on Software Engineering in Baltimore, Maryland, in 1993 [31] made the following points on the relationship between software engineers and "real" engineering:

- Engineering is defined as "the use of science and technology to build useful artifacts."

- Classical engineers use mathematics to describe their products (e.g., calculus, PDEs, and nonlinear functions);

- Computer systems designers should use engineering methods if they are to deserve the name "software engineers." This will include the use of mathematics.

References

[1] Hayes, I. J., *Specification Case Studies,* Englewood Cliffs, NJ: Prentice Hall, 1987.

[2] Jones, C. B., *Systematic Software Development Using VDM,* Englewood Cliffs, NJ: Prentice Hall, 1986.

[3] Dijkstra, E. W., *A Discipline of Programming,* Englewood Cliffs, NJ: Prentice Hall, 1976.

[4] Morgan, C. C., *Programming from Specifications, Second Edition,* Englewood Cliffs, NJ: Prentice Hall, 1994.

[5] Ward, M., "Derivation of a Sorting Algorithm," Durham University, Durham, U.K., Technical Report, 1990 (http://www.dur.ac.uk/~dcs0mpw/martin/papers/sorting-t.ps.gz).

[6] Morgan, C. C., "The Specification Statement," *Trans. Programming Lang. Syst.,* Vol. 10, 1988, pp. 403–419.

[7] Morgan, C. C., and K. Robinson, "Specification Statements and Refinements," *IBM J. Res. Develop.,* Vol. 31, No. 5, 1987.

[8] Morgan, C. C., and T. Vickers, *On the Refinement Calculus*, Berlin: Springer-Verlag, 1993.

[9] Ward, M., "Foundations for a Practical Theory of Program Refinement and Transformation," Durham University, Durham, U.K., Technical Report, 1994 (http://www.dur.ac.uk/~dcs0mpw/martin/papers/foundation2-t.ps.gz).

[10] Karp, C. R., *Languages with Expressions of Infinite Length*, Amsterdam: North-Holland, 1964.

[11] Scott, D., "Logic with Denumerably Long Formulas and Finite Strings of Quantifiers," in *Symposium on the Theory of Models*, J. Addison, L. Henkin, and A. Tarski (eds.), Amsterdam: North-Holland, 1965, pp. 329–341.

[12] Engeler, E., *Formal Languages: Automata and Structures*, Chicago: Markham, 1968.

[13] Back, R. J. R., *Correctness Preserving Program Refinements* (Mathematical Centre Tracts), Vol. 131, Amsterdam, the Netherlands, Mathematisch Centrum, 1980.

[14] Back, R. J. R., "A Calculus of Refinements for Program Derivations," *Acta Informatica*, Vol. 25, 1988, pp. 593–624.

[15] Morgan, C. C., *Programming from Specifications, Second Edition*, Englewood Cliffs, NJ: Prentice Hall, 1994, p. 180.

[16] Back, R. J. R., and J. von Wright, "Refinement Concepts Formalized in Higher-Order Logic," *Formal Aspects of Computing*, Vol. 2, 1990, pp. 247–272.

[17] Ward, M., "A Definition of Abstraction," *J. Software Maintenance: Research and Practice*, Vol. 7, No. 6, November 1995, pp. 443–450 (http://www.dur.ac.uk/~dcs0mpw/martin/papers/abstraction-t.ps.gz).

[18] Bull, T., "An Introduction to the WSL Program Transformer," *Conference on Software Maintenance*, San Diego, CA, November 26–29, 1990.

[19] Ward, M., and K. H. Bennett, "A Practical Program Transformation System for Reverse Engineering," *Working Conference on Reverse Engineering*, Baltimore, MD, May 21–23, 1993 (http://www.dur.ac.uk/~dcs0mpw/martin/papers/icse.ps.gz).

[20] Ward, M., F. W. Calliss, and M. Munro, "The Maintainer's Assistant," *Conference on Software Maintenance*, Miami, Florida, October 16–19, 1989 (http://www.dur.ac.uk/~dcs0mpw/martin/papers/MA-89.ps.gz).

[21] Ward, M., *Proving Program Refinements and Transformations*, Oxford University, Oxford, U.K., Ph.D. thesis, 1989.

[22] Ward, M., "A Recursion Removal Theorem—Proof and Applications," Durham University, Durham, U.K., Technical Report, 1991 (http://www.dur.ac.uk/~dcs0mpw/martin/papers/rec-proof-t.ps.gz).

[23] Ward, M., "A Recursion Removal Theorem," New York-Heidelberg-Berlin: Springer-Verlag, *Proc. of the 5th Refinement Workshop*, London, January 8–11, 1992 (http://www.dur.ac.uk/~dcs0mpw/martin/papers/ref-ws-5/ps.gz).

[24] Ward, M., "Recursion Removal/Introduction by Formal Transformation: An Aid to Program Development and Program Comprehension," *Comput. J.*, Vol. 42, No. 8, 1999, pp. 650–673.

[25] Ward, M., "Derivation of Data-Intensive Algorithms by Formal Transformation," IEEE Trans. on Software Engineering, Vol. 22, No. 9, September 1996, pp. 665–686 (http://www.dur.ac.uk/~dcs0mpw/martin/papers/sw-alg.ps.gz).

[26] Arsac, J., "Transformation of Recursive Procedures, in *Tools and Notations for Program Construction*, D. Noel (ed.), Cambridge, U.K.: Cambridge University Press, 1982, pp. 211–265.

[27] Arsac, J., "Syntactic Source-to-Source Program Transformations and Program Manipulation," *Comm. ACM*, Vol. 22, No. 1, January 1982, pp. 43–54.

[28] Knuth, D. E., "Structured Programming with the GOTO Statement," *Comput. Surveys*, Vol. 6, No. 4, 1974, pp. 261–301.

[29] Taylor, D., "An Alternative to Current Looping Syntax," *SIGPLAN Notices*, Vol. 19, No. 12, December 1984, pp. 48–54.

[30] Hoare, C. A. R., "The Emperor's Old Clothes: The 1980 ACM Turing Award Lecture," *Comm. ACM*, Vol. 24, No. 4, February 1981, pp. 75–83.

[31] Parnas, D. L., *Presentation at the International Conference on Software Engineering*, Baltimore, MD, May 21–23, 1993.

CHAPTER 5

The FermaT Evolution Workbench

Contents

5.1 Introduction
5.2 Previous transformation tools
5.3 Analyzing assembler code
5.4 The FermaT workbench
5.5 Results
    References

Chapter 4 gave an overview of the WSL language and transformation theory. One major application of the theory has been the development of the FermaT program transformation system, which forms a central component of the FermaT Evolution workbench.

5.1 Introduction

Recent research into the activities of software engineers [1] has shown the need for tools capable of both semantic-based searching and browsing through hierarchical structures. Other studies [2–4] provide strong evidence that software engineers desire tools to help them explore software. They use such tools heavily already and want improvements (the main search tools currently in use are text editors and regular expression search utilities such as **grep**). Top-down program comprehension requires browsing, while bottom-up comprehension require searching. Programmers use both strategies and frequently switch between them. The four most common search targets are the following:

1. Function definitions;
2. All uses of a function;
3. Variable definitions;
4. All uses of a variable [4].

The most common search motivations are as follows:

1. Defect repair;
2. Code reuse;
3. Program understanding;
4. Feature addition;
5. Impact analysis.

In [5], a design browser tool is described, for flexible browsing of a system's design-level representation and for information exchange with a suite of program comprehension tools, complemented with a retriever supporting full-text and structural searching. Source code is parsed to an intermediate ASCII representation, imported into a repository based on the UML metamodel, and accessed through an OO database management system (Poet 6.0). The elements in the database can be accessed like normal Java objects and used to build graphical representations in form of diagrams (information views).

The FermaT workbench is an industrial-strength assembler reengineering workbench consisting of a number of integrated tools for program comprehension, migration, and reengineering. It differs from these other tools in that FermaT is capable of a much deeper semantic analysis of the assembler source code.

5.2 Previous transformation tools

The first tool to be developed as a result of the authors' work on WSL and program transformation theory, was the maintainer's assistant (MA). This was a joint project involving the University of Durham, the Centre for Software Maintenance, Ltd., and IBM United Kingdom-Laboratories, Ltd. MA is implemented in Lisp and includes an X windows based front-end (XMA) that displays formatted WSL code. The user can select any point in the program and see a list of all the transformations that are applicable at that point. The user can then select a transformation from the list and see the result immediately.

MA includes a large number of transformations but is very much an academic prototype whose aim was to test the ideas rather than be a practical tool. In particular, little attention was paid to the time and space efficiency of

5.2 Previous transformation tools

the implementation. Despite these drawbacks, the tool proved to be highly successful and capable of reverse-engineering moderately sized assembler modules into equivalent high-level language programs.

The next tool, the Generic REverse Engineering Tool (GREET) [6] was a complete reimplementation of the transformation engine using Lisp and a commercial CASE tool builder. The transformations in GREET are implemented in $\mathcal{M}\varepsilon\mathcal{T}\mathcal{A}$WSL, an extension of WSL that includes high-level features for writing program transformations [7–9]. The extensions include an abstract data type for representing programs as tree structures and constructs for pattern matching, pattern filling, and iterating over components of a program structure. The "transformation engine" of GREET is implemented entirely in $\mathcal{M}\varepsilon\mathcal{T}\mathcal{A}$WSL. The implementation of $\mathcal{M}\varepsilon\mathcal{T}\mathcal{A}$WSL involves a translator from $\mathcal{M}\varepsilon\mathcal{T}\mathcal{A}$WSL to LISP, a small LISP run-time library (for the main abstract data types) and a WSL run-time library (for the high-level $\mathcal{M}\varepsilon\mathcal{T}\mathcal{A}$WSL constructs such as **ifmatch** and **foreach**, **fill**).

GREET contains parsers for IBM 370 Assembler and JOVIAL and can generate JOVIAL and C code as well as WSL. The user interface is similar to MA in that the user is presented with formatted WSL code and can click on a section of code and apply transformations.

One of the claims made in [7] is that implementing a large system in a very high-level domain-specific language (such as $\mathcal{M}\varepsilon\mathcal{T}\mathcal{A}$WSL) will greatly simplify maintenance and portability. This has proved to be the case with GREET: The entire transformation engine was ported to a very different version of Lisp (Scheme) by a single programmer in a few weeks. Several factors prompted this porting exercise:

- The transformation technology had reached such a level of maturity that the whole transformation process, from the raw WSL generated directly from the parsed assembler to high-level WSL suitable for translation to C or COBOL, could be carried out automatically with no human intervention.

- Transferring from the proprietary Lisp to highly portable Scheme code made the new transformation system completely platform independent. The same source code can be compiled to run on Solaris, AIX, Linux, Windows 98, Windows 2000 and many other operating systems.

- Automation of many transformation processes means that the user does not necessarily need to understand WSL or transformation theory. Transformation processes such as restructuring, extracting call graphs and migration to a different programming language can be carried out automatically with no human intervention (other than a small amount of hand-tuning of the generated code).

The new transformation engine is called FermaT and forms a central component of the FermaT workbench.

A practical system for reverse engineering has to deal with real programs, not laboratory or toy examples. More specifically, the following requirements were identified:

- The tool must cope with the usual programming constructs and their uses (and abuses) including gotos, global variables, aliasing, recursion, pointers, and side effects.

- It is not acceptable to assume that the code has been developed or maintained using structured methods. Real code must be acceptable, and major restructuring may be required before proper reverse engineering can start. This should be carried out automatically (or semiautomatically) by the system.

- Transformations in the library must be proven correct, so that the user can employ them with confidence, but also so that the user does not have to undertake such proofs. The transformations need applicability conditions, and these must be mechanically checked by the tool. In this way, all responsibility for correctness lies with the tool—there are no generated "proof obligations" that the user must discharge before correctness can be guaranteed.

- It must be possible to select a subcomponent of a large existing system and to guarantee to preserve the interactions of the subcomponent with the rest of the system. This permits attention to maintenance hot spots and permits a piecemeal approach to reverse engineering.

- The correctness of the implementation must be well-established.

The core of the tool is a library of proven transformations together with the transformation engine. The transformations in the library were proven before the tool was built. They allow a construct in WSL to be recast into another WSL construct while ensuring that the semantics are preserved. The software engineer using the tool has only to select a transformation and apply it. He or she does not have to do the proof; the system's transformation engine checks that the transformation is applicable.

5.2 Previous transformation tools

The first stage is to load the source code into the tool, and this is achieved by the source language to WSL translator. The WSL code is stored internally as an abstract syntax tree (together with ancillary information to aid applicability checking). Further details are given in [10–12].

The user is able to apply any transformation at any point in the program, and the system automatically checks the applicability conditions of a transformation before it is applied. This means that the correctness of the resulting transformed program is guaranteed by the system rather than being dependent on the user. When analysis of a program fragment is required (for example, computing the set of variables used in the fragment), the system stores the results of its analysis as part of the program, so that recalculation of the analysis is avoided wherever possible.

Presenting the programmer with a variety of different but equivalent representations of the program can greatly aid the comprehension process, making best use of human problem-solving abilities (i.e., visualization, logical inference, and kinetic reasoning).

The theoretical foundation work that proves that each transformation in the system preserves the semantics of any applicable program is *essential* if this method is to be applied to practical software maintenance or reverse engineering. It must be possible to work with programs that are poorly (or not at all) understood, and it must be possible to apply many transformations that drastically change the structure of the program (as in the examples in Chapter 8) with a very high degree of confidence in the correctness of the result.

Finally, the tool is also capable of computing standard complexity metrics for a selected region of the WSL program and presenting them in graphical form to show changes with time. Currently, McCabe, structural, size, control flow, data flow and branch-loop metrics may be computed [6].

The system is constructed as a hierarchy of abstract machines, each of which is formally specified. Additionally, the fact that the FermaT transformation engine is implemented almost entirely in *MetaWSL*, makes it possible for the developers to use the tool in the maintenance of its own source code.

It has been learned through experience that a user often employs a pattern of transformations, and it is easy within the tool to group such transformations into more powerful single transformations. Since transformations are implemented in *MetaWSL*, it is possible for users to develop their own transformations (as combinations of existing transformations) and add them to the system. Provided the new transformations are limited to invoking existing transformations, and are prevented from carrying out unrestricted editing operations, the new transformations are guaranteed to be correct.

5.3 Analyzing assembler code

Assembler presents a number of unique challenges to automated (and human!) analysis. The code is typically completely unstructured with branches and labels allowed in arbitrary positions. Even where structured macros are in use (such as **IF...THEN...ELSE** and **WHILE...DO**) there are no restrictions on branching into or out of structures; thus, the apparent surface structure provided by the macros cannot be relied upon. Subroutines are called by storing a return address in a register and then branching to the start of the subroutine. A subroutine returns by loading the register and branching to the address is contains; however, there is nothing to stop the programmer from overwriting or modifying the return address, or branching from the middle of one subroutine to the middle of another, or branching directly back to the main program or any number of other practices. As a result, even determining the boundaries of a subroutine body can be a challenge! Jump tables are yet another problem: The program carries out some computation and then treats the result as an address and branches to it. Self-modifying code is commonly used in legacy assembler code; rather than wasting a byte by using a flag, clever programmers would overwrite a branch instruction with a **NOP** instruction, or vice versa. The IBM 370 architecture also includes an execute instruction (**EX**); this contains the address of an instruction elsewhere in the program and a register that is used to modify the target instruction before executing the modified instruction.

These difficulties also show why assembler, especially legacy assembler, is so much more difficult and costly to maintain, compared to modern high-level languages. All of these complications need to be addressed by any practical tool for assembler reengineering. In addition, the need for comprehensive semantic analysis tools is much greater for assembler than for high-level languages. For example, a crude form of data flow analysis is possible in COBOL simply by searching for names of variables. If a variable, say **INTEREST-TOTAL**, is referenced in one statement, then a search for all assignments to **INTEREST-TOTAL** will quickly enable the programmer to determine where **INTEREST-TOTAL** gets its value. However, the heavy use of registers and work areas in assembler, and the lack of data type enforcement, combined with the lack of control flow structure, make these scanner-based techniques much less useful. A search for all references to register **R3**, or work area **WORK1** might return hundreds of hits, almost all of which are irrelevant. However, is very difficult to determine if there is an execution path from one line of assembler to another distant line. What is required is a detailed and thorough data flow analysis of the whole program. Such an analysis will also require a detailed and thorough control flow analysis of the whole program—for example to determine all possible return points for a subroutine call.

Data flow analysis is also needed for the following:

1. *Debugging*: Search backwards through data flow from the point where the value of an item is known to be invalid in order to find the code that sets the value;

2. *Enhancement*: Search forward from an area of code that is about to be changed in order to determine the impact of the proposed change.

These are some of the considerations that led to the development of the FermaT workbench.

5.4 The FermaT workbench

The FermaT workbench was designed specifically for analyzing, maintaining, and migrating assembler code (including mainframe assembler and x86 assembler) but the technology on which it is built is applicable to many other languages; for example, the transformation engine works directly on WSL and is not specific to WSL generated from assembler. Research projects, migration projects, and case studies have been carried out in C, COBOL, JOVIAL, BASIC, and other languages.

The various tools comprising the FermaT workbench are accessed via a toolbar and consist of the following:

- Function catalog;
- Function call graph;
- Text editor;
- Program flowchart;
- Data catalog;
- Control flow analyzer;
- Data flow analyzer;
- Program slicer;
- Migration tools.

Each tool is an independent executable, or set of executables, that communicates with the thin client workbench toolbar via TCP/IP connections and shared data files. This design has several advantages:

1. The tools do not all need to run on the same machine. For example, the processor-intensive analysis tools can run on a separate high-power workstation and communicate with the workbench across a local network (or even across the Internet).

2. One tool will not freeze the whole workbench while carrying out a time-consuming activity. The user can switch to another tool and carry on working while waiting for output from the first tool.

3. Tools can be tested independently of the rest of the workbench via a direct TCP/IP connection (such as Telnet). This also provides a simple way to automate regression testing.

Source files in FermaT are organized into directories called *projects*. Each FermaT project consists of a collection of assembler source, macro, and copybook files, typically comprising an assembler system or subsystem. The project also contains all the working files produced by the workbench.

5.4.1 The function catalog

A module is either a source file a macro file, or a copybook file. Modules are grouped into functions, and functions can be nested inside other functions. The function catalog (see Figure 5.1) shows a hierarchical view of the function tree, with modules as the leaves of the tree, plus a detailed view of the currently selected function. The detailed view shows which functions call this function, plus which functions are called by this function [including external modules (i.e., calls to modules that are not available in the current project, macro, or copybook library)].

5.4.2 The function call graph

The function call graph (see Figure 5.2) provides a graphical view of the calling relationships between modules. The call graph is computed by scanning the individual modules for calls to other modules and constructing a graph structure. Copybooks and macros can be included or excluded from the graph for clarity.

5.4 The FermaT workbench

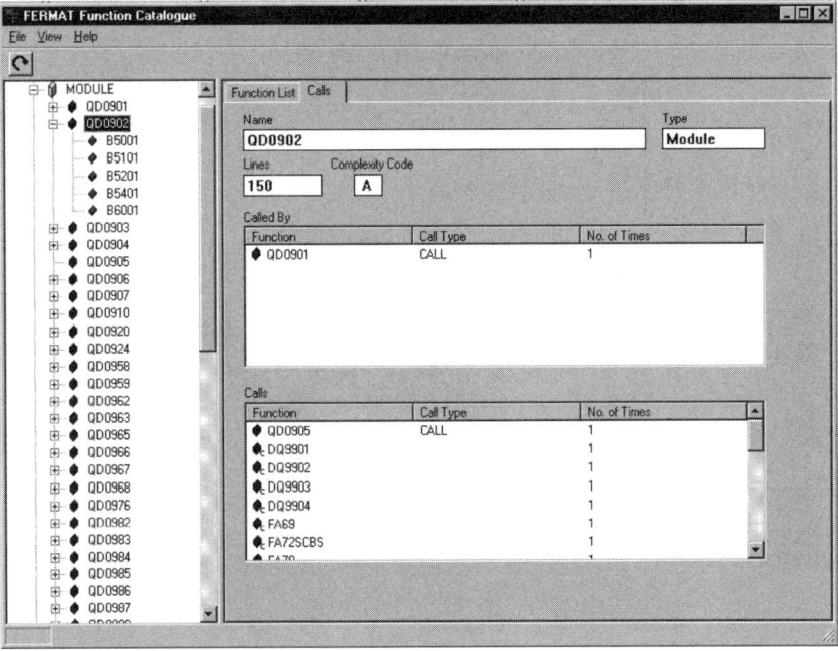

Figure 5.1 The function catalog.

5.4.3 The text editor

The text editor is a fully featured assembler-aware editor that is closely integrated with the other tools in the workbench. Comments are shown in green, and other lines may be highlighted in different colors to show the result of a search or other action. The text editor parses each line of assembler and therefore knows which symbols are data items (such as variables, constants, and data structures), which are mnemonics and so on. Any data item can be selected for tracking via the data tracker; this gives a list of all modules which use or reference that data item.

5.4.4 The program flowchart

Computing a flowchart (see Figures 5.3 and 5.4) requires parsing the assembler and breaking the list of instructions down into basic blocks. A *basic block* is a sequence of instructions that is entered at the top and that is exited at the bottom via a conditional or unconditional branch or by "falling through" to the next block.

The next stage is to compute all the links and possible links between basic blocks; this is not as easy as it sounds because there may be **EX**ecute

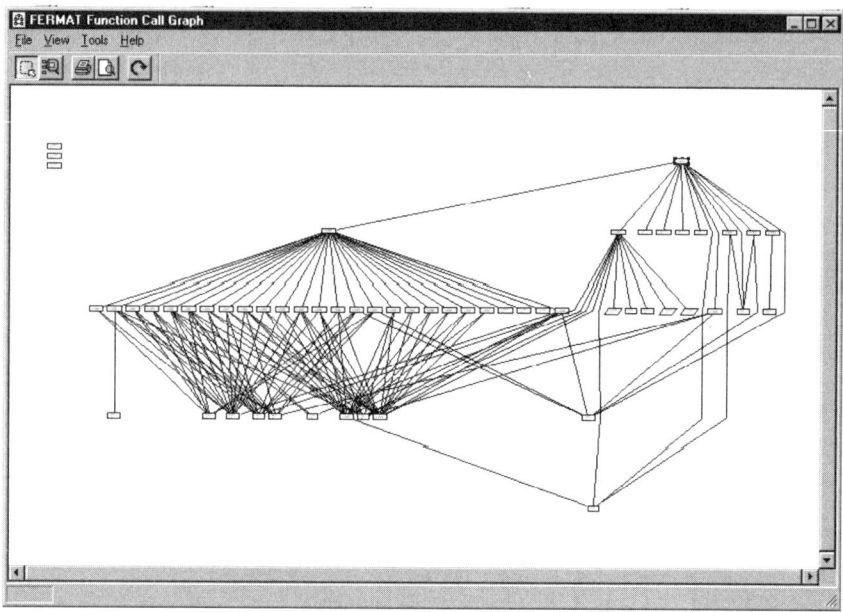

Figure 5.2 The function call graph.

statements, jump tables, and system and user macros, any of which may cause transfer of control, and the target of the transfer may not be a label-listed on the source line—the target may not be labeled at all! For example, the standard IBM system macro **GET**, which is used to read a record from a file, has two parameters, a record buffer and a **DCB** (data control block) pointer. However, the macro will cause a transfer of control on an end of file condition. The label to branch to on end of file is listed in the **DCB** and not on the macro line. The **DCB** may also list another label that the macro will branch to on a system error condition.

To deal with user-defined structured macros, FermaT uses a macros table that lists macros of each type (including the **GOTO** macro, **LABEL** macro, **IF** structure, and **WHILE** loop). This is used to interpret the macros in the source file and determine which lines are conditional or unconditional branches, which lines can "fall through" to the next line, and what are the targets for each branch.

The assembler-to-WSL translator uses a separate macros table, which provides WSL code equivalent to the macro expansion. If a macro is not listed in the latter table, then the macro expansion is translated directly to WSL.

The flowchart tool depicts the control flow of a module in a graphical form. The user can jump from a selected line in the editor to

5.4 The FermaT workbench

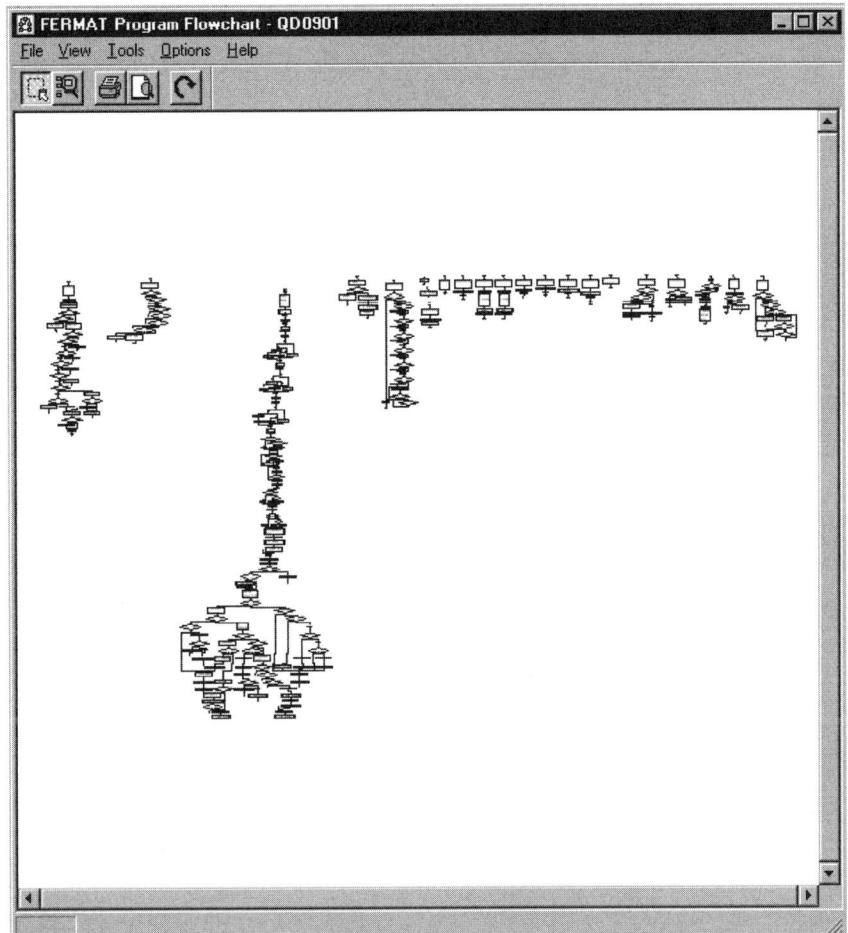

Figure 5.3 Flowchart (whole program).

the corresponding node in the flowchart and vice versa. In addition, a block of code can be selected in the editor and highlighted, and the corresponding flowchart nodes will be highlighted. A set of nodes in the flowchart can be highlighted and the corresponding lines in the editor will be highlighted.

Switching between two different views of the same program (textual and graphical) is a powerful way of improving program comprehension—details that are hard to spot in one view become more visible in the alternate view. For example, in the graphical view it is easy to spot loops in the code and determine which lines of code form the body of the loop.

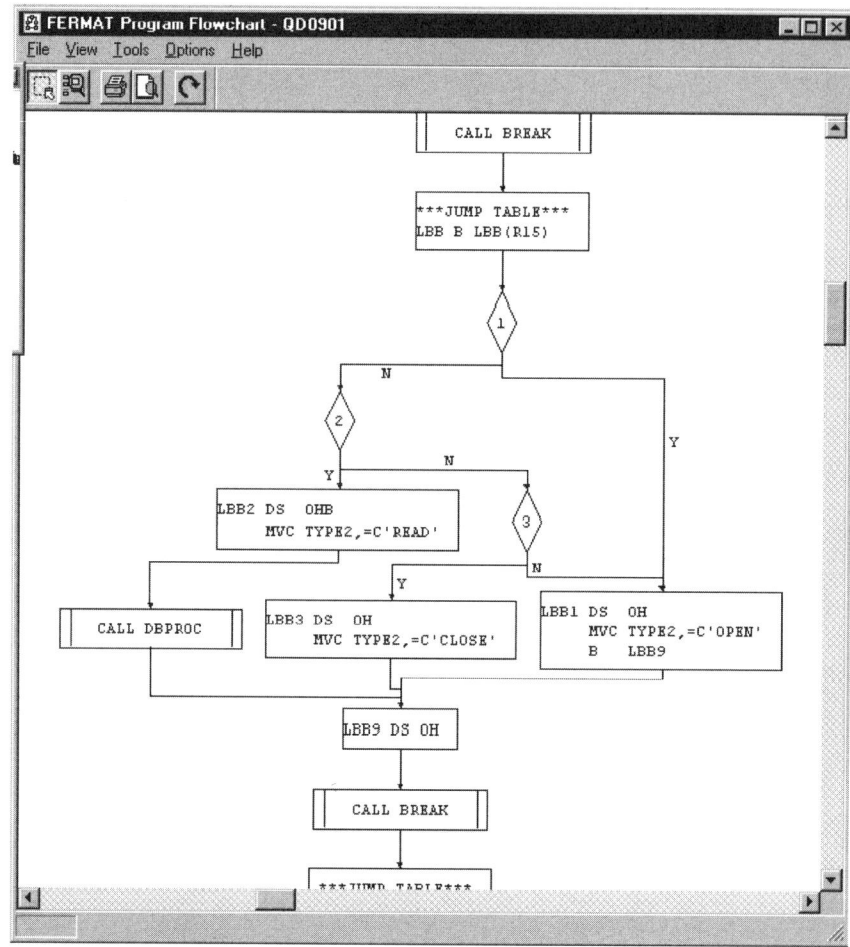

Figure 5.4 Flowchart (zooming in on part of the program).

Assembler-specific features in the flowcharter include the following:

- The executed instruction is found and copied in after the line containing the **EX** instruction.
- Relative branches are computed and the branch target determined where possible.
- Jump tables are detected automatically and converted to a list of conditional branches.
- Subroutines (internal and external) are detected automatically and highlighted.

- Data declarations are ignored in the flowchart.
- Structured macros are interpreted directly.

Any block of code in either the editor or flowchart can be highlighted and annotated. The block can then be collapsed to a single node in the flowchart. This is used for incremental redocumentation of the source and as an aid to reverse engineering the system.

5.4.5 The data catalog

The data catalog (see Figure 5.5) shows a hierarchical view of the data layout for the current module, showing which data items are structures containing other data items and which are atomic data elements. If the relevant macros and copybooks have been imported to the project, or are present in a library, then the data catalog can also show the data structures that are external to the current module. The data catalog also displays the details of the currently selected data items.

5.4.6 Analysis tools

The next four tools (control flow analysis, data flow analysis, slicing, and migration) require a much more detailed semantic analysis of the assembler. Because of this, these tools require an assembler listing file as input (rather than just the source file), since the listing contains macro expansions, copybook expansions, relative addresses for all code and data labels, and other important information. For the tools to derive all this information directly from the source files they would need to replicate much of the functionality of an assembler. Thus it makes better sense to reuse existing technology.

The analysis tools make use of the FermaT transformation engine; assembler code is translated into WSL, then a sequence of transformations is applied to restructure and simplify the WSL code and remove low-level assembler features. The resulting high-level WSL code is then analyzed for control flow and data flow and is sufficiently high-level that it can be translated directly into C or COBOL. See Chapter 8 and [10] for a case study of the automated migration of assembler to efficient and maintainable C code. The high-level WSL also forms the basis for reverse engineering an assembler program to an abstract specification in [13].

The assembler-to-WSL translator includes the following features:

- *Standard opcodes:* Each assembler instruction is translated into WSL statements that capture all the effects of the instruction. The machine

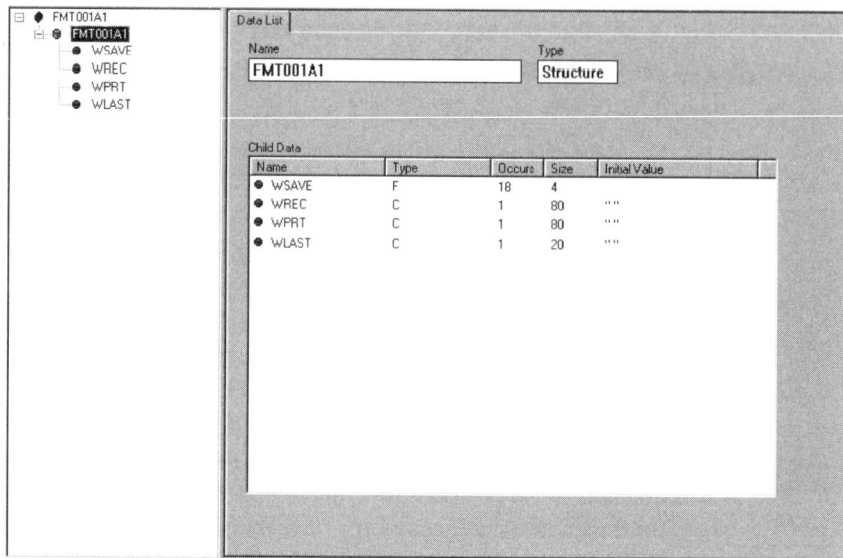

Figure 5.5 The data catalog.

registers and memory are modeled as arrays, and the condition code as a variable. Thus, at the translation stage we do not attempt to recognize **if** statements as such; we translate into statements that assign to **cc** (the condition code variable), and statements that test **cc**.

- *Standard system macros for file handling and other tasks:* When translating a **GET** macro, for example, the system determines the error label (if any) and end-of-file condition label (by searching for the data control block declaration) and inserts the appropriate tests and branches.

- *User macros:* These are added to the translation table with an appropriate WSL translation. If a macro is found that is not in the translation table, then the macro expansion is translated. If there is no macro expansion, then a suitable procedure call is generated.

- *Structured macros:* These are handled by simply translating the macro expansion. This replaces the structure by equivalent branches and labels, but our restructuring transformations are powerful enough to recover the original structure in each case.

- *The condition code:* This is implemented as a variable (**cc**). This is because when a condition code is set it is not always obvious exactly where it will be tested, and it may be tested more than once. Specialized transformations convert conditional assignments to **cc** followed by tests of **cc** into simple conditional statements.

- *BAL/BAS (branch and save) and branch to register:* This is handled by attempting to determine all possible targets of any branch to register instruction by determining all the places where a return address could be saved, or where a modified return address could end up. Each label is turned into a separate action with an associated value (the relative address). A store return address instruction stores the relative address in the register. A branch to register instruction passes the relative address to a **dispatch** action that tests the value against the set of recorded values and jumps to the appropriate label. This can deal with simple cases of address arithmetic (including jump tables) but may theoretically be defeated if more complex address manipulations are carried out before a branch to register instruction is executed.

- *Simple external branches (external subroutine calls):* These are detected.

- *Simple jump tables:* These are detected. The code for detecting jump tables can be customised and extended as necessary.

- *EXecute statements:* These are detected and generate the appropriate code (the executed statement is translated and then modified appropriately). The execute (**EX**) instruction in IBM assembler is a form of self-modifying code; it takes two parameters, a register number, and an address of the actual instruction to be executed. If the register number is nonzero, then the actual instruction is modified by the register contents before being executed. Execute instructions are typically used to create a variable-length move or compare operation (by overwriting the length field of a normal move or compare instruction).

- *Data declarations:* All assembler data (**EQU**ates, **DS**, **DC**, **DCB**, etc.) are parsed and restructured into C unions and structs, where appropriate.

- *DSECTs:* These are converted into pointers to structs (whenever the **DSECT**'s base register is modified, the appropriate pointer is modified to keep it in step).

- *EQUates:* These are translated as **#defines**, apart from (1) "EQU *" in a data area, which is translated as an appropriate data element, and (2) "FOO EQU BAR," which is recorded as declaring **FOO** as a synonym for **BAR**. (If the C translation of **BAR** is **baz.bar**, for example, then the C translation for **FOO** will be **baz.foo**.)

- *Self-modifying code:* Cases where a **NOP** or branch is modified into a branch or **NOP** are detected and translated correctly (using a generated flag). When an instruction is detected that modifies a **NOP** or branch instruction, then the translator generates a new flag that is initialized to zero or one (depending on whether the modified instruction was a **NOP** or branch). The modified instruction is translated as a conditional branch instruction that tests the flag and branches if the flag is set. The instructions that modify the **NOP** or branch are translated into code to set or reset the flag, as appropriate. More complex cases of self-modifying code (e.g., overwriting a block of code with another block of code generated on the fly) can usually be detected but cannot be translated other than by emulating the entire source machine and its environment! These cases are, however, extremely rare.

- *C header files:* These are generated automatically, one for the main program and separate header files for each **DSECT** referenced.

- *Structured and unstructured CICS calls (the **HANDLE AID** and **HANDLE CONDITION** CICS macros set up conditions under which other CICS macros can transfer control to labels listed in the **HANDLE** macro):* These are translated into the appropriate high-level code. Unstructured CICS calls are translated into equivalent structured code through a mechanism that can be extended to other macro packages (e.g., databases and SQL).

The aim of the assembler-to-WSL translator is to generate WSL code that models as accurately as possible the behavior of the original assembler module—without worrying too much about the size, efficiency or complexity of the resulting code. Typically, the raw WSL translation of an assembler module will be three to five times bigger than the source file and have a very high McCabe cyclomatic complexity (typically in the hundreds, often in the thousands). This is, in part, because every branch to register instruction branches to the dispatch action, which in turn contains branches to every possible return point.

However, the FermaT transformation engine includes some very powerful transformations for such tasks as simplifying WSL code, removing redundancies, and tracking dispatch codes. In most cases FermaT can automatically unscramble the tangle of branch and save and branch to register code to extract self-contained, single-entry single-exit procedures and so eliminate the dispatch action. In addition, FermaT can nearly always eliminate the **cc** variable by constructing appropriate conditional statements. Chapter 4 shows how program transformations are used to eliminate code that sets and tests flag variables; these and similar transformations are applied extensively and automatically to replace references to the **cc** flag by the appropriate conditions and to remove redundant assignments to the **cc** flag.

The resulting WSL code, after automatic transformation, can then be processed by several analysis tools. Analysis of the transformed WSL code provides much more information, and more accurate information, than could be provided by a direct analysis of the original assembler. For a start, there are fewer nodes in the control flow graph for the WSL code. There are also considerably fewer edges in the control flow graph. For example, the raw WSL contains edges from every branch to register instruction to the dispatch procedure, which in turn has an edge to every possible return point. The transformed CFG has usually eliminated the dispatch procedure and replaced all the save return address and branch to register code by a hierarchy of single-entry single-exit subroutines. The result is much more accurate control and data flow information.

5.4.6.1 Control flow analysis

The control flow analysis tool breaks up the structured WSL into basic blocks and uses these to construct the nodes of the control flow graph. From this graph we can calculate the dominator tree [14] and control dependence information [15]. The control dependencies of an instruction are those branch statements that control whether or not the given instruction is executed. To be precise, if one arm of the branch is taken, then the given instruction will eventually be executed (provided the program terminates at all), while if the other branch is taken then the program may terminate without executing the given instruction.

The user can see a graphical display of the dominator tree and control dependence graph, as well as displaying and browsing control dependence information in the editor.

5.4.6.2 Data flow analysis

The dominator tree is used to compute the static single assignment (SSA) [16, 17] form of the basic blocks computed from the restructured WSL program. From this, a dataflow file is computed; this lists in a concise form all the dataflow and control dependence information for the assembler module with links back to each symbol in the assembler module.

5.4.6.3 Program slicer

The dataflow file contains all the information needed to compute forwards and backwards static slices of the original program [18]. Any instruction or data item in the program can be selected and a program slice computed and displayed.

5.4.6.4 Migration tools

Chapter 8 includes a case study using FermaT migration tools to migrate assembler to C.

5.5 Results

The results from using the FermaT Workbench on major reengineering projects have so far been very encouraging. A simple application of the technology is using FermaT for Euro assessment.

Euro assessment With the introduction of the Euro currency throughout much of Europe, banks and other financial organizations have had to make some major enhancements to their software systems. A Euro project involves much more than simply adding another currency to the system: There are complex rules to determine how to convert to and from the Euro, and these rules are enforced by legislation. As a result, a Euro conversion is likely to be an order of magnitude more complex than a Y2K conversion.

The first stage in a Euro conversion project is the assessment phase, where the aim is to determine precisely which lines of code need to be changed. Assessment involves the following steps:

1. First collect the source and run an automatic inventory report. Depending upon how many missing dependencies there are this may take several passes to obtain a full inventory.

2. Then, scan the copybooks/macros for details of all data declarations.

3. Then enter the seek table utility, which uses details of the data declarations to assist the user to dynamically (i.e., without requiring a rescan of the source) produce a base seek table, based upon comments and data types.

4. The rest of the source modules are scanned for data declarations, and this information is again passed onto the seek table utility.

Where there are distinct business areas (with few shared data names and structures), the rest of the assessment project can be conducted in parallel for each business area.

5. The base seek table is then further tweaked for the source modules in each business area.

6. The seek table utility then exports a matched field list for every module, to take into account fields with the same names but different uses within different modules (e.g., work fields). The data impact scanner then reads in these matched field lists and finds every instance of every required field in every module. Reporting information is output that can be imported into databases/spreadsheets.

In two Euro projects the whole assessment process was completed in about five days for a typical 500K LOC system. Larger systems do not require proportionately more effort because there are usually common library modules containing a large proportion of data declarations.

References

[1] Singer, J., et al., "An Examination of Software Engineering Work Practices," *Proc. of CASCON'97,* Toronto, Canada, 1997.

[2] Elliott, S., et al., *Browsing and Searching Software Architectures.*

[3] Lethbridge, T. C., and J. Singer, "Understanding Software Maintenance Tools: Some Empirical Research," *IEEE Workshop on Empirical Studies of Software Maintenance (WESS'97),* Bari, Italy, October 1997.

[4] Sim, S. E., C. L. A. Clarke, and R. C. Holt, "Archetypal Source Code Searches: A Survey of Software Developers and Maintainers," *International Workshop on Program Comprehension,* 1998.

[5] Robitaille, S. R. Schauer, and R. K. Keller, "Bridging Program Comprehension Tools by Design Navigation," *IEEE International Conference on Software Maintenance,* San Jose, CA, October 2000.

[6] Bennett, K. H., T. Bull, and H. Yang, "A Transformation System for Maintenance—Turning Theory into Practice," *Conference on Software Maintenance,* Orlando, Florida, 1992.

[7] Ward, M., "Language-Oriented Programming," *Software-Concepts and Tools,* Vol. 15, 1994, pp. 147–161 (http://www.dur.ac.uk/~dcs0mpw/martin/papers/middle-out-t.ps.gz).

[8] Ward, M., "Foundations for a Practical Theory of Program Refinement and Transformation," Durham University, Durham, U.K., Technical Report, 1994 (http://www.dur.ac.uk/~dcs0mpw/martin/papers/foundation2-t.ps.gz).

[9] Ward, M., "Specifications from Source Code-Alchemists' Dream or Practical Reality?" *4th Reengineering Forum,* Victoria, Canada, September 19–24, 1996.

[10] Ward, M., "Assembler to C Migration Using the FermaT Transformation System," *International Conference on Software Maintenance,* Oxford, U.K., August 30–September 3 1999.

[11] Ward, M., and K. H. Bennett, "Formal Methods to Aid the Evolution of Software," *International Journal of Software Engineering and Knowledge Engineering,* Vol. 5, No. 1, 1995, pp. 25–47 (http://www.dur.ac.uk/~dcs0mpw/martin/papers/evolution-t.ps.gz).

[12] Ward, M., and K. H. Bennett, "Formal Methods for Legacy Systems," *J. Software Maintenance: Research and Practice,* Vol. 7, No. 3, May 1995, pp. 203–219 (http://www.dur.ac.uk/~dcs0mpw/martin/papers/legacy-t.ps.gz).

[13] Ward, M., "Reverse Engineering from Assembler to Formal Specifications via Program Transformations," *7th Working Conference on Reverse Engineering,* Brisbane, Queensland, Australia, November 23–25, 2000 (http://www.dur.-ac.uk/~dcs0mpw/martin/papers/wcre2000.ps.gz).

[14] Lengauer, T., and R. E. Tarjan, "A Fast Algorithm for Finding Dominators in a Flowgraph," *Trans. Programming Lang. and Syst.*, Vol. 1, No. 1, July 1979, pp. 121–141.

[15] Pingali, K., and G. Bilardi, "Optimal Control Dependence Computation and the Roman Chariots Problem," *Trans. Programming Lang. and Syst.*, May 1997 (http://www.cs.cornell.edu/Info/Projects/Bernoulli/papers/toplas97.ps).

[16] Bilardi, G., and K. Pingali, "The Static Single Assignment Form and Its Computation," Cornell University, Ithaca, NY, Technical Report, July 1999 (http://www.cs.cornell.edu/Info/Projects/Bernoulli/papers/ssa.ps).

[17] Cyhtron, R., et al., "Efficiently Computing Static Single Assignment Form and the Control Dependence Graph," *Trans. Programming Lang. and Syst.*, Vol. 13, No. 3, July 1991, pp. 451–490.

[18] Weiser, M., "Program Slicing," *IEEE Trans. on Software Engineering,* Vol. 10, No. 4, July 1984, pp. 352–357.

CHAPTER 6

An Integrated Evolution Framework

Contents

6.1 Characteristics of legacy systems

6.2 The expanded evolution approach

6.3 EWSL

6.4 Summary

References

Having addressed the evolution of procedural legacy programs in Chapters 4 and 5, we would like to discuss our approach to evolving a broader range of programs, including object-oriented programs and real-time programs.

6.1 Characteristics of legacy systems

6.1.1 Typical problems

Legacy systems present a fundamental challenge to those who own and operate them. These systems have begun to age but continue to provide vital services [1, 2]. They were designed to follow requirements and an implementation approach that existed earlier in the organization's life cycle. Then they were released into an environment, possibly different from the planned environment, or an environment that changed significantly over several years. Now, after many years or even decades, they are still expected to operate efficiently, solve problems, and incorporate changes in technology and business practices for many years to come [3].

Because legacy software systems are so critical to an organization's survival, they are not retired or substituted with newly developed systems without compelling reasons. Major changes require a huge investment in new technology, with a significant risk that the new systems may fail to deliver the required services. Therefore, organizations maintain functionality, correct defects, and upgrade legacy systems to keep up with changing business or technical conditions.

Legacy systems share many negative characteristics, or in another word, problems. Some of the worst, and lamentably typical ones, are described as follows:

- Legacy systems are large, with hundreds of thousands or even millions of lines of codes.

- They are written in legacy languages, such as COBOL.

- They are built around a legacy environment [e.g., IBM's IMS (a DBMS from IBM)].

- They are autonomous. Applications operate independently, with little or no interface with other applications. If interfaces are present, they are often badly designed, and haphazard at best according to modern criteria. For example, some interfaces were based on export/ import models or lack data consistency.

To complicate matters, these legacy systems are often *mission-critical* (i.e., essential to the organization's business) and must be operational at all time.

6.1.2 Structure and data dependency

A legacy system is, under most circumstances, composed of nested procedures and functions. This chapter uses the term *component* to mean "procedure" or "function." If the system is monolithic, then we apply various restructuring techniques; for example, FermaT can restructure monolothic assembler modules into a hierarchy of single-entry, single-exit procedures. According to the nested structure, these components have different visibility (scope) levels. The components that nest at the top layer (i.e., components with no parent, such as **main()** in C programs) are assumed to have the highest visibility level: level 0. This means that those components are in a most general position in the whole system. Similarly, the direct subprocedures and subfunctions of a level-0 component have the visibility level 1. And for a component of level i, the visibility level of its direct subprocedures and subfunctions is level $i + 1$. A depiction of visibility levels is given in Figure 6.1. All data items are associated with the same component's visibility (scoping) level at which they were first declared. Therefore, the top global components and their data items have the highest visibility level, which is marked level 0, and those at the nth nested layer below the top level have visibility level n. In ideal cases, a component at level i only has direct access to components at level $i + 1$. Components

6.1 Characteristics of legacy systems

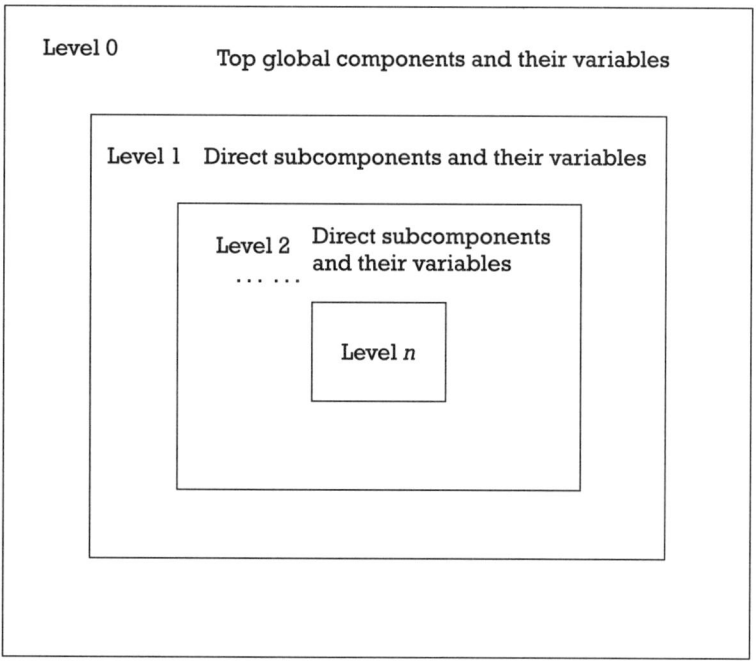

Figure 6.1 Visibility levels of system components and their data items.

distributed over several levels can be treated as a system composed of subcomponents at different levels.

The functional effect of a component can be interpreted as changing part or all of the data items at a higher level than this component (i.e., the relative global variables to this component) and giving them new values with the aid of data items belonging to this component (i.e., this component's local variables). Therefore, a component can be viewed as a mapping function between the old and new values of its relative global data items. The effect of a component is embodied in the change of its relative global variables. Figure 6.2 shows this mapping relation. The rectangle with rounded corners represents a component; the circles represent local variables of the component, and the rectangles represent global variables to the components. Variables at the left side form the original state, and those at the right are the new state after invocation of the component.

For an object-oriented system, the data fields of an object and those accessible to the object can be considered to be global data items, and other data items used by its methods are local ones of the object.

Based on the above concepts of visibility level and mapping function, Figure 6.3 shows the typical structure and data dependency of a legacy

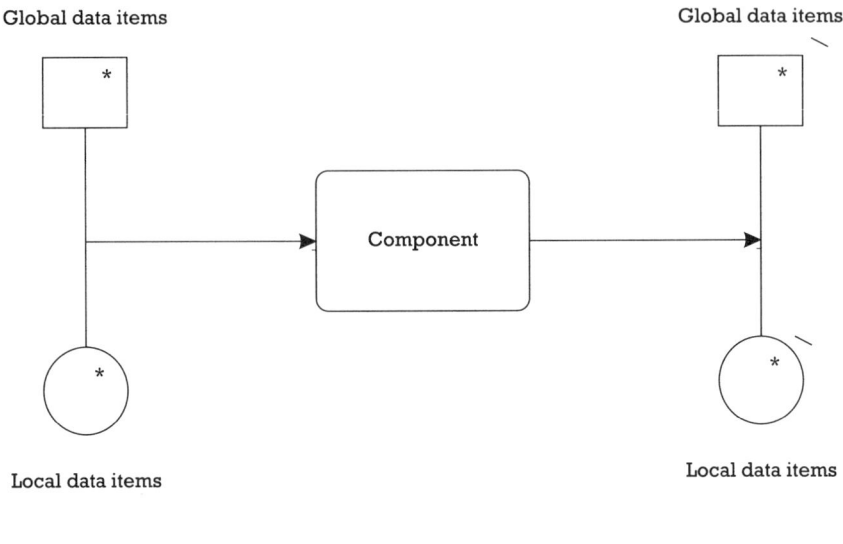

Figure 6.2 Functional mapping of a system component.

system. Here, primary data items are the global data items with visibility level 0, and secondary data items are those data items whose visibility level is deeper than 0. The primary data items at the top are initial states of the legacy system, and those at the bottom are the final states. Those in the middle are intermediate states. The nested rectangles are the components at various visibility levels in the legacy system.

6.2 The expanded evolution approach

6.2.1 Extending WSL

The study in previous chapters has shown that using a WSL is the most suitable and efficient approach to the evolution of computing systems because of its various abstraction levels and the integrity of these levels.

Based on the characteristics of legacy systems, a unified approach for software evolution is developed. The approach is based on the extension of

6.2 The expanded evolution approach

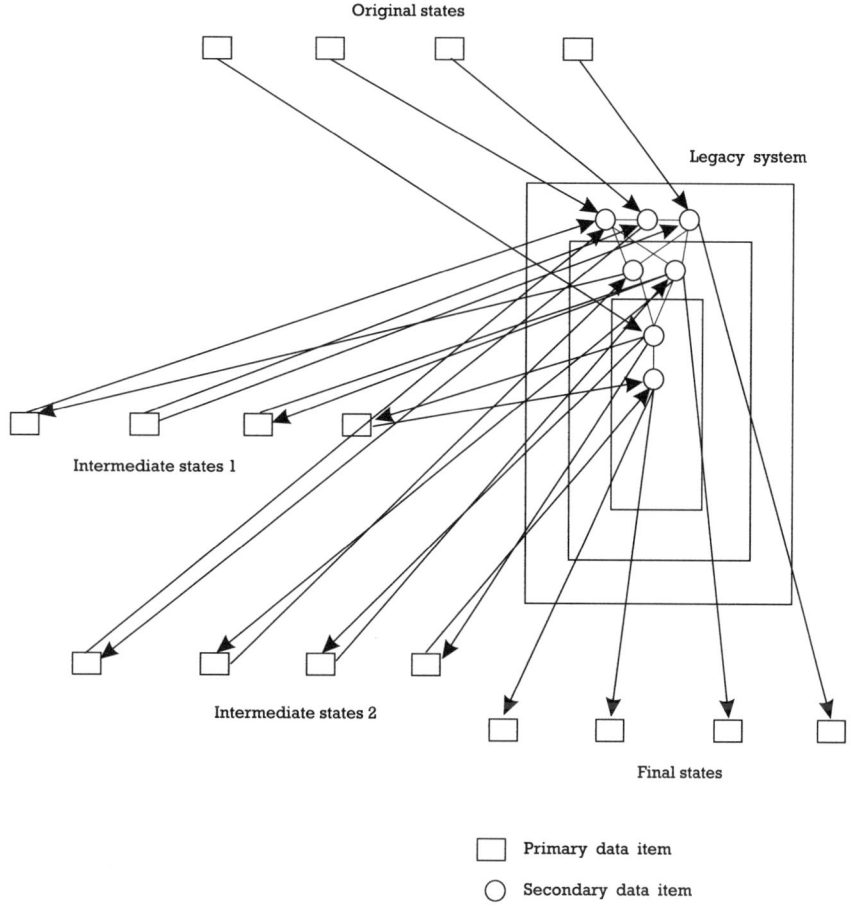

Figure 6.3 Global and local data dependency.

the WSL, which enjoys a sound formal semantics. An integrated framework for evolution has been constructed to support the proposed approach.

For the reverse engineering stage, we endeavor to extract a formal specification from the legacy source code. There are two reasons to support this approach:

1. Specifications are more compact than source code; they are expressed in a more problem-oriented notation and are easier for the software engineer to understand. Therefore, extracting specifications can greatly facilitate the software engineers' understanding of the legacy system, both in efficiency and accuracy, and therefore

facilitate further redesign and respecification of the original system. The benefit is worth the cost, especially for critical legacy systems.

2. From the new specification, executable code can potentially be generated automatically or semiautomatically. Using formal notations could assure more precise system description and increase the automation of the whole evolution process.

6.2.2 Architecture of extended WSL (EWSL)

Extended WSL (EWSL) is a multilayered WSL with sound formal semantics. Due to the distinct advantage of ITL [4–8], we use it as the semantic foundation of EWSL.

Figure 6.4 shows the architecture of EWSL. The top part is the object-oriented section, which includes three layers, namely ITL specification, object-oriented TAM (ObTAM) and common object-oriented language (COOL). ObTAM is an extension of TAM language [9–11] with object-oriented features. The most concrete layer of the object-oriented section is COOL, which provides structures as those in an ordinary object-oriented language.

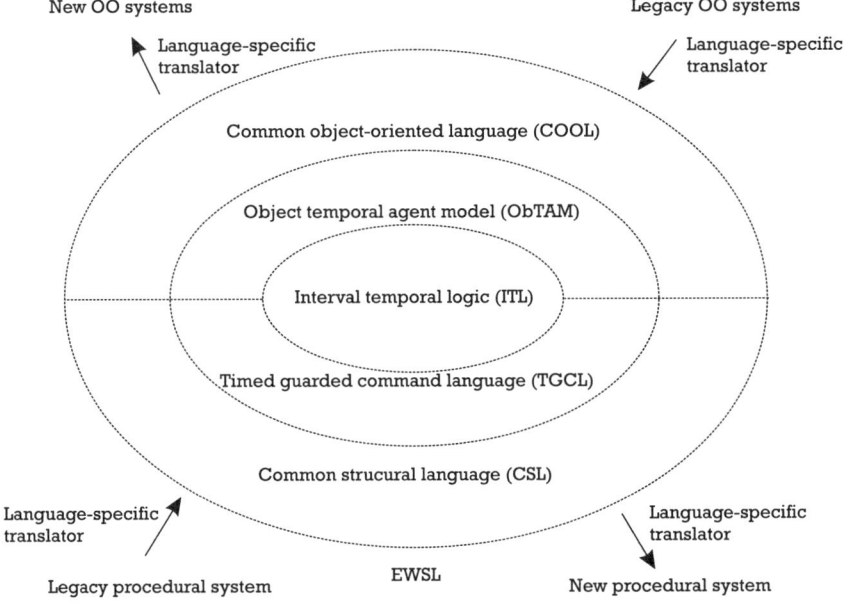

Figure 6.4 EWSL: general architecture.

6.2 The expanded evolution approach

The bottom part is the structural (procedural) section, which also includes three layers: ITL specification, timed guarded command language (TGCL) and CSL. TGCL is an extension of Dijkstra's guarded command language [12, 13] with time and concurrency features. Both TGCL and CSL are at the code level, while in CSL, operators and concepts are implemented in common programming elements, such as shunts.

Both the object-oriented and procedural systems are specified with ITL formulae. The semantics of the other layers of EWSL, together with the abstraction and object extraction rules, are defined in ITL.

6.2.3 Working flow of EWSL

Figure 6.5 shows the possible process when using EWSL to evolve legacy systems. The approach may be used as follows: The source code of

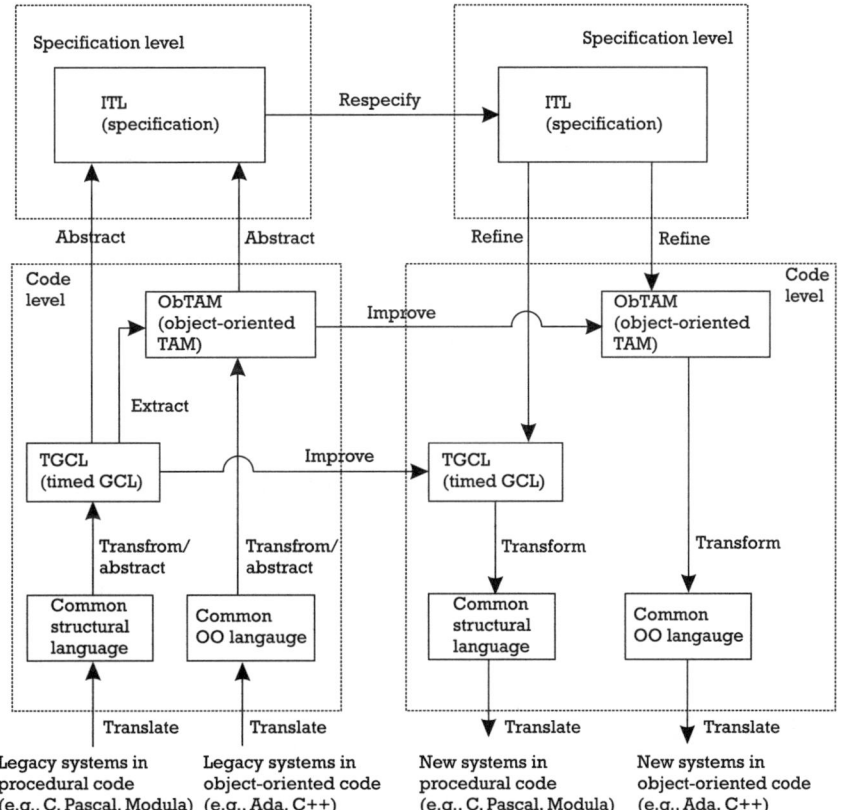

Figure 6.5 EWSL: working process for evolution.

a procedural or object-oriented legacy system is first translated into CSL or COOL through a language specific translator. This translates between a source and target language to and from EWSL (an example is the COBOL-to-EWSL translator in [14]). Such a translation ensures standardization, since legacy systems may have come in various languages, such as C, C++, Modula, or COBOL. This is followed by transformation to TGCL or ObTAM through successive applications of correctness-preserving transformation rules.

There are three possible paths for reengineering (Figure 6.5):

1. TGCL and ObTAM code can be improved or extended by adding the required extra functionalities. The TGCL and ObTAM code can be then transformed into an equivalent programming language (either through transformation or straight forward translation). In this path, the procedural nature of a procedural legacy system is kept.

2. If the object-oriented paradigm is sought, object extraction is performed to obtain an equivalent ObTAM code from the procedural TGCL code. Then the ObTAM code is extended or improved. Subsequently, this is transformed to an object-oriented language, such as ADA, JAVA, or C++.

3. If a high level of abstract specification is needed, then following the construction of TGCL code or ObTAM code or both, semantics calculation is performed to produce an ITL specification. The specification will be subsequently used as a basis for forward engineering through refinement.

ITL specifications are abstract enough for the software reengineer to carry out redesign and respecification of the target system. Therefore, at the specification level, improvements such as the addition of new functions and services will be introduced to make the legacy system more suitable for the new requirements. After these improvements, forward engineering can be carried out by using refinement rules to refine the new target system into a new concrete form, for example, in ADA.

6.3 EWSL

6.3.1 ITL

ITL forms the most abstract and logical layer in our language. It is used to give a specification-oriented semantics for TGCL and ObTAM. Furthermore, all transformation, object extraction, abstract, and refinement relations and rules are precisely described and proved within ITL. The choice of ITL is based on a number of reasons. It is a flexible notation for both propositional and first-order reasoning about periods of time found in descriptions of hardware and software systems. Unlike most temporal logics, ITL can handle both sequential and parallel composition and offer powerful and extensible specification and proof techniques for reasoning about properties involving safety, liveness and projected time. Timing constraints are expressible and furthermore most imperative programming constructs can be viewed as formulae in a slightly modified version of ITL [4]. Tempura [6], an executable subset of ITL, provides an executable framework for developing, analyzing, and experimenting with suitable ITL specifications.

6.3.1.1 Syntax

An interval σ is considered to be a (in)finite sequence of states $\sigma_0\sigma_1...$, where a state σ_i is a mapping from the set of variables *Var* to the set of values *Val*. The length $|\sigma|$ of an interval $\sigma_0...\sigma_n$ is equal to n [one less than the number of states in the interval, (i.e., a one-state interval has length 0)].

ITL syntax is defined as follows: Expressions in ITL include constants, static variables (which do not change within an interval), state variables (which can change within an interval), functions applied to expressions, and the notation $\iota a : f$ where a is a static variable and f is a predicate. This returns a value for a such that $f(a)$ holds. If there is no such value, then $\iota a : f$ returns any value from a's range.

Formulae in ITL include predicates $p(e_1,...,e_n)$ (where the e_i are expressions) and the following compositions of formulae:

- $\forall v \cdot f$ is true if $f(v)$ holds for all values of v;

- **skip** is true over any unit interval (any σ with $|\sigma| = 1$);

- $f_1;f_2$ holds if the interval can be decomposed ("chopped") into a prefix and suffix interval, such that f_1 holds over the prefix and f_2 over the suffix, or if the interval is infinite and f_1 holds for that interval;

- f^*: holds if the interval is decomposable into a finite number of intervals such that for each of them f holds, or the interval is infinite and can be decomposed into an infinite number of finite intervals for which f holds.

6.3.1.2 Specification

The syntax of specification statement is $W : f$ where W is a set of variables and f an ITL formula. The set W is the frame of the specification; only those variables listed in W can be changed. The specification statement represents a blackbox description of the behavior of the required system. When we specify agents that require a minimum execution interval, care must be taken in regard to the feasibility of the specification. This is to ensure that the written specification indeed conforms with whatever restricted computational (executable) model chosen.

6.3.2 Timed guarded command language (TGCL)

Based on the basic structures of Dijkstra's guarded command language [12], TGCL introduces time, concurrency, and communication. This gives TGCL the necessary power for tackling time-critical concurrent systems. A TGCL variable is either an atomic variable, a structural variable, or a data field of a structural variable (written $x.d$).

TGCL also adopts the concept of shunt in TAM. *Shunts* are shared variables via which communication between agents is performed. In TGCL, a TAM agent is implemented as an executable program segment. A shunt contains two values: The first one is a stamp that records the time of the most recent write, and the second one is the value that was most recently written.

The informal semantics of TGCL are described as follows:

- $x := e$ evaluates expression e and stores the result into variable x.
- $\mathscr{A};\mathscr{A}'$ is the sequential composition of $\mathscr{A}$ and $\mathscr{A}'$.
- **if** $\prod_{i \in I} g_i$ **then** $\mathscr{A}_i$ **fi** is a conditional statement. If any guard g_i is true then one of the corresponding $\mathscr{A}_i$ will be chosen for execution.
- **while** g **do** $\mathscr{A}'$ **od** is the loop statement.
- **skip** is empty operation statement.
- $T = \{x_i : T_i\}$ is the structure building declaration. It defines a structure named T, which has data fields x_i of type T_i, $i \in 1..n$.
- $x : T$ defines x as a variable of type T, where T can be a simple data type or a structure.
- **proc** $P(\text{In } \mathbf{pin}_i : T_i, \text{Out } \mathbf{pout}_j : T'_j)\{\mathscr{A}'\}$ defines a procedure in TGCL. The procedure is named P, which has $\mathbf{pin}_i$ as its input parameters,

and **pout**$_j$ as its output parameters. The input parameter passing convention is **call by value**, which means that the values of the practical parameters are passed into the procedure; and the output parameter passing convention is **call by reference**, which means that the address references of the practical parameters are passed into the procedure, and therefore any change made will take effect on practical parameters themselves. $\{\mathcal{A}'\}$ is the procedure body of P.

- $P(\text{In } e_i, \text{Out } x_j)$ means the invocation of procedure P with parameters p_i, while e_i are input parameters and values of x_j are output parameters.

- $x.d$ is field selection. x is a structure, and d is a field of x.

- *parbegin* $\mathcal{A}_1 \| \mathcal{A}_2 \|, ..., \| \mathcal{A}_n$ *parend*. Here $\|$ is introduced as the parallel operator. This statement means that $\mathcal{A}_1, ..., \mathcal{A}_n$ execute concurrently, and the construct terminates when all of the $\mathcal{A}_i$ have terminated.

- $[t].\mathcal{A}'$ means that the execution of $\mathcal{A}'$ should be completed within t time units (deadline).

- $\mathcal{A}_1 \trianglerighteq_s^t \mathcal{A}_2$. The given shunt s is treated as a signal and is monitored from the release time for t time units. If s is written to in that interval then the agent $\mathcal{A}_2$ is released with a release time equal to the end of the interval; otherwise the agent $\mathcal{A}_1$ is released at the end of the interval.

- *delay n* will cause a delay of the system for n time units.

- $(t, x) \leftarrow s$ is the input statement with time feature, which reads the timestamp and value from a shunt s at the same time. The timestamp is read into t and the value into x.

- $x \rightarrow s$ is the output statement with time feature, which writes the value given into shunt s.

6.3.3 Object-oriented TAM

TAM aims to be a realistic software development method for real-time systems. It has sufficient power for time, concurrency and communication. ObTAM extends TAM with object-oriented features, (e.g., object hierarchy and inheritance).

6.3.3.1 Syntax

ObTAM syntax is the same as the syntax of TGCL without the procedural part, but with an additional object-oriented portion.

A variable of ObTAM can be an atomic variable, an object variable, or a data field $x.d$ of an object variable x.

The informal semantics of ObTAM are described as follows:

- *General elements*: same as those for TGCL.

- *Object-oriented elements*:

    - $x : T$ means defining x as a variable of type T, where T can be a simple data type or a class.

    - $T <_{sub} T'$ can be used to build the object hierarchy. It declares that class T is a subclass of class T'. As the consequence, T will inherit all the data fields and methods in T' if they are not redefined in T. On the other hand, all the data field and methods in T' will be overridden with the counterparts in T if they are redefined in T.

    - $T = \{x_i : T_i,\ m_j(\textbf{In pin}_{j_k} : T_k, \textbf{Out pout}_{j_l} : T'_l)[\mathscr{A}_j]\}$ is the class-building declaration. It defines a class named T, which has data fields x_i of type T_i, $i \in 1..n$, and methods m_j, $j \in 1..r$. The behavior of a class is a sequence of method invocations. $\textbf{pin}_{j_k}$ stands for the input parameters of method m_j, and $\textbf{pout}_{j_l}$ stands for the output parameters of method m_j. The input parameter passing convention is **call by value**, and the output parameter passing convention is **call by reference**. $\mathscr{A}_j$ is the methods body of method m_j.

    - $x.d$ is object field reference. x is an object, and d is a field of x.

    - $x.m(\textbf{In } e_k : T_k, \textbf{Out pout}_l : T'_l)$ is method invocation. It invocates the method m in object x.

- *Real-time elements*: same as those for TGCL.

6.3.4 Common structural language (CSL)

CSL is developed to enrich the statements in TGCL and make EWSL compatible to WSL in FermaT. Statements in CSL are more program-like. CSL can be viewed as an extension of WSL in FermaT with time, concurrency, and type, or a variation of TGCL with a more program-like format and diversity in statements. CSL is the most concrete procedural layer of EWSL, and statements described in Chapter 4 belong to this category.

6.3.5 Common object-oriented language (COOL)

The syntax of COOL is the same as the syntax of CSL without the procedural part, but with the following additional object-oriented portion:

1. Class definition:

   class T
   $$\{$$
   $$\quad T_i : x_i;$$
   $$\quad m_j(\textbf{In } \textbf{pin}_{j_k} : T_k, \textbf{Out } \textbf{pout}_{j_l} : T'_l)$$
   $$\quad\quad \{\mathscr{A}_j\}$$
   $$\}$$
   $$\stackrel{\wedge}{=} T = \{x_i : T_i, \; m_j(\textbf{In } \textbf{pin}_{j_k} : T_k, \textbf{Out } \textbf{pout}_{j_l} : T'_l)[\mathscr{A}_j]\}$$

   This statement is the class-building declaration. It defines a class named T, which has data fields x_i of type T_i, $i \in 1..n$, and methods m_j, $j \in 1..r$. $\textbf{pin}_{j_k}$ stands for the input parameters of method m_j, and $\textbf{pout}_{j_l}$ stands for the output parameters of method m_j. The input parameter passing convention is **call by value**, and the output parameter passing convention is **call by reference**. $\mathscr{A}_j$ is the body of method m_j.

2. Class hierarchy:

   $T \textbf{ extends } T' \stackrel{\wedge}{=} T <_{sub} T'$

   This statement is used to build the object hierarchy. It declares that class T is a subclass of class T'. Therefore, T inherits the properties of T'.

3. Field reference:

   $x.d \stackrel{\wedge}{=} x.d$

   This is object field reference. x is an object, and d is a field of x.

4. Method invocation:

   $x.m(\textbf{In } e_k, \textbf{Out } y_l) \stackrel{\wedge}{=} x.m(\textbf{In } e_k, \textbf{Out } y_l)$

   This invokes the method m on object x.

5. Object declaration:

   $T : x \stackrel{\wedge}{=} x : T$

This statement defines x as a variable of type T. If T is a class, x will be an object of class T.

6.4 Summary

WSL has been extended to EWSL, which forms the foundation of using a formal approach to evolve a broader range of software systems, and the developed framework provides a flexible and reliable system of evolution. Evolution can be carried out at different levels, so the software engineer can select the approriate level for the task in hand, and formal methods can be applied throughout the process, at every level of abstraction [15].

References

[1] Schneidewind, N. F., and C. Ebert, "Preserve or Redesign Legacy Systems," *IEEE Software*, Vol. 15, No. 4, 1998.

[2] Sneed, H. M., "Planning the Reengineering of Legacy Systems," *IEEE Software*, Vol. 12, No. 1, January 1995.

[3] Abelson, H., G. J. Sussman, and J. Sussman, *Structure and Interpretation of Computer Programs*, Cambridge, MA: MIT Press, 1985.

[4] Cau, A., and H. Zedan, "Refining Interval Temporal Logic Specification," *Fourth AMAST Workshop on Real-Time Systems, Concurrent and Distributed Software (ARTS'97)*, Mallorca, Spain, May 1997.

[5] Cau, A., "Compositional Verification and Specification of Refinement for Reactive Systems in Dense Time Temporal Logic," De Montfort University, Leicester, U.K., Technical Report, January 1996.

[6] Moszkowski, B., *Executing Temporal Logic Programs*, Cambridge, U.K.: Cambridge University Press, 1986.

[7] Moszkowski, B., "A Temporal Logic for Multilevel Reasoning About Hardware," *IEEE Computer* Vol. 18, No. 2, February 1985, pp. 10–19.

[8] Zedan, H., and H. Heping, "An Executable Specification Language for Fast Prototyping Parallel Responsive Systems," *EUROMICRO Working Conference of Software Maintenance and Engineering*, Florence, Italy, March 1998.

[9] Scholefield, D., *A Refinement Calculus for Real-Time Systems*, Ph.D. thesis, 1992.

[10] Scholefield, D., and H. Zedan, "TAM: A Formal Framework for the Development of Distributed Real-Time Systems," *Symposium on Formal Techniques in Real-Time and Fault-Tolerant Systems*, Nijmegen, the Netherlands, January 1992.

[11] Scholefield, D., H. Zedan, and J. He, "A Specification-Oriented Semantics for the Refinement of Real-Time Systems," *Theoretical Computer Science*, Vol. 30, August 1994.

[12] Dijkstra, E. W., *A Discipline of Programming*, Englewood Cliffs, NJ: Prentice Hall, 1976.

[13] Dijkstra, E. W., and C. S. Scholten, *Predicate Calculus and Program Semantics*, Berlin: Springer-Verlag, 1990.

[14] Kwiatkowski, J., I Puchalski, and H. Yang, "Preprocessing COBOL Programs for Reengineering," in *Object Technology and System Reengineering*, Chichester, U.K.: Horwood Publishing Limited, 1999, pp. 91–110.

[15] Yang, H., X. Liu, and H. Zedan, "Abstraction: A Key Notion for Reverse Engineering in System Reengineering Approach," *Journal of Software Maintenance: Research and Practice*, Vol. 12, No. 5, 2000, pp. 197–228.

CHAPTER 7

Process for Evolution

Contents

7.1 A process for evolution
7.2 Implementing the process
7.3 Translating into EWSL
7.4 Restructuring
7.5 Abstracting
7.6 Understanding with the support of the domain knowledge-based analysis (DKBA) tool
7.7 Reusing components
7.8 Retargeting
7.9 Measuring software evolution
References

This chapter shows how the languages and methods introduced in Chapter 6 form the basis for a practical process for evolving object-oriented, real-time and parallel systems.

7.1 A process for evolution

Over the last several years a practical process of evolution has been developed and experimented with; it takes the following stages [1–3]:

1. Translate source code into EWSL;
2. Restructure (including clustering and visualizing code);
3. Abstract;
4. Understand with the support of a cognitive tool;
5. Reuse components;
6. Retarget;
7. Measure evolution.

Sections 7.2 to 7.9 discuss these stages.

7.2 Implementing the process

The reengineering assistant (RA) is a semiautomatic tool that aims at helping reengineers through the whole process of reengineering legacy systems. RA is a rule-based intelligent system. Automation is a goal of RA, but with the understanding that human intervention is crucial in reverse engineering. Figure 7.1 shows the general system architecture of RA. The architecture reflects the working flow of EWSL in Chapter 6.

The legacy source code is firstly translated into CSL or COOL, and then the CSL/COOL code is parsed and displayed in the browser interface. An internal LISP database of the code is meanwhile generated. The internal database is in a form of syntax tree, which is convenient for transformation and abstraction. Once the CSL/COOL is parsed and stored, the user can go through the evolution processes with the help of the following tools:

- Translating source code into EWSL is done by a language specific translator.

- Restructuring is done by the program transformer. CSL/COOL code is improved through program transformation. New required functionalities can also be added. The new CSL/COOL code can then be translated into an equivalent programming language via a language-specific translator. Graphic models may also be introduced in RA to help understand the legacy system, for example, entity-relation (ER) diagrams, data flow diagrams (DFDs), and structure charts (SCs).

- Abstracting is done by the abstractor. To seek a high-level specification, the abstractor extracts it from CSL or COOL code with abstraction techniques (see below in this chapter). The extracted specification could subsequently be used as a basis for respecification, redesign, and forward engineering through refinement.

- Understanding is carried out with the support of a cognitive tool, DKBA tool.

- Reusing components is first done by the componentizor, the reuse libraries, and the synthesizer. If an object-oriented paradigm is sought, object extraction is performed on CSL code to obtain an equivalent COOL code. Then the COOL code can be extended or improved or left unchanged. Subsequently, the new code can be transformed into an object-oriented language, such as ADA, JAVA, or C++. Reuse libraries are used to store reuseable components, which may form a library.

- Retargetting is mainly done by the synthesizer, which builds up new systems by integration of components in the reusable library.

7.2 Implementing the process

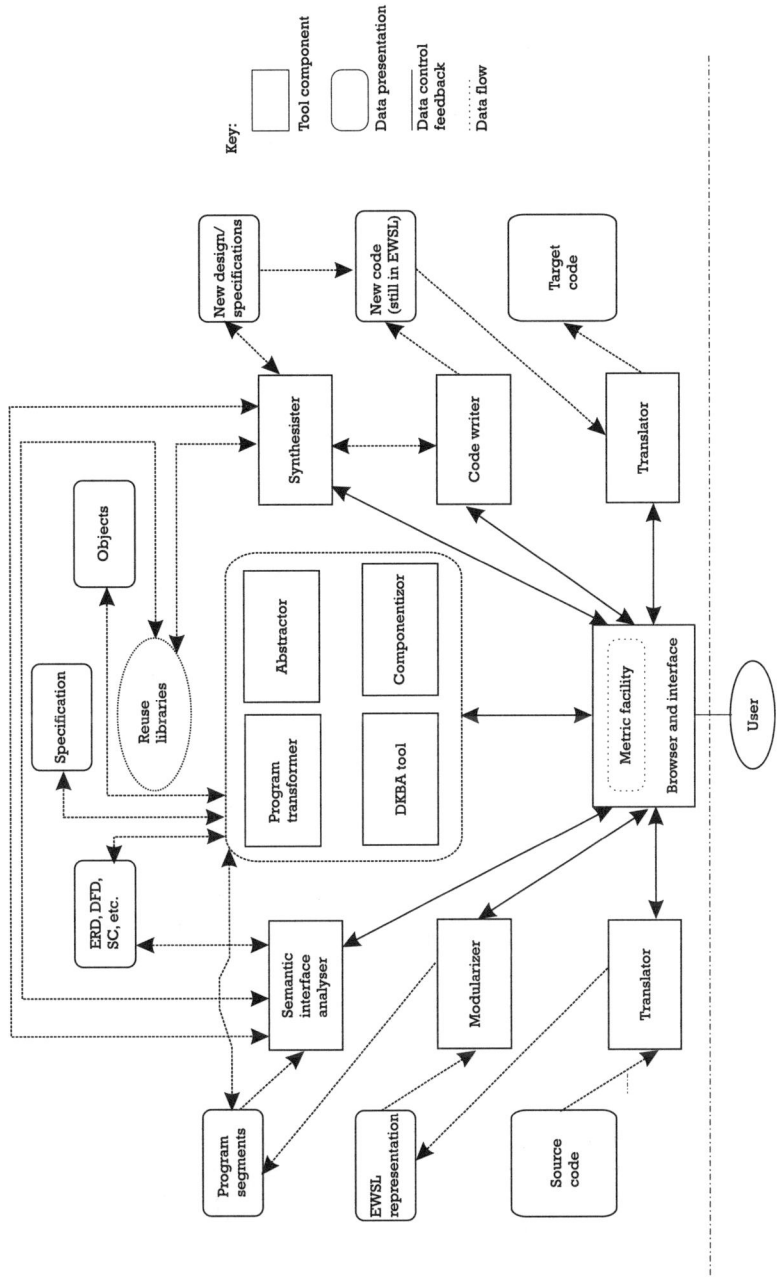

Figure 7.1 General system structure of Reengineering Assistant (RA).

> Measuring reengineering/evolution is done through the metric facility.

The sole interface between software engineers and RA is the browser-interface. It has the following functions:

> To display the translated legacy source code in CSL/COOL;

> To accept process command from software reengineers;

> To accept necessary information that must be acquired from software reengineers;

> To display process results, including extracted specification, new object-oriented COOL program, and transformed source code;

> To display the metric results.

Figure 7.2 shows more detailed tool structure of the reverse engineering part in RA (i.e., extraction of ITL specification from legacy source code).

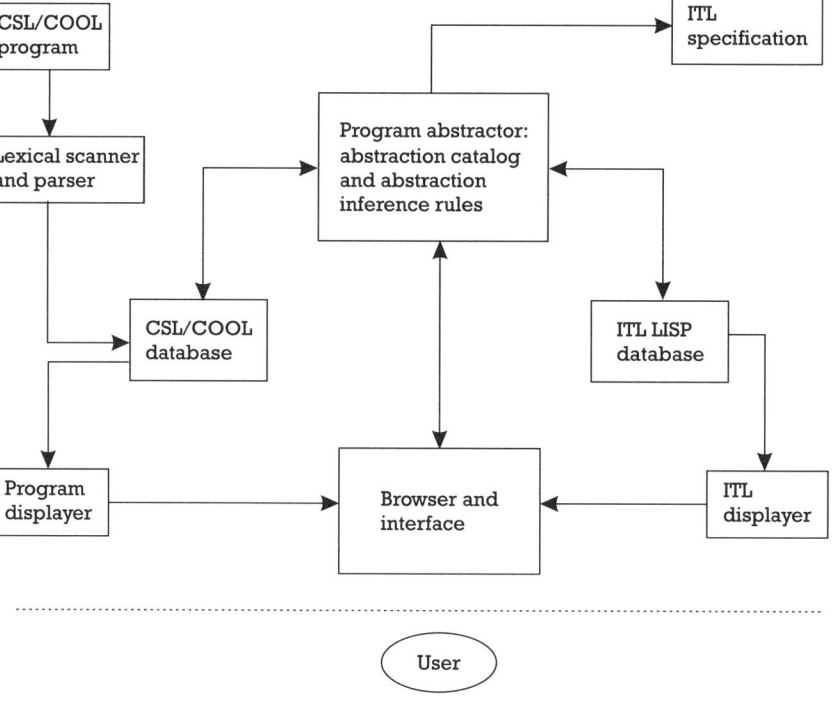

Figure 7.2 Structure of the reverse engineering part of reengineering assistant.

The lexical scanner and parser are used to check the syntax of the CSL/COOL code; errors will be reported to the user through the browser-interface for correction. Correct programs are stored in the CSL/COOL LISP database in a specially designed syntax tree structure. Meanwhile, the program displayer is started to display the program in the browser-interface in a pretty print format (i.e., with indentation and different fonts).

The program abstractor is an inference engine. Various abstractions are classified into corresponding catalogs, and abstraction rules are implemented as inference rules. The extracted ITL specification is stored in the ITL LISP database, in a syntax tree structure specially designed for logic formulae. During abstraction inferencing, the CSL/COOL LISP database and ITL LISP database provide the necessary data. In a knowledge systems sense, they are the databases backing the inference engine. For the extracted ITL specification, further abstraction may also be applied to make it more concise. During the abstraction process, the extracted specification is pretty printed in the browser-interface with the ITL displayer, and the process information is displayed in the LISP dialog window.

CSL/COOL programs are at source code level, and ITL specifications are at the specification level. The program abstractor is an inference machine to cross various abstraction levels with the aid of human interactions.

7.3 Translating into EWSL

A language-specific translator takes code in the source language and translates it into equivalent EWSL code. The translator does not need to be concerned to preserve the structure of the original source code or to generate efficient or readable EWSL [4]. The primary concern is to capture the precise semantics of the source program. For example, the IBM 370 assembler to EWSL translator works by translating each assembler instruction into a block of EWSL code, which captures all the side effects of the instruction (including setting the condition codes and assigning to registers) regardless of whether or not these side effects are used.

7.4 Restructuring

Once the source program has been captured in EWSL there are a large number of restructuring and simplifying transformations (as described in Chapters 4 and 5) that can be applied automatically to clean up the code, unscramble the structure, and delete redundant code (such as redundant assignments to condition code variables). The result is a structured program consisting of a hierarchy of single-entry, single-exit procedures.

A class of transformations have been dedicated to program clustering, which groups relevant control statements and data definitions to form clusters for further restructuring. This is very useful when the code was not written in a structured or object-oriented programming language. In this type of application, it is useful to restructure the code into abstract data types (ADTs) and then later these ADTs can be good candidates to become objects if the code is to be evolved into an object oriented system. For example, an ADT usually involves a set of data items and a number of operations on the set of data items. The operations are implemented in terms of procedures and functions. Clustering transformations can automatically group these data items and operations together. Clustering transformation techniques are also used in mining reusable components (Section 7.7).

Software visualization is often the first step for understanding and deciding which program segments should be selected for a further restructuring. Visualization techniques have been employed in both the FermaT workbench and the RA tool (Figures 5.1–5.5). The workbench includes tools to visualize data structures, module interrelationships (intermodule call graphs), and the control flow within a module. A detailed flowchart of a large module can easily be too large to fit on the screen all at once. Zooming in on a part of the graph is possible, and it is also possible to scroll the viewing window around the large graph. However, a better approach is to use FermaT's clustering facility to collapse groups of flowchart nodes to a single annotated node. This makes it easy to visualize the module's high-level structure while still allowing the user to drill down to low-level details.

7.5 Abstracting

An implementation (code), a design, and a specification of a software system are usually at different levels of abstraction. To move from code to design and then to specification involves a process of raising the level of abstraction (see Chapter 3).

Abstraction is the crucial technique to reverse engineering [5–9]. Without tackling abstractions properly, any design or specification recovery methodology cannot succeed. To achieve correct and practical abstraction, two fundamental problems need to be solved:

1. It is necessary to identify what abstraction is. Although abstraction technology has been used in quite a few research projects [10–15],

the definition of abstraction remains a disputed issue. Most existing definitions adopt ad hoc methods and only cover special aspects of the problem. This results in definitions of abstraction that are ambiguous, incomplete, or even incorrect in some cases. This chapter proposes a taxonomy of abstraction. Within this taxonomy, abstractions are formally defined under different conditions in a reverse engineering environment. Monotonicity and relations between these abstractions are discussed and then described in a formal notation. Healthiness obligations are developed as axioms to guarantee correct and sensible abstraction during reverse engineering.

2. Once abstractions are identified in reverse engineering, the next question is how to perform the abstraction (i.e., how to cross levels of abstractions). This research issue has not been properly addressed, and practical solutions with precisely defined semantics are urgently needed. To solve this problem, a group of abstraction rules for conducting abstraction in the above process are proposed. These rules aim at extracting formal specification from legacy source code and are formally defined and proven sound in ITL, which assures precision and correctness.

7.5.1 Abstraction and abstraction patterns

Our approach first identifies all data items and their visibility levels, where visibility level 0 is the highest. Thereafter it makes the subject system more abstract by removing some data items (those of visibility level > 0) whilst expressing their contribution to the overall functional behavior of the system in terms of the remaining data items. Such a contribution will be expressed (encoded) within the specification statement of EWSL, which is an ITL formula (see Chapter 8 for details).

The approach therefore can be described as follows:

1. Identify all components in a system. There is an obvious correlation between the structure of the legacy code and the structure of the resulting formal specification. The more structured the formal specification is, the easier it is to understand, to improve, and to be used as an appropriate starting point for forward engineering. If the system is very monolithic or unstructured, then engage existing restructuring techniques [11, 16, 17] to decompose the system into subsystems and restructure them.

2. Associate visibility levels for each component. These levels reflect the nesting structure in the system (see Figure 6.1).

3. All data items are associated with the visibility level of the component in which they were first declared.

4. Identify the central data structures and items of the system (i.e., those with level 0).

5. For each ith-level component with $i > 0$ do the following:

   a. Identify all data items local to the component.

   b. Record the effect of the data item, identified in step 5.a, on any data items in levels Q with $Q < i$, in a specification statement of EWSL, and introduce a procedure definition if necessary. Elementary abstraction rules are mostly used, and the procedure name should reflect the functionality of the procedure as closely as possible. Avoid introducing new procedures whenever possible.

   c. Abstract away unnecessary implementation details and trivial functionality within the generated specification. This will be done via corresponding further abstraction rules.

The correctness is achieved through the soundness of the applied abstraction rules.

Abstraction is a process of generalization, removing restrictions, eliminating detail, and removing nonessential information [18]. Unlike transformation, which keeps the semantics unchanged, abstraction endeavors to weaken the original semantics of system implementation. Thus the abstractions cannot be applied without a clear idea of which information contained in the program refers simply to the implementation, and not to the function of the program. In the general case, this information cannot be determined automatically within the system, so user guidance is needed.

To solve this problem, a set of abstraction patterns are proposed based on already developed further abstraction rules as an efficient means to let the software reengineer inform the computer system about his or her observations of the legacy system. Then the computer system will perform abstraction with the aid of these observations and the relevant abstraction rules. These abstraction patterns appear in EWSL and the supporting tool as abstraction pattern assertions.

7.5.2 Definitions

In a software system, the specification is different from source code in the following aspects:

- The source code has implementation details that are not needed in a specification.
- The implementation is focused on how to do, while specification is focused on what to do.
- There can be more nondeterminism in a specification than in an implementation.

In a broad sense, abstraction corresponds to a weakening in semantics, and this weakening is due to the following:

- Inessential design/implementation details are omitted.
- Nondeterminism is increased.
- How to do is substituted by what to do.

The simplest interpretation of the notion of abstraction is that of hiding irrelevant details. Although simple, it leaves open to wider interpretation what constitutes "irrelevant." For this reason, we have decided to categorize abstraction in a way that hopefully makes it clear. We classify abstraction as follows:

1. Weakening abstraction (WA);
2. Hiding abstraction (HA);
3. Temporal abstraction (TA);
4. Structural abstraction (SA);
5. Data abstraction (DA).

These five kinds of abstraction form a fairly complete taxonomy of abstraction. The formal definition of abstraction will be given, and special cases will be discussed next.

The implementation of a software system is known as the concrete form of the system (e.g., source code), and the specification is known as the abstract description. To unify terminology, we use the term *representation* for both abstract and concrete forms. Therefore, an abstraction relation $\succcurlyeq$ is defined as a function relating two representations of one single system. A representation $\mathcal{B}$ is an abstraction of representation $\mathcal{A}$, written as $\mathcal{A} \succcurlyeq_f \mathcal{B}$ (read as $\mathcal{B}$ is an abstraction of $\mathcal{A}$ in respect of f) is defined as

$$\mathcal{A} \succcurlyeq \mathcal{B} \stackrel{\Delta}{=} f(\mathcal{A}, \mathcal{B})$$

where f is defined according to the type of abstraction, namely WA, HA, TA, SA and DA.

WA WA is quite broad in sense. Here, "weakening" refers to semantics weakening of representations during abstraction. If some information is taken out from the original representation, and the new result representation does not contradict with the original, (that is, the semantics of the original representation implies that of the new representation), then a semantics weakening sequence is present and the new representation is a WA of the original one.

HA HA focuses on the simplification of data space. It emphasizes that a part of the data space of the original representation is to be considered as irrelevant or unnecessary and is therefore omitted from the representation. However, the resulting representation should still be a semantic weakening of the original one. In practical reverse engineering, HA is often used to get rid of local variables and hide internal communication channels. This is because these details become unimportant or too local and should not be observed outside the black box when a software system is viewed from a more abstract point of view.

TA TA is abstraction that relates to time. It is useful and popular when tackling the reverse engineering of real-time systems. For the representation of a fragment of software systems, namely $\mathcal{A}$, its duration is defined as the time span from the beginning of its execution to the end of its execution. Temporal abstraction reflects the variation of this duration while abstraction is conducted.

SA SA is so named because it endeavors to make structural simplification in system representation. There are two kinds of composition structures: sequential composition and parallel composition. With SA, these compositions are reduced and their effects are recorded in a more abstract representation. Two basic conditions determine whether a change in system representation is a structural abstraction: first, whether there are any sequential or parallel compositions that have been reduced in the new representation, and second, whether the semantics of the new representation represent a weakening of the original.

DA   DA is a general technique by which one can change the state space of a program. DA allows the software engineer to extend and change the original data types in legacy code to more high-level and domain-specific data types. In the absence of DA, data structures identified from legacy code remain unchanged during the whole reverse engineering process although it will help to acquire better specification if the data structure is mapped to a more suitable one. DA is a quite complex means to reverse engineering. Correct DA can improve the resulting specification greatly, while improper DA may result in degraded specification.

In a DA, a DA relation must be defined first to map the original data structures to new data structures and therefore the original data states to new data states. The condition of DA is that the semantics of the new representation must be a weakening of the original representation. If it is difficult to judge, then the data states of the original representation need to be mapped over the data abstraction relation. The ghost variables technique, discussed in Chapter 8, is one way to break down a complex DA into smaller steps.

7.5.3 Healthiness obligation

Healthiness obligations are conditions that must hold for the abstraction to be valid. Different abstractions have different healthiness obligations. These are similar to Dijkstra's healthiness conditions [19, 20] for his guarded command language. One can think of them as axioms or invariants.

- *HA*
  - Shared variables between different representations should not be hidden. These shared variables connect different representations and involve important design or functional information.
  - Variables with a visibility level of zero should not be hidden. This is because such variables are global variables in structured legacy systems and are crucial to the design and specification.

- *WA*
  - Any representation should not be abstracted to **TRUE** or **FALSE** (trivial specification or starting from scratch). Although abstraction throws away irrelevant or unimportant details, it does not make sense to throw away everything!

- *TA*
  - An infinite action cannot be performed in a finite interval.
  - Any representation cannot be abstracted to an agent with a negative time interval.

- *SA*
  - Two finite representations in sequential or parallel composition can not be structurally abstracted to an infinite representation. This means that if there is any contention between the two representations (for example, resource deadlock), then the sequential or parallel composition can not be reduced.

- *DA*
  - A DA operation must not map variables to themselves; otherwise the result reduces to weakening abstraction.

7.5.4 Relations between abstractions

The partial ordering relations between the five categories of abstractions discussed in Section 7.5.2 are shown in Figure 7.3.

The following conclusions have been proven sound in formal logic:

1. TA, SA, and HA are also WAs. This means that WA is the basis of all these abstractions. In other words, TA, SA, and HA are stronger in semantics than WA. The reason is that semantics weakening forms a part of the definitions of other abstractions. Abstraction is different from both transformation and restructuring, and there should be a consistency between the original semantics and the abstracted semantics.

2. TA, SA, and HA are independent of each other. There is no partial ordering or overlap between them.

7.5 Abstracting

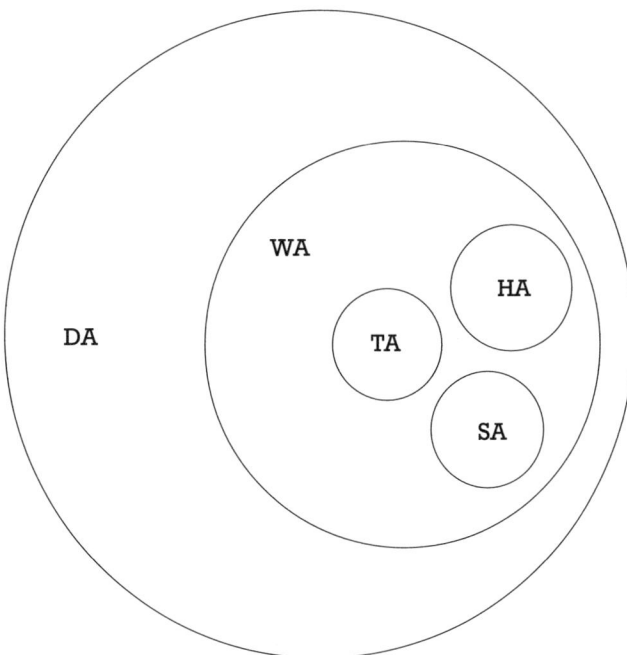

Figure 7.3 Subset relations between abstractions.

3. DA is the most general. If the variable set of $\mathscr{A}$ remains to be the same of $\mathscr{B}$ (i.e., the DA relation r maps to itself) then DA reduces to WA.

7.5.5 Elementary abstraction rules

We classify abstraction rules into two categories: (1) elementary abstraction rules to abstract source statements into logic formulae that may be very redundant and specific, and (2) further abstraction rules, which extract a more concise and abstract specifications from the formulae through composition and semantic weakening. Also, abstraction rules fall into different sections according to the domain with which the rules deal. For example, when dealing with an object-oriented (time-critical) system, the abstraction rules consist of general abstraction rules, object-oriented abstraction rules, and time critical rules.

Abstraction rules in this category aim to abstract the statements in TGCL and ObTAM to formulae in ITL (initially, the formulae may be redundant or even too specific) and these rules can transform source statements into logic formulae, which is a kind of specification. So, in further abstraction, logic composition and semantic weakening will be applied through further abstraction rules to abstract these formulae to a more concise and abstract specification.

The statements in TGCL and ObTAM consist of two sets: (1) simple statements such as assignment, input, and output, and (2) composite statements, which are a composition of simple statements and composite statements through composition structures, such as condition, loop, and procedure. Therefore, elementary abstraction rules fall into two sets correspondingly: the first set, which is named *primitive abstraction rules*, converts the simple statements to ITL formulae, and the second set, which is named *compound abstraction rules*, deals with the composite statements.

7.5.6 Further abstraction rules

Further abstraction rules aim to extract more concise and abstract specifications from the formulae obtained through applying the elementary abstraction rules. Logic composition and semantics weakening are the basis of further abstraction. During further abstraction domain knowledge may be applied by software engineers to give the software system a more concise and domain-specific description.

There is no object combination during further abstraction (i.e. objects may be abstracted but not combined).

7.6 Understanding with the support of the domain knowledge-based analysis (DKBA) tool

Program understanding is the process of acquiring knowledge from a computer program. Current methods that support automatic program understanding can be classified into the following categories:

- *Basic analysis* in which only programming language syntax and semantic are used;

- *Formal analysis*, which deals with formal and structural program properties;

- *Informal reasoning* where heuristics and domain knowledge are used to extract domain model or other program properties from source code.

7.6 Understanding with the support of the DKBA tool

Informal reasoning can be further classified into

- Structurally oriented heuristic analysis [21];
- DKBA [13, 22–30].

As the demand for software evolution is increasing dramatically, there is a growing realization that the design of effective software evolution tools must be smarter, and this motivates artificial intelligence (AI) researchers to search for better solutions. We use a clarity-guided belief revision appoach to domain knowledge recovery in legacy system [31–36] in our evolution process. More specifically, solutions are given to three key issues:

1. *Knowledge representation*, where the concrete semantic network is separated from the abstract semantic network;
2. *Uncertainty and nonmonotonic reasoning*, which is based on confirmation theory and belief revision;
3. *Heuristic search techniques*, which owe their development to programming psychology.

The most difficult part of the evolution process is understanding the system [37]. Program understanding is a complex and difficult task especially for analyzing the source code of large legacy systems. Full automation is not practical, and close cooperation between program analyst and DKBA tool is needed. A number of requirements for DKBA tool are identified:

- *Uncertainty:* To deal with such problems as ambiguity and incompleteness, of source code or the domain knowledge that prevails in legacy systems, the ability to tolerate and deal with uncertain information and knowledge is the first requirement for DKBA tools. This is important because only through tolerating uncertainty can continuous reasoning be achieved.
- *Nonmonotonic reasoning:* In the real world, nonmonotonic reasoning frequently occurs. For example, a program analyst may refute a conclusion made by a DKBA user in the light of new evidences found, and therefore, revised reasoning and propagating the change through the knowledge space is needed. A good knowledge representation in which nonmonotonic reasoning can be carried out is needed.

- *Quality of conclusions:* The quality of conclusions provided by a DKBA user is important because bad conclusions may mislead programmers into wrong judgement paths leading to future refutations of the conclusions. This is extremely adverse to the productivity of the knowledge recovery process.

- *Response time:* In a human-machine interactive environment, a quick response from the DKBA tool to an analyst's query is obviously important. A certain kind of prediction from the DKBA assistant for program analyst's intention is desirable. There is sometimes a trade-off between the quality of the conclusion and the response time. However, a high-quality oriented search can sometimes lead to a reduction in response time in the future because high-quality results can help in producing further high-quality results, and this increases the probability of users' hitting an existing result. The governing principle here is whenever basic quality can be assured, do it quickly. Good heuristic knowledge can help to achieve this.

7.6.1 Knowledge representation

We use a semantic network as the domain knowledge representation in our approach. The definition of a semantic network is as follows:

A semantic network, SN is a pair (N, E), where N denotes the set of nodes and E the set of interrelationships among nodes. N can be classified into two kinds of nodes, named object nodes and action nodes. Object nodes can represent class, instance, and features, for example, while action nodes can represent operations or events that occur among several objects. E can be classified into object-object, object-action, and action-action relationships. Table 7.1 gives a description of the possible occurrence of interrelationships in each category.

As the semantic network is used to discover knowledge from programs, we enhance the ordinary semantic network representation by importing the concept of a knowledge slice. In order to implement this idea, we give two

Table 7.1 Interrelationships Among Nodes in a Semantic Network

	Possible Interrelationships
Object–object	Instance of, part of, etc.
Object–action	Receiver of, sender of
Action–action	Subplan of, precedent of, etc.

7.6 Understanding with the support of the DKBA tool

layers of description of semantic network (i.e., the abstract semantic network and the concrete semantic network, respectively). Figure 7.4 shows an abstract semantic network for network application domain. In this abstract semantic network, no detailed interrelationships among nodes can be found. It is designed for the purpose of showing knowledge slices in the application domain where the nodes and edges grouped by an arc (if more than two nodes involved) form a single slice of domain knowledge. By using an abstract semantic network to gather knowledge slices, all these knowledge slices can be highly interconnected, which can facilitate continuous reasoning, uncertainty propagation, and nonmonotonic reasoning (to be introduced in later sections). Concrete semantic networks cover objects, actions, and the concrete interrelationships among them. Figures 7.5 to 7.7 give examples for concrete semantic networks in the situation where interrelationships for action-action, object-object, and action-object exist respectively.

The normal reasoning process for domain knowledge recovery during the preparation stage is descibed as follows:

1. Collect domain concepts and the interrelationship among these concepts from the program by matching the whole program against the total set of domain concepts.

2. Pick up all the candidate domain knowledge that has the potential of matching with the collected domain concepts and the interrelationships among the concepts.

During the reasoning stage, iterate on the following steps until there is no candidate domain knowledge:

1. Pick up a candidate domain knowledge item.

2. Check whether this candidate domain knowledge can be successfully matched.

3. Propagate the matched result both at the domain knowledge level and the program level in order to discover more candidate domain knowledge.

7.6.2 Uncertainty reasoning and nonmonotonic reasoning

There are two issues to be addressed:

1. Names in programs can have ambiguous meanings, particularly when abbreviated (the same abbreviation can have several different interpretations).

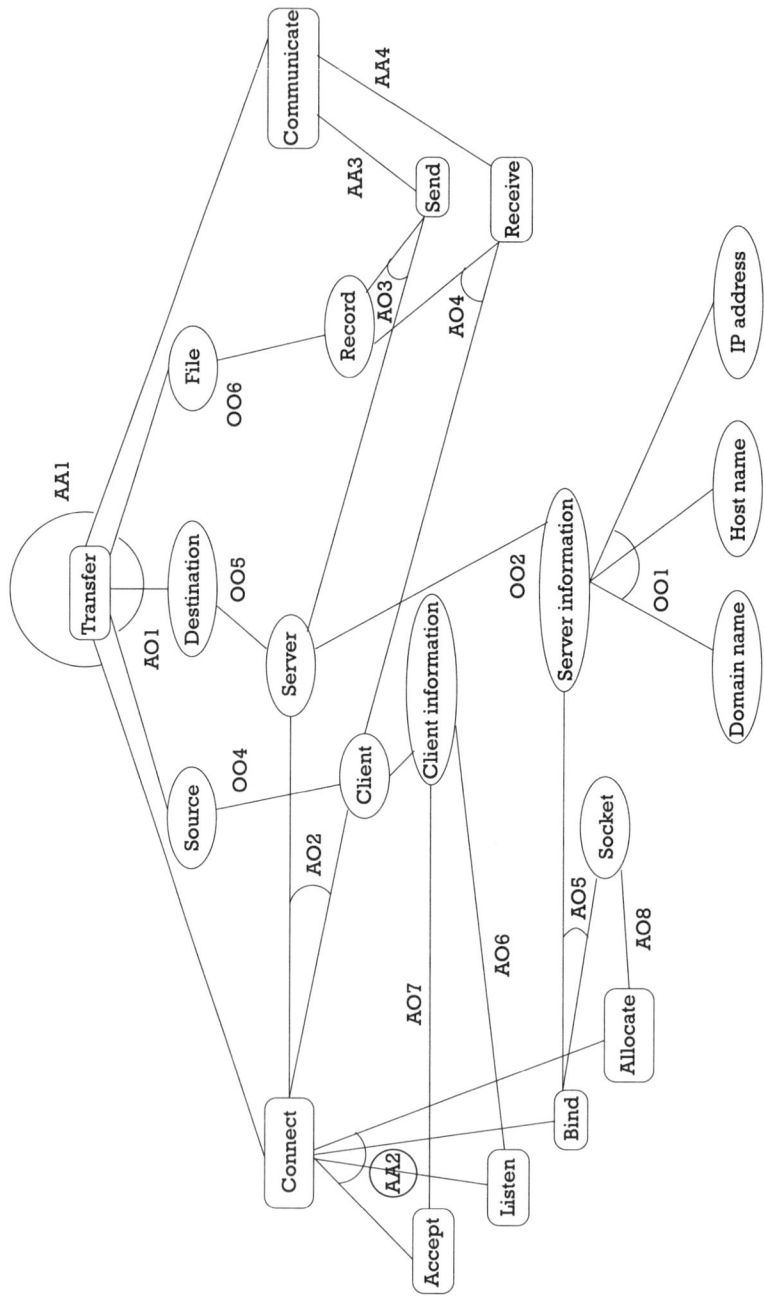

Figure 7.4 An example of abstract semantic network in the network application domain.

7.6 Understanding with the support of the DKBA tool

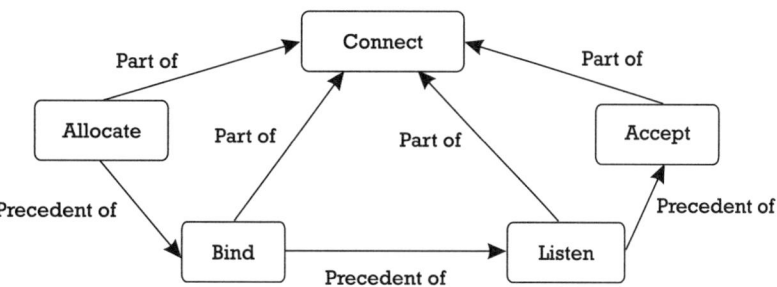

Figure 7.5 An example of concrete semantic network for an action-action interrelationship.

2. In the reasoning stage, there may be insufficient evidence to get a 100% match against domain knowledge slices.

Our solution to uncertainty issues is based on the principles of confirmation theory [38]. Although we build our uncertainty reasoning model on a semantic network that is quite different from MYCIN, the rule-based expert system in which confirmation theory was deployed, it is still useful to give a brief introduction to the principles of confirmation theory.

MYCIN and confirmation theory In MYCIN, production rules are used as knowledge representation. A single production rule takes the form: $E \xrightarrow{CF(H,E)} H$. E stands for evidences and H stands for hypotheses. Both E and H are propositions. $CF(H, E)$ stands for the strength of the rule (i.e., the degree by which E has effect on H).

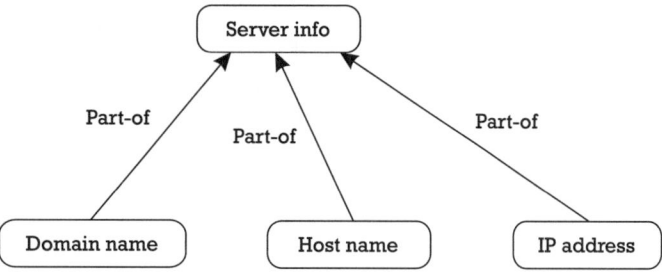

Figure 7.6 An example of concrete semantic network for an action-object interrelationship.

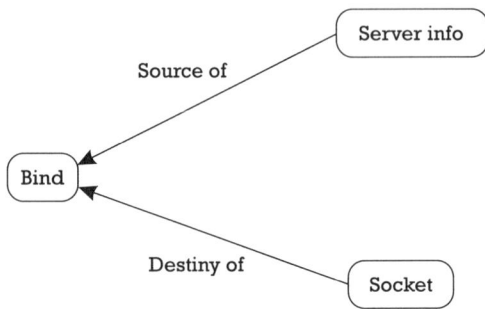

Figure 7.7 An example of concrete semantic network for an action-object interrelationship.

Uncertainty description of rules The most important concepts in confirmation theory are the multiplication rate of belief (MB) and multiplication rate of disbelief (MD). An exclusivity law holds between MB and MD:

Theorem 7.1

$$\begin{cases} \text{if} \quad \text{MB}(H, E) > 0, \quad \text{MD}(H, E) = 0 \\ \text{if} \quad \text{MD}(H, E) > 0, \quad \text{MB}(H, E) = 0 \end{cases}$$

Both MB and MD have their probability interpretation as follows:

Definition 7.1

$$\begin{cases} \text{MB}(H, E) = \dfrac{P(H|E) - P(H)}{1 - P(H)} & \text{if} \quad P(H|E) > P(H) \\ \text{MD}(H, E) = \dfrac{P(H) - P(H|E)}{P(H)} & \text{if} \quad P(H|E) < P(H) \\ \text{MB}(H, E) = \text{MD}(H, E) = 0 & \text{if} \quad P(H|E) = P(H) \end{cases}$$

The certainty factor (CF) is therefore defined as follows.

Definition 7.2 $\text{CF}(H, E) = \text{MB}(H, E) - \text{MD}(H, E)$

It is clear that that $-1 \leq \text{CF} \leq 1$. From Theorem 7.1, Definition 7.1, and Definition 7.2 we can also get

7.6 Understanding with the support of the DKBA tool

Definition 7.3

$$\mathrm{CF}(H, E) = \begin{cases} 1 & P(H) = 1 \\ \dfrac{P(H|E) - P(H)}{1 - P(H)} & P(H|E) > P(H) \\ 0 & P(H|E) = P(H) \\ -\dfrac{P(H) - P(H|E)}{P(H)} & P(H|E) < P(H) \\ -1 & P(H) = 0 \end{cases}$$

Uncertainty description of evidences In MYCIN, the uncertainty of E is still described by $\mathrm{CF}(E, E')$ where E' is called the virtual variable, which represents all the evidences related to E. From Definition 7.3 we can see: if E is true, $\mathrm{CF}(E, E') = 1$; if E is false, $\mathrm{CF}(E, E') = -1$; if E has just been initialized with no related evidence obtained, $\mathrm{CF}(E, E') = 0$.

Other descriptions of uncertainty processing In MYCIN, uncertainty issues are also discussed in such situations as propagation of uncertainty through in a rule, synthesis of multiple results, and dealing with compound evidences. In this work we are dealing with the uncertainty processing in a semantic network, and therefore we have only introduced necessary knowledge about confirmation theory as background for discussion in this chapter. Interested readers can refer to [38] for more information.

Identifying names In the name dictionary where all the concepts in a specific domain are held, a single domain concept can be represented by either an atomic name or a compound name. An atomic name is an indivisible lexical unit whereas a compound name constitutes several atomic names. If all the user-defined names in a program are given as full names, then the domain concepts can be obtained directly. However, in reality, programmers always use naming abbreviation rules by which names of such factors as variables, types, procedures, are only meaningful for the programmers who wrote the program (not for others). This ambiguity pushes us to find solutions to recover the original names. For atomic names, the ambiguity results mainly from the abbreviation methods programmers used. We therefore give two classifications to atomic name abbreviation rules: regular abbreviation rules and irregular abbreviation rules. The regular abbreviation rules can be "first three letters (0.15)" or "first letter + last two letters (0.2)," which can be applied to all the atomic names. The number in brackets attached to each rule indicates the strength of this rule. The irregular abbreviation rules are mainly involved in the pronunciation of a particular word. For simplicity, we collect as many irregular abbreviation cases as possible for each atomic name. Apart from regular abbreviation rules, the match for an atomic name having irregular abbreviation rules is done by checking every case. Each irregular abbreviation rule has a real number indicating its rule strength. Generally, the strength of irregular abbreviation rules is much higher than that of regular abbreviation rules. A portion of atomic name dictionary is shown in Table 7.2.

A single compound name is made up of several atomic names with or without connection symbols linking them together. The connection symbols can be "-", "_", etc. The cases without a connection symbol could be capitalized words, which may not be found in the atomic name dictionary. The ambiguity in a compound name mainly comes from the ambiguity in the atomic names that compose the whole name. We describe two classes of compound abbreviation rules: regular compound abbreviation rules and irregular compound abbreviation rules. The regular compound abbreviation rule is as follows: Match each atom name from a compound name in a program against corresponding compositions of a particular compound name in compound name dictionary. The certainty factor of the match is the minimum of all the certainty factors result from the match of atomic names. The irregular compound abbreviation rules are embodied in a set of irregular cases collected as ordinary abbreviations for commonly used compound names. According to the number of atomic names in each name,

Table 7.2 Atomic Name Dictionary

Atomic Name	Irregular Cases
...	
Accept	Acpt (0.85)
...	
Client	
...	
Destiny	
...	
Information	info (0.90), infor (0.85)
...	
Receive	Recv (0.90), Rec (0.60)
...	
Record	Rec (0.60)

7.6 Understanding with the support of the DKBA tool

the compound names can be classified into a pair compound name dictionary or a triple compound name dictionary, for example. Table 7.3 shows a pair compound name dictionary.

The procedure of recovering an atomic/compound name in program is comprised of the following steps:

1. Decide whether the input name is a compound name or an atomic name by checking for connection symbols (for those without connection symbol, try another rule mentioned above) in order to select a suitable name dictionary. For a compound name, check the number of components to decide which compound name dictionary to use.

2. **LOOP** on all the records in the dictionary. For each record, check the following:
   - Whether the full name can be matched;
   - Whether irregular abbreviation rules apply;
   - Whether regular abbreviation rules apply.

3. **IF** none of the three cases above apply or the overall certainty factor is 0, **THEN** ignore this name. **ELSE** choose a match with the highest certainty value.

Several match examples for atomic/compound names can be found in Table 7.4.

Uncertainty reasoning in semantic networks The obtained names together with their uncertainty values are put into an abstract semantic network from which candidate domain knowledge slices can be selected. Specifically, such issues will be discussed as how to decide the degree of

Table 7.3 Pair Compound Name Dictionary

Compound Name	Compositions	Irregular case
...		
Client-Information	Client, Information	
...	...	
Domain-Name	Domain, Name	DN (0.70)
...		

Table 7.4 Match Examples for Atomic/Compound Names

Name in Source Code	Domain Concept (Certainty Factor)
Client	Client (1.0)
Info	Information (0.95)
Des	Destination (0.15)
Rec	Receive (0.6), Record (0.6)
Client-info	Client-Information (0.9)
DN	Domain-Name (0.7)

matching in a domain knowledge slice, and how the resulting matching degree affects the belief of each participating domain concept. Also, it is necessary to determine how to control the search in the net, and what if a previously confirmed (refuted) conclusion is, in the light of new information, now refuted (confirmed).

Contribution strength and refutation strength A candidate domain knowledge slice is composed of domain concepts and interrelationships among these concepts as shown in Figures 7.6 to 7.7. Part (or all) of the knowledge slice can match with evidences collected from the program being analyzed. However, as generally is the case, within one knowledge slice, each domain concept or interrelationship will make a different contribution to the recognition of this knowledge slice. Take Figure 7.6, for example, the actions of connect, listen, and accept will contribute more than allocate and bind to recognize this scenario where subactions are taken to fulfill the task of connect. Moreover, the absence of a domain concept or interrelationship would totally refute the existence of a particular knowledge slice in program. We hereby introduce two concepts: contribution strength (CS) and refutation strength (RS). CS indicates the strength the presentation of a domain concept or interrelationship has to build up more belief in the knowledge slice. RS indicates the destructive power that the absence of a domain concept or interrelationship has to refute the knowledge slice. Both CS and RS are real numbers in the range 0 to 1. Their role will be exemplified by the formulae in the next section. By default, CS and RS are set to 0. Table 7.5 shows an example. Since interrelationships are built on domain concepts, we give relatively lower contribution strength to interrelationships. However, although domain concepts can present themselves in a knowledge slice, the key interrelationships among them may be absent from the program. This suggests that those domain concepts may be the constituents of other knowledge slices rather than this one. That is the reason why a higher RS can be given for interrelationships than for domain

7.6 Understanding with the support of the DKBA tool

Table 7.5 Contribution Strength, Refutation Strength, and Decision Weight

Domain Concept and Interrelationship	CS	RS
Connect	0.90	0.90
Allocate	0.15	0.15
Bind	0.30	0.30
Listen	0.90	0.90
Accept	0.90	0.90
(Allocate) ⇔ (Bind)	0.15	0.20
(Bind) ⇔ (Listen)	0.30	0.50
(Listen) ⇔ (Accept)	0.30	0.90
(Connect) ⇔ (Allocate)	0.25	0.25
(Connect) ⇔ (Bind)	0.25	0.30
(Connect) ⇔ (Listen)	0.30	0.40
(Connect) ⇔ (Accept)	0.30	0.40

concepts. The initial source of refutation is usually from the user, and therefore refutation should have a higher authority than acceptance.

Calculation of the matching degree of a domain knowledge slice
Let $SN = (n_1, ..., n_m, e_1, ..., e_k)$ be a domain knowledge slice and $[(CS_1, RS_1), ..., (CS_{m+k}, RS_{m+k})]$ be the contribution strength and refutation strength of each element in SN respectively, $CF = (CF_1, ..., CF_{m+k})$ be the current certainty factors of each element in SN and MV be the matching degree of SN. The algorithm of calculating the matching degree MV of SN is as follows:

$MB := 0;$
for $i := 1$ **to** $m + k$ **do**
    if $CF_i > 0$
        then $MB := MB + (1 - MB) * CF_i * CS_i$ **fi od**;
$MD := 0;$
for $i := 1$ **to** $m + k$ **do**
    if $CF_i < 0$
        then $MD := MD + (1 - MD) * (-CF_i) * RS_i$ **fi od**;
$MV := (1 - MD) * MB - MD$

Belief updating The purpose of computing the matching degree of domain knowledge slices is to re-evaluate the certainty of participating knowledge concepts (note, not interrelationships). The formulae below are designed for calculating updated belief on each node. Let CF'_i be the updated certainty for node i. The other terms used in this algorithm are accorded with the definition in the last section.

$$MB = \begin{cases} CF_i & CF_i > 0 \\ 0 & CF_i \leq 0 \end{cases}$$

$$MD = \begin{cases} -CF_i & CF_i < 0 \\ 0 & CF_i \geq 0 \end{cases}$$

$$MB' = \begin{cases} MV \times CS_i & MV > 0 \\ 0 & MV \leq 0 \end{cases}$$

$$MD' = \begin{cases} 0 & MV > 0 \\ -MV \times RS_i & MV \leq 0 \end{cases}$$

$$CF'_i = \begin{cases} MB + (1-MB) * MB' & MB > 0 \wedge MB' > 0 \\ -(MD + (1-MD) * MD') & MD > 0 \wedge MD' > 0 \\ MB - MD' & MB > 0 \wedge MD' > 0 \\ MB' - MD & MD > 0 \wedge MB' > 0 \end{cases}$$

An example   An example of a computation of MV is shown in Table 7.6. We can see although the information on connect hasn't initially been given due to such factors as the mismatching of names, it can still be reasoned out by the presence of other evidences, and the results will in turn benefit other domain concept recognition through certainty propagation in the network.

Table 7.6 An Example for Computation of MV

Domain Concept and Interrelationship	CS	RS	CF	CF'
Connect	0.90	0.90	0.00	0.89
Allocate	0.15	0.15	0.00	0.15
Bind	0.30	0.30	0.00	0.30
Listen	0.90	0.90	1.00	1.00
Accept	0.90	0.90	1.00	1.00
(Allocate) ⇔ (Bind)	0.15	0.20	0.00	0.00
(Bind) ⇔ (Listen)	0.30	0.50	0.00	0.00
(Listen) ⇔ (Accept)	0.30	0.90	1.00	1.00
(Connect) ⇔ (Allocate)	0.25	0.25	0.00	0.00
(Connect) ⇔ (Bind)	0.25	0.30	0.00	0.00
(Connect) ⇔ (Listen)	0.30	0.40	0.00	0.00
(Connect) ⇔ (Accept)	0.30	0.40	0.00	0.00
MB=0.99, MD=0.0, MV=0.99				

7.6 Understanding with the support of the DKBA tool

Table 7.7 Network Search Algorithm

ADC := null;
CDC := knowledge slices affected by initial evidences from program;
while CDC $\neq \emptyset$ **do**
    Epi := a selected candidate from CDC;
    STACK $\overset{push}{\longleftarrow}$ ⟨Epi, 1⟩;
    while STACK $\neq$ ⟨⟩ **do**
        ⟨Epi′, layer⟩ $\overset{pop}{\longleftarrow}$ STACK
        if Epi′ is not marked $\wedge$ layer $\leq$ DC
            then Compute matching degree of Epi′;
                and update the belief of nodes;
            if matching degree of Epi′ > AT
                then CDC := CDC − Epi′;
                      ADC := ADC + Epi′ **fi**;
            Mark Epi′ as 'processed';
            in the abstract semantic network;
            CDC′ := the candidate knowledge slices
                affected by Epi′;
            CDC := CDC + CDC′;
            STACK $\overset{push}{\longleftarrow}$ ⟨CDC′, layer + 1⟩ **fi od** ;
    Clear all the marks in this "earthquake" **od**

Network search algorithm   If we imagine a recently matched knowledge slice as an epicenter of an earthquake, then by updating the certainty of domain concepts within it, the neighboring knowledge slices that share common domain concepts in the abstract semantic network (see Figure 7.4) can now become candidate knowledge slices to be matched and ready to pass on the seismic wave. Empirical experience suggests that several layers of knowledge slices away from the epicenter are involved in the seismic wave and together are likely to form a highly coupled knowledge group and thus produce more high-quality knowledge concepts. We therefore set a depth constant (DC) to limit the depth of search in a single "earthquake." We give higher priority to those candidates involved in the "earthquake" than other existing candidates. In order to stop further matching on an already satisfactory conclusion, we introduce an acceptance threshold (AT) to pick out good conclusions with certainty value higher than AT. Table 7.7 shows the general search algorithm, with a global candidate domain concept (CDC) and accepted domain concept (ADC).

From the algorithm we can see that a potentially good conclusion may be iteratively built-up by first selecting a good epicenter and evaluating DC layers around it to build up more certainty. In the next iteration, the same epicenter or the layers around it must be selected since they have higher certainty than before (and also higher than other candidates). When a good conclusion is accepted and deleted from the candidate knowledge slices, the selection of another good candidate is in turn needed. The question here is how to make an efficient evaluation of which candidate is good.

Nonmonotonic reasoning Nonmonotonic reasoning occurs when a user refutes a conclusion made by the DKBA assistant. It requires a re-evaluation of knowledge slices directly or indirectly involved. From the discussion in Section 7.6.2 it is seen that nonmonotonic reasoning can be naturally included in the normal uncertainty reasoning procedures without extra effort. The only thing needed is to select those knowledge slices whose participating domain concept was refuted as a "good" candidate.

7.6.3 Program space partitioning

The DKBA tool in RA uses programming psychology to find computationally simple and empirically effective heuristic rules for candidate selections. A large software program is generally cowritten by a group of programmers. Each programmer is responsible for only one part of the program, which is usually a self-contained component with relatively independent functionality. Even within each module, submodules can be written by particular programmers to fulfill self-contained functions, (for example, a back office processing module can have such submodules as telephone line maintenance and phone-bill). All those components are connected with common well-defined interfaces for passing parameters. Empirical studies [37] suggests that each programmer, with a different training background and character from the others, tends to use a particular and consistent code-writing style. These styles usually affect the readability of the code they write. If different programming styles in a program can be identified, how many programmers contributed to the final program can be recognized. The benefits of this heuristic rule are twofold: (1) The search for good candidates can be focused in a single functional submodule that is more efficient and

7.6 Understanding with the support of the DKBA tool

desirable, and (2) priority can be given to program regions with good readability to improve the effectiveness of knowledge recovery.

7.6.4 Programming style and program partitioning

Three key features in source code can be used to distinguish different programming styles. They are style of comments, style of names, and style of indent. We give taxonomy to each feature. Some examples can be found in Table 7.8.

A, B, etc. in the category class of Table 7.8 are not referring to particular styles, but only used for the purpose of distinguishing different styles. Algorithms for creating sampling functions of programming styles are given in Table 7.9. Some abbreviations are programming style (PS), current program line (CPL), sampling function (SF), and sample interval (SI).

The partitioning of program is based on the programming style of sampling function. We know a programmer's programming style is consistent regardless of the function of the code he or she is writing. We also know that it is possible that different users share the same programming style. However, what can be decided is that the program points where the new program style comes up or the old program style disappears will be the watershed of different programmers. An algorithm is hereby designed to partition a program on the basis of this principle. Some abbreviations are

Table 7.8 Programming Styles

Feature	Example	Class	Pattern
Comment	//******************** //* This is my module * //********************	A	//*
	//++++++++++++++++++++ //+ This is my module + //++++++++++++++++++++ ...	B	//+
Name	Client-info	A	*-*
	Client_info ...	B	*_*
Indent	if (i<0) return;	A	?????*
	if (i<0) return; ...	B	??*

Table 7.9 Algorithm for Creating Sampling Function of Programming Styles

PS := null;
CPL := 1;
SF := null;
while CPL $\neq$ END_OF_PROGRAM **do**
    ps := programming style in CPL;
    if ps $\in$ PS
      then PS[ps] := PS[ps] + 1
      else PS := PS $\cup$ {ps}
          PS[ps] := PS[ps] + 1 **fi**;
    if CPL mod SI = 0
      then SF := (SF, PS);
           PS := null **fi**;
CPL := CPL + 1 **od**

sample pointer (SP), sample number (SN), programming style number (PSN), and partition (Par).

Following the algorithm in Table 7.10, the program is linearly divided into small program sections. It is possible that several program sections are written by the same programmers. We hereby regroup the program sections by checking the programming styles obtained within them (i.e., if two program sections have exactly the same programming styles, they will be put into one group).

Table 7.10 Algorithm for Partitioning Program Based on Programming Styles

Sp := 1;
Par := null;
while Sp $\neq$ SN **do**
    ps := 1;
    while ps $\neq$ PSN **do**
      if PS[ps] = 0 $\wedge$ PS[ps + 1] > 0 $\vee$ PS[ps] > 0 $\wedge$ PS[ps + 1] = 0
        then Par := (Par, Sp) **fi**;
      ps := ps + 1 **od** ;
Sp := Sp + 1 **od**

Evaluating the quality of program sections Let Qua_i be the quality of program section i, **CW** and **NW** be the weights for comment and name respectively where $CW > 0$, $NW > 0$, $CW + NW = 1$, CD_i and ND_i be the density of comments and names in program section i respectively. Both CD_i and ND_i can be easily calculated based on the algorithm in Table 7.10. We will not give its algorithm separately. We have $Qua_i = CW \times CD_i + NW \times ND_i$.

Search heuristic revisited Now we can look at the question of how to efficiently select a good candidate knowledge slice. To calculate the quality of candidate knowledge slices, let **CKS** be a candidate knowledge slice, **PSS** be be the set of program sections where the participating domain concepts of each knowledge slice comes from, **QPSS** be the set of metric with each element being the quality of corresponding program section, and **QCKS** be the quality for **CKS**; we have: $QCKS = \min\{QPSS\}$. The priority of choosing a good candidate knowledge slice is therefore given to the knowledge slice (1) with the highest **QCKS**; (2) in the same program partition with previous **Epi** (see Table 7.7) if still can be decided by (1); (3) with highest previous matching degree if it still can not be decided by (1) and (2); (4) if all else fails randomly choose one.

7.6.5 The DKBA tool

In Figure 7.8, there are both control flow and data flow. The user is able to check the reasoning results from the the DKBA tool. When necessary, the user can issue a confirmation or a refutation of the relationship between a variable and a domain concept. To naturally integrate this function into DKBA tool's own reasoning procedure, the user has control over the good knowledge slice selector to perform his or her command immediately.

7.7 Reusing components

Reusing components in a reengineering process involves using a reverse engineering method to expose components from the existing system and a library to store and manage the components. Then the new system is restructured and integrated with reusable generic components and newly built components by forward engineering. In our approach reusable components are mined from legacy systems and made potentially reusable. New systems can be made by the integration of both mined and newly build components (Figure 7.9).

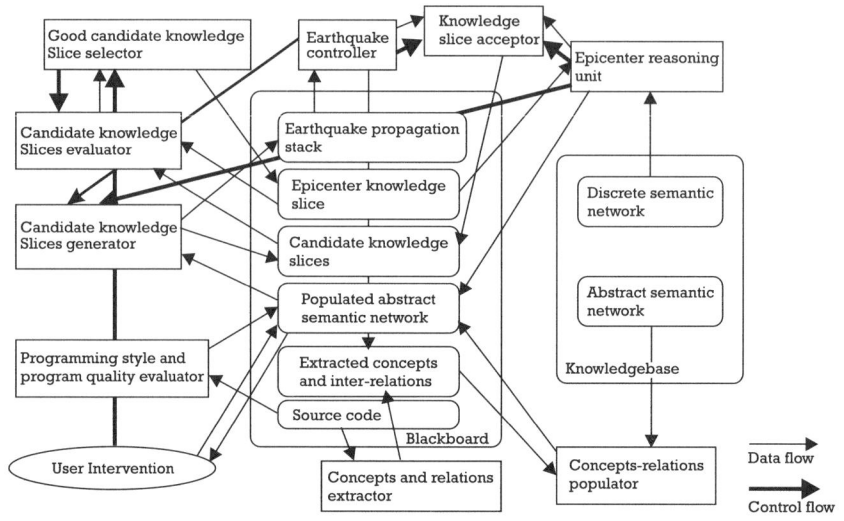

Figure 7.8 Architecture of the DKBA tool.

It is important that an efficient and feasible way to extract components from the legacy systems is employed. This section explicitly defines components and described a method.

Component-based development (CBD) is the industrialization of the software development process based on the assembly of prefabricated

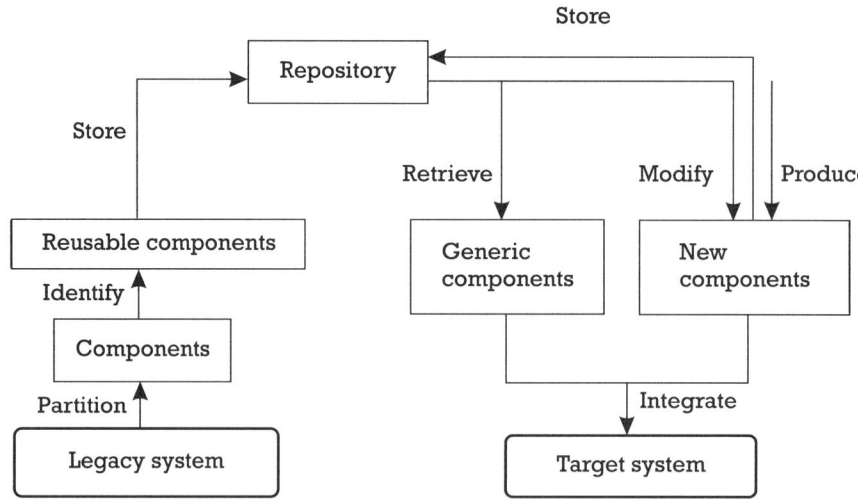

Figure 7.9 Process of component-based evolution.

7.7 Reusing components

software components [39]. Two basic ideas underlie CBD. First, application development can be significantly improved if applications can be quickly assembled from prefabricated software components. Secondly, an increasingly large collection of interoperable software components will be made available to developers in both general and specialist catalogs.

Manufacturing industries long ago learned the benefits of moving from custom development to assembly from prefabricated components. Modern manufacturing has evolved to exploit two crucial factors underlying today's market requirements: reducing cost and time-to-market by building from prebuilt, ready-tested components, but adding value and differentiation by rapid customization to targeted customers.

7.7.1 Definition of component

Components were defined in [40] as "bits of software that can be replicated and, often with modifications, assembled repeatedly to form any number of applications." In this definition, components are not regarded as off-the-shelf black boxes—modification of the components may be made before they can be reused. More flexible and adaptable components will only require configuration (rather than modification) before they can be reused. Another view is that "a reusable software component is a logically cohesive, loosely coupled module that denotes a single abstraction" [41]. High cohesive and low coupling are the basic features of components because of the variation in levels of abstraction, but it is also important to mention the context in which a component can be used. A further view is that "A software component is a static abstraction with plugs" [42]. Here, *static* means that a software component is a long-lived entity that can be stored in a software base, independent of the applications in which it has been used; *abstraction* means that a component puts a more or less opaque boundary around the software in encapsulates; and *with plugs* means that there are well-defined ways to interact and communicate with the component (such as parameters, ports, and messages).

A typical component-based software reengineering process should contain steps of identification, classification, storing, retrieval, adaptation, and composition, such as the following:

- Mine components from the legacy systems;
- Wrap up components with well-defined interfaces;

- Store the components in a component library;
- Build new reusable components if needed;
- Develop new systems by integrating components.

When we consider the components of a software system, the following come to mind: program design documents, source code modules, object code modules, copy libraries, file descriptions, screen definitions, and user manuals, among others. Functions, macros, procedures, templates, and modules may all be valid examples of components [43], and component software may standardize interfaces and generic code for various kinds of software abstractions. Furthermore, components in a system may be entities other than just code (e.g., specifications, documentation, test data, and example applications).

The importance of a precise definition of what constitutes a software component and how to describe it have become a critical issue. Components are larger than classes, can be in any programming language, can include their own meta data, are assembled without programming, and need to specify what they require to run.

Compared to objects, components are larger sized, physical entities, instead of conceptual entities, and support encapsulation with defined interfaces. A component's strength is integration, so flexibility is key, and components should also be highly scalable.

Thus, we regard a software component as follows:

> A coherent and configurable software package, independent of the applications in which it has been used, with well-defined interfaces in different contexts to interact and communicate with other components, in order to compose a larger system.

7.7.2 Mining components

Today, complex and high-quality computer-based systems need to be built in a very short time period. This strongly demands a more organized and more systematic approach to building software by reuse.

A great advantage of extracted components is that they have already been tested to be reliable. By borrowing an existing suitable software development method that has been well-developed, forward engineering can then be carried out more easily in the process of building target systems. The extracted components are more domain-specific than the newly built ones and can be reused directly and efficiently. In our approach,

7.7 Reusing components

a component consists of five elements: code, specification, interface, design, and documentation [44–47]. Source code is the most elementary part of a component, which can be used to extract other elements.

A component is more packaged than an ordinary object. The assumption is that it will be used in many contexts unknown to its own designers. It should be robust in anticipation of abuse from other components, complaining rather than collapsing.

In addition to the executable code itself, there should be a specification documenting its behavior unambiguously, using a suitable modeling and design notation. Since a typical component will be used in more than one product, it is worth investing in good specification and design even more than usual. The specification is essential because clients do not have access to the design and should not have to waste time experimenting. A clear specification also tends to prolong the life of the designers' original vision, even through many updates and enhancements.

Components are identified by their interface. An interface should be defined in different context to interact and communicate with other components.

The term *black box* conveys the idea of a component whose internal workings are hidden, and so inaccessible, with the complementary notion that what is important about such a component are the ways in which it interacts with other components over some well-defined interface: its behavior.

It is important to consider how components fit together, rather than how each performs its particular function. They should be functionally self-contained (see Figure 7.10).

Finally, a well-structured library is needed to store all those elements, where all associated software components may then be classified, stored, compared, and retrieved, by software composition techniques.

These five elements can be obtained through reverse engineering in RA. They are described as follows:

1. *Code:* This is straightforward EWSL code.

2. *Specifications:* These are usually formal and written in EWSL.

3. *Documentation:* The whole point is to make the program understandable by other people. Natural language is clearly a rich source of conceptual information and is used in the documentation in the form of manual pages or comments, usually associated with the code.

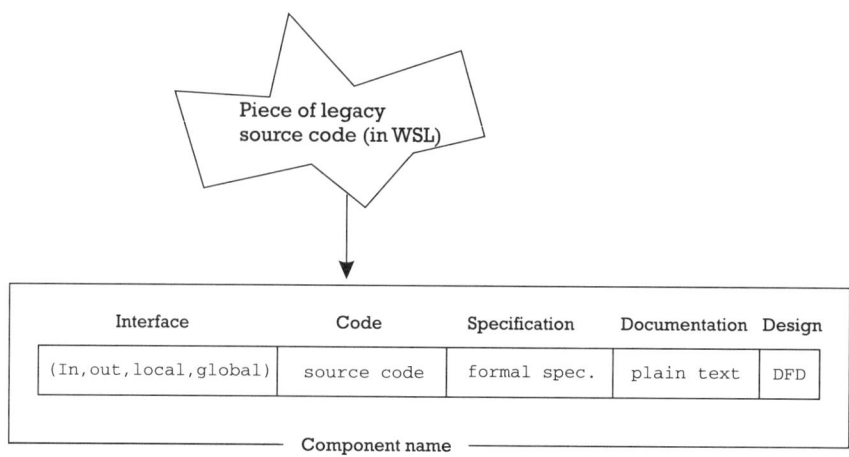

Figure 7.10 Five elements of a component.

4. *Interface:* This is represented in terms of input/output variables [e.g., (In: var *VarName*, Out: var *VarName*, Local: var *VarName*, Global: var *VarName*)].

5. *Design:* We present the design by DFDs.

7.8 Retargeting

Retargeting involves activities at the turning point between reverse engineering and forward engineering. If we recall the three stages of reengineering (i.e., reverse engineering, functional restructuring, and forward engineering) retargeting involves functional restructuring and the start of forward engineering.

Normally, the users' new requirements are added on top of the existing system when the system is reengineered, and these new requirements are implemented in a small number of program functions (compared with the total number of functions in the system). This small number of functions can ideally be implemented using reusable components from the reuse library. If not, new components will have to be developed. Since adding new requirements to the new system is carried out at the specification level, this stage is called functional restructuring.

In general, reverse engineering is the main thrust of reengineering because it addresses a very difficult problem: program comprehension.

Forward engineering can always be undertaken with a sound and existing software development method. Nevertheless, in the case of our reengineering approach, we are mainly concerned with intergrating existing reusable components and newly developed components, and retargeting should put component integration in the right direction (i.e., retargeting is to use the RA to check whether reusable components in the reuse library are sufficient to cover the new requirements and to indicate what new components need to be developed).

7.9 Measuring software evolution

Due to the high risk and lack of approaches and methods to reverse–engineer legacy systems, it is important that evolution processes be properly assessed and controlled. The assessment of resources, products, and processes when reverse engineering is a crucial activity that which needs the development of software metrics for reverse engineering. Software metrics are a key technology for managing reverse engineering projects. Well-developed software metrics for reverse engineering will be a great aid to software engineers.

The history of software metrics is not so long: About 30 years ago, Maurice Halstead published his first paper, which was the beginning of the first long-term software metrics research effort [48]. Thus software metrics became a significant part of software engineering.

Metrics are critical to any engineering discipline, and software engineering is no exception. Software metrics can be used throughout the software life cycle to assist in cost estimation, quality control, productivity assessment, and project control and can be used to help assess the quality of technical work products and to assist in tactical decision making as a project proceeds.

In the definitions of software metrics, three terms, *measure, measurement*, and *metrics*, must be noticed and distinguished, because definitions of these terms can easily become confusing. Within the software engineering context, these terms are defined as follows:

- A *measure* provides a quantitative indication of the extent, amount, dimensions, capacity, or size of some attribute of a product or process [49].

- *Measurement* is the act of determining a measure [49]. It is the process of empirically and objectively assigning numerical results to the attributes of software in such a way as to describe the software.

- A software *metric* is a quantitative measure of the degree to which a system, component, or process possesses a given attribute.

There are three classes of software properties whose attributes should be measured [50]:

1. *Processes* are collections of software-related activities.
2. *Products* are any artifacts, deliverables, or documents that result from a process activity.
3. *Resources* are entities required by a process activity.

For example, in reverse engineering, it is mainly the product attributes that will be measured. The products in reverse engineering are existing systems.

Among these entities, a distinction between internal attributes and external attributes can be made [50]:

- *Internal attributes* can be measured in terms of the entity itself, either directly or indirectly.
- *External attributes* can be indirectly measured with respect to how the entity relates to its environment; even its environment is important, rather than the entity itself.

Other important definitions are listed as follows following classical texts in the science of measurement [51–53].

- *An attribute* is a feature or property of an entity.
- *Direct measurement* of an attribute is measurement that does not depend on the measurement of any other attribute.
- *Indirect measurement* of an attribute is measurement that involves the measurement of one or more other attributes. (It is often useful in making visible the interactions between direct measurements.)

7.9.1 Software metrics for reverse engineering

Reverse engineering metrics are clearly a much neglected area. First, people fail to set measurable targets for their final reverse engineering products, such as specifications. Second, in many reverse engineering projects, people fail to understand and quantify the component costs of these projects, since excessive cost is a frequent complaint from many customers and software engineers themselves. We cannot hope to control costs if we are not measuring the relative components of cost. Third, we are not always told how measures were designed and executed, or which entities were measured and how. Without this additional information, we remain skeptical and unable to decide whether to apply the results to situations found in reverse engineering projects. In general, the lack of measurement of reverse engineering is compounded by the lack of a rigorous approach and the lack of wide acceptance by people.

As the motivation of software metrics, Tom Demarco said [54], "You cannot control what you cannot measure." Software metrics are necessary for achieving reverse engineering.

Reverse engineering includes abstractions and transformations to change the code to a higher abstraction level, in some cases to more abstract object-oriented code, step by step until the final specification of the raw code is reached. This is the main stage in the entire reverse engineering process. In this stage, the most important entity is the abstraction level of the code (i.e., abstractness). By measuring the abstraction level, engineers can identify the extent to which irrelevant information about the code has been omitted or hidden and whether the code is abstract enough to understand. Also, engineers should control transformations and abstractions following the economic way. The economic way reflects another entity that is important for not only engineers but also clients and managers. It is the cost factors of the reverse engineering process. Every step will cause an increase in the cost of the entire reverse engineering project. Following the abstractions and transformations, engineers should try to reduce the increasing rate of growth in the costs. When assessing the quality of the specification gained from the abstractions and transformations, engineers and managers also want to obtain a value for the cost to the entire process. In conclusion, it can be seen that the main properties that need to be determined in reverse engineering are understandability, complexity, reusability, abstraction level, and cost.

7.9.2 Adaptation and development

Concrete measures for reverse engineering can be developed hierarchically. First, numbers of selected measures for forward engineering can be adapted for reverse engineering. Then, new software measures for reverse engineering can be developed, based on existing measures for forward engineering, or from scratch. For example, complexity measures are a major part of software metrics. Much of the early research in the metrics field was focused on measuring software complexity [55]. Some of these metrics can be used for both forward engineering and reverse engineering. The difference is that numerical results of complexity measures for forward engineering tend to become larger as development progresses whilst results of complexity measures for reverse engineering should become smaller. New reverse engineering measures can also be produced based on some of the existing measures for forward engineering [56–58].

7.9.3 Five categories of measures

Complexity measures Complexity is (1) the degree to which a system or component has a design or implementation that is difficult to understand and verify and (2) pertains to any of a set of structure-based metrics that measure the attribute in (1) [59].

Complexity is one of the most pertinent characteristics of computer software. Complexity measures comprise a fundamental element of software metrics. This can be verified by the large number of existing complexity measures for forward engineering: More than 200 complexity measures can be found in the literature [60].

In forward engineering, complexity measures are mainly used to indicate the quality of software. In a reverse engineering process, people mainly want to understand an existing program through reverse engineering from the original program to less complex specifications, because the less complex a program is, the easier it is for people to understand it. In general, the complexity measures indicate the understandability of software—that is, the difference between the use of complexity measures in forward engineering and reverse engineering. Some existing complexity measures can meet the needs of reverse engineering. Normally, these measures are all direct measures and give internal attributes of programs or systems.

Before starting a reverse engineering process, complexity measures can help people to know the general complexity level of the object program and to predict how hard it will be to carry out the next steps. When carrying out abstractions and transformations, complexity measures can ensure that reverse engineers carry out operations with the aim of always reducing the complexity of the object program by hiding irrelevant information. However, the main use of complexity measures lies in their ability to give an overview of the raw code to managers and engineers (i.e., as an overall indicator). Several complexity measures are used for reverse engineering. They are presented below.

7.9 Measuring software evolution

Complexity metric 1: McCabe complexity (MCCM)

Definition 7.4 The number of linearly independent circuits in a program flowgraph [61]. This measure is calculated as the number of predicates plus one.

Complexity metric 2: Structural (STRUCT)

Definition 7.5 The sum of the weights of every construct in the program. The construct is defined subjectively according to experience gained by engineers and managers. See Table 7.11 for an example.

Complexity metric 3: Lines of code (LOC)

Definition 7.6 The number of statements in the program.

Complexity metric 4: Number of node (NON)

Definition 7.7 The number of nodes in the abstract syntax tree.

Complexity metric 5: Control-flow and data-flow complexity (CFDF)

Definition 7.8 The number of edges in the flowgraph (CF) plus the number of times that variables are used (defined and referenced) (DF).

Complexity metric 6: Branch-loop complexity (BL)

Definition 7.9 The number of nonloop predicates plus the number of loops. This is a modification of the measure defined by Moawad and Hassan [62] and modified by Yang [57].

Table 7.11 Sample Weight Values of Constructs

Construct	Weight	Construct	Weight	Construct	Weight
+	1	-	2	*	2
/	3	**	3	=	0
<>	0	<	0	>	0
<=	0	>=	0	Min	1
Max	1	Div	2	Mod	2
If	4	And	1	Or	2
Not	2	Push	10	Abort	10
Array	0	Proc	20	For	10

Complexity metric 7: Recursion and nesting complexity (RNC)

Definition 7.10 The number of instances of recursion and nesting in the program.

Complexity metric 8: Function points (FPs) interface complexity (FPIC)

Definition 7.11 The weighted adjusting functions that count for the external interface files through which data is stored elsewhere by another application. The function complexity scores are simple, average, and complex. This is a modification of the function points measure defined by Albrecht [63] and modified by Banker [64].

Abstractness measures Abstractness measures are in a central position for both reverse engineering measures and the five categories, because abstraction and transformation are significant notions in reverse engineering, crossing the entire reverse engineering process. Both abstraction and transformation are used to enhance the abstraction level of the software.

Abstractness measures are mainly used to measure the abstractness of an object program, which is related to characteristics of complexity. In reverse engineering, abstractness measures are concentrated on structural abstraction, which shows the abstraction level of the program by analyzing the structure of the program (i.e., by accounting and processing the internal mechanism of a system or program). This includes control flow (connections among nodes, branches, and loops) and data flow (the degree of abstraction of the data). Also, abstractness is a direct index of the understandability, which relates to cognitive complexity (measuring the weight of high abstract-level constructs in the program). The main property of abstractions and transformations in the reverse engineering process is hiding irrelevant information. Therefore, to represent hidden irrelevant information numerically is a means of measuring the indicated abstractness. Also, values of abstractness are always increasing following reducing the number of pieces of irrelevant information (i.e., reflecting the raising abstract level as indices).

Abstractness metric 1: Abstractness based on McCabe's cyclomatic complexity measure (ABST-MCCM)

Definition 7.12 The reciprocal of the number of linearly independent circuits in a program flowgraph, which is calculated based on McCabe's cyclomatic complexity measure [61].

7.9 Measuring software evolution

Abstractness metric 2: Abstractness based on lines of code (ABST-LOC)

Definition 7.13 The quotient of the number of statements (LOC) over the number of nodes (NON) in the abstract syntax tree.

Abstractness metric 3: Abstractness based on data-flow complexity (ABST-DF)

Definition 7.14 The reciprocal of the number of times variables are referenced in procedures and functions plus the number of times that variables are defined. This is a modification of the measure defined by Oviedo [65].

Abstractness metric 4: Abstractness based on loop complexity (ABST-LOOP)

Definition 7.15 The reciprocal of the number of loops plus one. This is a modification of the measure defined by Moawad and Hassan [62]. The reciprocal of the original measure is used because it is believed that the fewer loops there are in a program, the higher the abstraction level of the program.

Abstractness metric 5: Abstractness in statement (ABST-STAT)

Definition 7.16 The percentage of statements at higher abstract levels over the total statements.

Abstractness metric 6: Abstractness in vocabulary (ABST-VOC)

Definition 7.17 The percentage of constructs at higher abstract levels in the total constructs in the programs.

Abstractness metric 7: Abstractness based on the weight of declaration statements (ABST-WOS)

Definition 7.18 Measures the weight of special declaration statements that are defined by different systems and requests.

Object-orientedness (OO) measures Object orientedness is the degree to which a system or its components has a design or implementation that is expressed in terms of objects and messages via encapsulation, inheritance, and polymorphism between the objects.

Following the strong trend toward object-oriented technology, object orientedness measures have become an unavoidable subset of software metrics required for reverse engineering. Nowadays, many software managers and engineers want to reengineer their huge number of conventional procedural systems into object-oriented systems. OO measures for reverse engineering can be helpful to managers and engineers.

OO measures measure OO characteristics including inheritance (mechanism allowing the reuse of class specifications), encapsulation (information hiding supported by objects), and polymorphism (to hide different implementations behind a common interface) [66]. Some OO measures are also helpful to assess the pre-object-oriented characteristics of procedural codes, but it is not the main aim of OO measures for reverse engineering. These measures are highly relevant to OO applications.

In reverse engineering, OO measures give the complexity of classes (templates for creating objects—that is, packets containing data and procedures [66]) and relationships between classes (e.g., the class hierarchy, which is a tree structure representing inheritance relations [66]). OO measures can be used to measure source programs, transitional programs, and specifications, which can help to reverse-engineer OO legacy systems effectively and efficiently. Kemerer and Chidamber (KC)'s object-oriented metrics suite has been adapted for reverse engineering measures [67], that are suitable to measure the reverse engineering processes of OO legacy systems. They are listed below along with an example of using some of those measures to measure a program segment.

OO metric 1: Weighted methods per class (WMC)

Definition 7.19 Consider a class C_1, with methods $M_1,...M_n$ that are defined in the class. Let $c_1,...c_n$ be the complexity of the methods. Then

$$\text{WMC} = \sum_{i=1}^{n} c_i$$

If all method complexities are considered to be unity, then WMC $= n$, the number of methods. Here the number of methods is calculated as the summation of McCabe's cyclomatic complexity of all local methods.

OO metric 2: Depth of inheritance tree (DIT)

Definition 7.20 Depth of inheritance of the class is the DIT metric for the class. In cases involving multiple inheritance, the DIT will be the maximum length from the node to the root of the tree.

7.9 Measuring software evolution

OO metric 3: Number of children (NOC)

Definition 7.21 Calculates the number of immediate subclasses subordinated to a class in the class hierarchy.

OO metric 4: Coupling between object classes (CBO)

Definition 7.22 As for a class, it is a count of the number of other classes to which it is coupled. It relates to the notion that two classes are coupled when methods in one class use methods or instance variables defined by another class.

OO metric 5: Response for a class (RFC)

Definition 7.23 $RFC = |RS|$ where the RS is the response set for the class. The response set of a class is a set of methods that can potentially be executed in response to a message received by an object of that class.

OO metric 6: Number of variables per class (NVC)

Definition 7.24 Calculated as the average number of public variables and private variables per class.

OO metric 7: Average parameters per method (APM)

Definition 7.25 Calculated as the number of method parameters divided by the total number of methods.

OO metric 8: Number of objects (NOO)

Definition 7.26 The number of objects extracted from source code.

Economic/cost estimation measures Economics is mainly the characteristics of the duration, effort, and productivity of a reverse engineering process.

The main aim of economics (cost estimation) measures is to indicate the cost of reverse-engineering the existing code tactically and strategically. In reverse engineering, effort, duration and productivity can be measured. Effort in reverse engineering is a measure of the productive work to extract specifications from raw code in the process of reverse engineering. Duration is the time to reverse engineer a system. Productivity is the ratio of the quantity and quality of specifications and information produced from the reverse engineering process per unit of time. In fact, as the name of this category suggests, the main use of these measures is to supply several estimated results of both reverse engineering products and process. Then, by comparing actual results and estimated results, engineers can obtain a view of the cost level and try to control the cost of their project to bring it closer to estimated values obtained from economic measures. In order to control the reverse-engineering process and reduce the cost of obtaining specifications, engineers and managers must be able to estimate relevant quantities. Economic measures are mainly based on the reduction in the number of source code instructions, called the size reduction rate (SRR). Concrete measures are presented below:

Economics metric 1: Cost ratio value in relation to lines of code (CRVL)

Definition 7.27 The cost unit of specifications in relation to the cost of raw code.

Economics metric 2: Size reduction rate (SRR)

Definition 7.28 Source lines of code divided by lines of specification.

Economics metric 3: Cost ratio value in relation to SRR (CRV)

Definition 7.29 Gives a cost unit of specifications compared to reverse engineered lines.

Economics metric 4: Effort assessment based on person-days (EPD)

Definition 7.30 *Effort:*
$$\text{Person-days} = I_r \times 2.4(\text{SRR}/1{,}000)^{1.05} \times 19$$

This measure is a modification of the basic COCOMO model defined by Boehm [68].

Economics metric 5: Reverse engineering duration (RED)

Definition 7.31
$$\text{Reverse engineering duration (days)} = 2.5 \times (\text{EPD})^{0.38}$$

This measure is a modification of the COCOMO model defined by Boehm [68].

7.9 Measuring software evolution

Economics metric 6: One specification per hour (SPH)

Definition 7.32

$$SPH = \frac{SRR \times 8}{\text{Lines of specification} \times RED \times 1{,}000}$$

This measure is an adaption of the COCOMO model defined by Boehm [68]. Eight work hours per day is used here.

Economics metric 7: Productivity of reverse engineering (REP)

Definition 7.33

$$REP = \frac{SRR}{EPD \times 1{,}000}$$

This measure is another modification of the COCOMO model [68, 69].

Economics metric 8: Duration (scheduling time) for obtaining each object (TFO)

Definition 7.34 This measure gives the scheduling duration for gaining one object equally.

$$TFO = \frac{RED}{NOO}$$

Reusability measures The last category of the five categories is reusability measures. The main attributes of reusability are generality, transportability, and retrievability. Understandability is also reflected by the feature of reusability. Highly reusable components of a system are normally easy to understand. Generality measures estimate whether the system or components of the system perform a broad range of functions so that they can be used in more than one computer program or software system. Transportability measures also give the ease of translating programs. Retrievability refers to the ease of design recovery.

One reason for using reusability measures in reverse engineering is that reverse engineering can indicate whether a component is reusable or not. This valuable information for reengineers is given by the reusability measures. Depending on the results of reusability, people can know what should be done after reverse engineering (i.e., when rebuilding the system based on specifications obtained from the reverse engineering process). Another reason is that it is believed that the direction of heuristics is along the trend of finding a component more reusable when reverse engineering.

The main basis of developing reusability measures is based on Selby's study [70]. The main rules of reusability in Selby's study are elaborated below. The characteristics of reusable components are listed as follows:

- Smaller size—generally less than 140 source statements;
- Simple interfaces;
- Few calls to other modules (low coupling);
- More calls to low-level system and utility functions;
- Fewer input-output parameters;
- Less human interaction (user interface);
- Good documentation, as shown by the comment-to-source statement ratio;
- Few design changes during implementation;
- Less effort to design and build needed;
- More assignment statements than logic statements per source statement.

Reusability measures are always used to measure resources and initial products in the initial stages of the reverse engineering process. Normally, reusability measures will not be supposed to measure the process and transitional products in reverse engineering. Several reusability measures are listed below.

Reusability metric 1: Weight of interfaces in relation to lines of code (WOIL)

Definition 7.35 This is a measure calculated by dividing the number of lines of interface code by the total number of lines of code.

Reusability metric 2: Human interaction level in relation to lines of code (HIL)

Definition 7.36 This calculates human action level by lines of commands.

7.9 Measuring software evolution

$$\text{HILL} = \frac{\text{Lines of users' commands}}{\text{Source lines of code}}$$

Reusability metric 3: Average module size (AMS)

Definition 7.37 This measure is calculated by number of statements over number of methods [71].

$$\text{AMS} = \frac{\text{LOC}}{\text{Number of methods}}$$

Reusability metric 4: Environment independence level (EIL)

Definition 7.38 This assesses the weight of parts that must run under the old environment in the object program.

$$\text{EIL} = \frac{\text{Lines of system-dependent code} + \text{lines of hardware-dependent code}}{\text{Source lines of code}}$$

Reusability metric 5: Documentation level (DL)

Definition 7.39 This evaluates the size of documentation affiliated to the program.

$$\text{DL} = \frac{\text{Number of comments/documentation}}{\text{Source lines of code}}$$

Reusability metric 6: Self-descriptiveness (SD)

Definition 7.40 This estimates the weight of on-line comments and statements with the self-descriptiveness characteristic in the program.

$$\text{SD} = \frac{\text{Number of on-line comments and special statements}}{\text{Total number of statements}}$$

Reusability metric 7: Error tolerance level (ETL)

Definition 7.41 This measures the weight of parts in the program that can be used to detect errors and remind errors.

$$\text{ETL} = \frac{\text{Lines of error detecting components}}{\text{Source lines of code}}$$

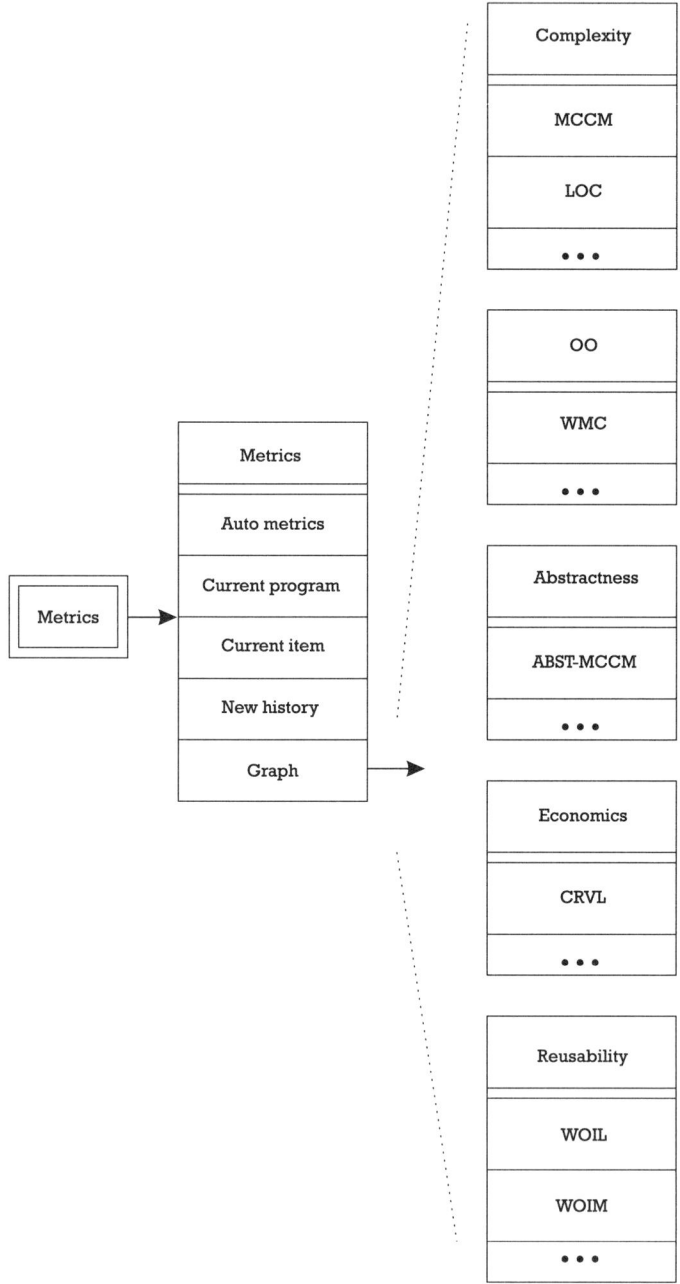

Figure 7.11 Menu buttons of the metric facility.

Reusability Metric 8: Weight of reuse on lines of code (WOR)

Definition 7.42 This assesses the weight of reused parts of the object program depending on documentation.

$$\text{WOR} = \frac{\text{Number of reused lines of code}}{\text{Source lines of code}}$$

7.9.4 The metric tool in RA

In the Reengineering Assistant, a tool called the "Metric Facility" was designed and built to measure the object program on which the user is working. The metric facility can be invoked by the user at any time to measure the object program. In this research, the tool component of the metric facility is used to implement reverse engineering measures. Also, the tool itself will be strengthened when developing reverse engineering measures.

By using the Metric Facility, a user can calculate any one, or all of the metrics, applied either to the current program item on which he or she is working or to the whole program. During the process of abstracting and transforming a program, the measures at each stage can be recorded and the results can be plotted when required. Menu buttons are shown in Figure 7.11.

The metric facility provides a function to plot graphs of metric results, using the record generated by the automatic mechanism. One of measures is plotted in one graph, including the name of the measure, the (index) number of the measure at each line, and the name of the abstraction or transformation applied. If by the time the graph is going to be plotted, the number of the abstraction or transformation applied exceeds the maximum number of characters that can be displayed in one line on the screen, the graph is plotted vertically. Also, as with deep analysis, the plots are always converted into smoothed curves. Then by analyzing the shape of the curves, the status of a reverse engineering process can be judged more explicitly and conveniently.

References

[1] Yang, H., *Acquiring Data Designs from Existing Data-Intensive Programs*, Durham University, Durham, U.K., Ph.D. thesis, 1994.

[2] Yang, H., "The Supporting Environment for a Reverse Engineering System—The Maintainer's Assistant," *IEEE Conference on Software Maintenance 1991*, Sorrento, Italy, October 1991.

[3] Yang, H., and K. H. Bennett, "Extension of a Transformation System for Maintenance—Dealing with Data-Intensive Programs," *IEEE International Conference on Software Maintenance (ICSM'94)*, Victoria, Canada, September 1994.

[4] Kwiatkowski, J., I Puchalski, and H. Yang, "Preprocessing COBOL Programs for Reengineering," in *Object Technology and System Reengineering*, Chichester, U.K.: Horwood Publishing Limited, 1999, pp. 91–110.

[5] Chen, Z., et al., "A Wide-Spectrum Language for Object-Based Development of Real-Time Systems," *Journal of Information Science*, 1999.

[6] Chen, Z., H. Zedan, and H. Yang, "Integrating Structured OO Approaches with Formal Techniques for the Development of Real-Time systems," *Journal of Information and Software Technology*, 1999.

[7] Liu, X., H. Yang, and H. Zedan, "Tackling the Abstraction Problem for Reverse Engineering in a Reengineering Approach," *IEEE International Conference on Software Maintenance (ICSM'98)*, Washington, D.C., November 1998.

[8] Yang, H., X. Liu, and H. Zedan, "Abstraction: A Key Notion for Reverse Engineering in a System Reengineering Approach" *Journal of Software Maintenance: Research and Practice*, Vol. 12, No. 5, 2000, pp. 197–228.

[9] Zedan, H., and H. Yang, "A Sound and Practical Approach to the Reengineering of Time-Critical Systems," *EUROMICRO Working Conference of Software Maintenance and Reengineering*, Florence, Italy, March 1998.

[10] Balmas, F., "PRISME: Formalizing Programming Strategies As a Way To Understand Programs," *Eighth International Conference on Software Engineering and Knowledge Engineering*, Lake Tahoe, Nevada: IEEE Computer Society, June 1996.

[11] Bennett, K. H., "Software Maintenance for the Year 2000," *Sixth European Workshop on Software Maintenance*, The Centre for Software Maintenance, Durham University, Durham, U.K., 1992.

[12] Cheng, B. H. C., "Applying Formal Methods in Automated Software Development," *Journal of Computer and Software Engineering*, Vol. 2, February 1994, pp. 137–164.

[13] Engberts, A., W. Kozaczynski, and J. Ning, "Concept Recognition–Based Program Transformation," *IEEE Conference on Software Maintenance-1991*, Sorrento, Italy, 1991, pp. 73–82.

[14] Gannod, C., and B. H. C. Cheng, "Strongest Postcondition Semantics as a Basis for Reverse Engineering," *Proc. of IEEE Working Conference on Reverse Engineering*, Toronto, Canada, July 1995, pp. 188–197.

[15] Howden, W. E., and S. Pak, "Problem Domain, Structural and Logical Abstractions in Reverse Engineering," *Proceedings of the International Conference on Software Maintenance-1992*, IEEE Computer Society Press, Orlando, Fla., November 1992, pp. 214–224.

[16] Griswold, W. G., and D. Notkin, "Architectural Tradeoffs for a Meaning-Preserving Program Restructuring Tool," *IEEE Trans. on Software Engineering,* Se-21, No. 4, April 1995, pp. 275–287.

[17] Korel, B., "Computation of Dynamic Program Slices for Unstructured Programs," *IEEE Trans. on Software Engineering,* SE-23, No. 1, 1997, pp. 17–34.

[18] Ward, M., "A Recursion Removal Theorem," Berlin: Springer-Verlag, *Proc. of the 5th Refinement Workshop,* London, January 8–11, 1992 (http://www.dur.ac.uk/~dcs0mpw/martin/papers/ref-ws-5/ps.gz).

[19] Dijkstra, E. W., *A Discipline of Programming,* Englewood Cliffs, NJ: Prentice Hall, 1976.

[20] Dijkstra, E. W., and C. S. Scholten, *Predicate Calculus and Program Semantics,* Berlin: Springer-Verlag, 1990.

[21] Jahnke, J. H., W. Schafer, and A. Zundorf, "Generic Fuzzy Reasoning Nets As a Basis for Reverse Engineering Relational Database Applications," *Proceedings of the European Software Engineering Conference,* Zurich: Springer, LNCS 1301, September 1997.

[22] Balmas, F., "Toward a Framework for Conceptual and Formal Outlines of Programs," *Fourth Working Conference on Reverse Engineering,* Amsterdam, the Netherlands: IEEE Computer Society, October 1997, pp. 226–235.

[23] Biggerstaff, T. J., B. G. Mitbander, and D. Webster, "The Concept Assignment Problem in Program Understanding," *Proceedings of the International Conference on Software Engineering,* Los Alamitos, CA: IEEE Computer Society Press, April 1993, pp. 482–498.

[24] Desclaux, C., and M. Ribault, "MACS: Maintenance Assistance Capability for Software—A KADME," *IEEE Conference on Software Maintenance-1991,* Sorrento, Italy, 1991, pp. 2–12.

[25] Fiutem, R., et al., "Understanding the Architecture of Software Systems," *Fourth Workshop on Program Comprehension,* Berlin: IEEE Computer Society Press, March 1996, pp. 187–196.

[26] Kontogiannis, K., et al., "Localization of Design Concepts in Legacy Systems," *Proceedings of the International Conference on Software Maintenance 1994,* Los Alamitos, CA: IEEE Computer Society Press, September 1994, pp. 414–423.

[27] Quilici, A., "A Hybrid Approach to Recognizing Programming Plans," *Proc. of the 1st Working Conference on Reverse Engineering,* Los Alamitos, CA: IEEE Computer Society Press, 1993, pp. 126–133.

[28] Quilici, A., and S. Woods, *Toward a Constraint-Satisfaction Framework for Evaluating Program-Understanding Algorithms,* Norwell, MA: Kluwer Academic Publishers, 1996.

[29] Rich, C., and R. C. Waters, "The Programmers' Apprentice," *IEEE Computer,* Vol. 21, November 1988, pp. 10–25.

[30] Wils, L., "Flexible Control for Program Recognition," *Proceedings of Working Conference on Reverse Engineering,* Baltimore, MD: IEEE Computer Society Press, Los Alamitos, CA, May 1993.

[31] Kitchenham, B., et al., "Towards an Ontology of Software Maintenance," *Journal of Software Maintenance: Research and Practice,* Vol. 11, December 1999, pp. 365–389.

[32] Li, Y., and H. Yang, "Simplicity: A Key Engineering Concept for Program Understanding," *International Workshop on Program Comprehension (IWPC'01),* Toronto, Canada, May 2001.

[33] Li, Y., H. Yang, and C. Chu, "Clarity Guided Brief Revision for Domain Knowledge Recovery in Legacy Systems," *Twelfth International Conference on Software Engineering and Knowledge Engineering (SEKE'00),* Chicago, Illinois, July 2000.

[34] Li, Y., H. Yang, and C. Chu, "Towards Building a Smarter Domain Knowledge Recovery Assistant," *IEEE Computer Software and Application Conference (COMPSAC'00),* Taipei, Taiwan, October 2000.

[35] Li, Y., H. Yang, and W. Chu, "A Concept-Oriented Brief Revision Approach to Domain Knowledge Recovery from Source Code," *Journal of Software Maintenance: Research and Practice,* Vol. 13, No. 1, 2001.

[36] Yang, H., Z. Cui, and P. O'Brien, "Extracting Ontologies from Legacy Systems for Understanding and Reengineering," *IEEE Computer Software and Application Conference (COMPSAC'99),* Phoenix, Arizona, October 1999.

[37] Rugaber, S., *White Paper on Reverse Engineering,* Software Engineering Research Center, Georgia Institute of Technology, Atlanta, Georgia 30332-0280, March 1994.

[38] Shortliffe, E. H., "A Model of Inexact Reasoning," *Medicine Mathematical Bioscience,* Vol. 23, 1975, pp. 351–379.

[39] Short, K., *Component-Based Development and Object Modeling,* February 1997, Version 1.0.

[40] Biggerstaff, T. J., and C. Ritcher, "Reliability Framework, Assessment, and Direction," *IEEE Software,* Vol. 14, No. 4, 1987, pp. 252–257.

[41] Booch, G., *Software Components with Ada,* Menlo Park, CA: Benjamin/Cummings, 1987.

[42] Nierstrasz, O., and D. Tsichritzis, *Object-Oriented Software Composition,* Englewood Cliffs, NJ: Prentice Hall, 1995.

[43] Bracha, G., "The Programming Language Jigsaw: Mixins, Modularity, and Multiple Inheritance," Department of Computer Science, University of Utah, Ph.D., March 1992.

[44] Chu, C., et al., "A Formal Approach for Component Retrieval and Integration Analyis," *Journal of Software Maintenance: Research and Practice,* Vol. 12, No. 6, 2000, pp. 325–342.

[45] Chu, C., and H. Yang, "Integration of Reusable Components for Software," *IEEE International Computer Software and Application Conference*, Dallas, Texas, August 1995.

[46] Tennet, R. D., "The Denotational Semantics of Programming Languages," *Comm. ACM*, Vol. 19, No. 8, August 1976, pp. 437–453.

[47] Yang, H., C. Chu, and Y. Sun, "A Practical System of COBOL Program Reuse for Reengineering," *IEEE International Workshop on Software Technology and Engineering Practice (STEP'97)*, London, July 1997.

[48] Halstead, M. H., "Natural Laws Controlling Algorithm Structure," *ACM SIGPLAN Notices*, Vol. 7, 1972.

[49] Pressman, R. S., *Software Engineering—A Practitioner's Approach*, New York: McGraw-Hill, 1987.

[50] Fenton, N. E., and S. L. Pfleeger, *Software Metrics—A Rigorous Approach, Second Edition*, London: International Thomson Computer Press, 1996.

[51] Krantz, D. H., and R. D. Luce, *Foundations of Measurement*, Academic Press, 1, 1971.

[52] Kyburg, H. E., *Theory and Measurement*, Cambridge, U.K.: Cambridge University Press, 1984.

[53] Roberts, F. S., *Measurement Theory with Applications to Decision Making, Utility, and the Social Sciences*, Reading, MA: Addison-Wesley, 1979.

[54] DeMarco, T., *Controlling Software Projects*, New York: Yourdon Press, 1982.

[55] Melton, A., Chapter 5 in *Software Measurement*, London: Thomson Computer Press International, 1996.

[56] Bennett, K. H., T. Bull, and H. Yang, "A Transformation System for Maintenance—Turning Theory into Practice," *Conference on Software Maintenance*, Orlando, Florida, 1992.

[57] Yang, H., P. Luker, and C. Chu, "Measuring Abstractness for Reverse Engineering in a Reengineering Tool," *IEEE International Conference on Software Maintenance*, Bari, Italy, October 1997.

[58] Zhou, S., and H. Yang, "Measuring Software Components Through Object Orientation and Abstraction for Reengineering," *ACM and IEEE International Symposium on Internet Technology (ISIT'98)*, Taipei, Taiwan, 1998.

[59] IEEE, *IEEE Standard Collection: Software Engineering*, New York: IEEE Inc., 1997.

[60] Zuse, H., *Software Complexity—Measures and Methods*, New York: Walter de Gruyter, 1991.

[61] McCabe, T. J., "A Complexity Measure," *IEEE Trans. on Software Engineering*, Vol. 2, 1976.

[62] Moawad, R., and M. Hassan, "Structural Approach Towards Software Reliability Evaluation," *Proc. of COMPSAC83*, 1983.

[63] Albrecht, A. J., and J. E. Gaffney, "Software Function, Source Lines of Code, and Development Effort Prediction—A Software Science Validation," *IEEE Trans. on Software Engineering*, Vol. 9, No. 6, 1983, pp. 639–648.

[64] Banker, R. D., and R. J. Kauffman, and C. Wright, "Automating Output Size and Reuse Metrics in Repository-Based Computer-Aided Software Engineering," *IEEE Transactions on Software Engineering*, Vol. 20, No. 3, 1994, pp. 169–187.

[65] Oviedo,E., "Control Flow, Data Flow, and Programmers' Complexity," *Proc. of COMPSAC80*, 1980.

[66] Eliens, A., *Principles of Object-Oriented Software Development*, Reading, MA: Addison-Wesley, 1995.

[67] Kemerer, C. F., and S. Chidamber, "A Metrics Suite for Object-Oriented Design," *IEEE Trans. on Software Engineering*, Vol. 20, No. 6, June 1994, pp. 476–493.

[68] Boehm, B. W., *Software Engineering Economics*, Englewood Cliffs, NJ: Prentice Hall, 1981.

[69] Conte, S. D., H. E. Dunsmroe, and V. Y. Shen, *Software Engineering Metrics and Models*, Menlo Park, CA: The Benjamin/Cummings Publishing Company, Inc., 1986.

[70] Selby, H., "Quantitative Management for Software Tests," in *Software Reusability*, Reading, MA: Addison-Wesley, 1989.

[71] Stalnane, T., "Development of a Model for Reusability Assessment," *Proc. of the Second Symposium on Software Quality Techniques and Acquisition Criteria*, Florence, Italy, 1995.

CHAPTER 8

Case Studies in Evolution

Contents

8.1 First case study: Book index generator

8.2 Second case study: Topological sorting algorithm

8.3 Third case study: Assembler reengineering

8.4 Fourth case study: A mass migration exercise

8.5 Fifth case study: Migrating a telecommunications system

8.6 Sixth case study: Mine drainage system

8.7 Summary

References

This chapter presents six case studies using the FermaT and RA tools to evolve from source code to specifications or to new source code in a different language.

Book index generator   This case study illustrates detailed steps for using our method. The purpose is to provide guidance to readers to use the FermaT tool in their own practice.

Topological sorting   After an extensive search of the literature, this algorithm by Knuth and Szwarcfiter, published in [1], was selected as being one of the most difficult and challenging programs for formal analysis, given its small size. It therefore makes an ideal stress test of the transformation technology: If we can handle this, then we can also handle the much larger but significantly less complex programs found in typical business computing systems.

Assembler reengineering   The third case study starts with an IBM 370 assembler module that is translated to WSL and reengineered to an equivalent high-level language program and ultimately to an abstract specification. The specification precisely describes the behavior of the program while abstracting away from the nonessential implementation details. As a result, the specification is considerably shorter and easier to understand than either the original assembler or even the high-level language program.

The original program was taken from "A Guided Tour of Program Design Methodologies" by G. D. Bergland [2], where is it used as an example of the complexities and poor structure that emerge after an incorrect program is patched and fixed over a period of time. This program was translated into assembler by a professional assembler programmer whose brief was to use many of the programming tricks (such as **EX**ecute statements and self-modifying code) that make assembler so much more difficult to maintain than high-level language code (the maintenance cost per function point for assembler has been measured to be 2.8 times higher than for COBOL).

The purpose of this study is to see if FermaT transformations can be used to cover the whole reengineering process from very low-level code (assembler) to abstract formal specifications and to a high-level program in a different programming language.

Mass migration exercise The fourth case study is a test of how well the migration technology will scale up to systems containing millions of lines of code and cope with different styles of assembler from many different sources. The study focuses on the code migration part of a migration project: taking the assembler modules, translating to WSL, applying thousands of individual restructuring, and simplifying transformations to each module, and finally translating into equivalent maintainable C code. The case study took a random selection of 1,925 assembler modules (comprising just over one million lines of source, which expands into over 5 million lines of listing) taken from over 25,000 modules provided by a number of large commercial assembler users.

Migrating a telecommunications system from assembler to C The fifth case study is a commercial migration project. The project is a fairly large embedded system, consisting of about 500,000 lines of Intel 186 assembler and 250,000 lines of C that runs on four different hardware platforms in 18 countries. The task was to use FermaT to migrate all the assembler code to efficient, structured and maintainable C code to enable migration to a more modern processor together with major enhancements to the functionality of the system.

Mine drainage system The sixth case study shows how a real-time system is reverse-engineered to obtain its specifications.

8.1 First case study: Book index generator

In this case study we give an example of how to use program transformations to extract a formal specification from source code and then develop two new programs in different programming languages from the specification. The example program is taken from a programming textbook [3], and was used by the textbook's author to generate the index for the book. The program was originally written in DataFlex (a database programming language); we have transcribed it to C while faithfully preserving the structure:

```
#include <stdio.h>
main()       /* DataFlex transcription */
{
  int morenum, filestat;
  char page[6], theline[51], item[31], lastitem[31];
  FILE *fopen(), *fp_in, *fp_out;
  fp_in = fopen("DIDB","r");
  fp_out = fopen("DID2INX.TXT","w");
  theline[0] = '\0';
  morenum = 0;
  filestat = fscanf(fp_in," %s%s",page,item);
  goto inhere;
  for(;;) {
    filestat = fscanf(fp_in," %s%s",page,item);
    if (filestat == EOF) goto alldone;
    morenum = 1;
    if (strcmp(item,lastitem)) {
        fprintf(fp_out," %s\n",theline);
        theline[0] = '\0';
        morenum = 0;
        inhere:
        strcpy(theline,item);
        strcat(theline," ");
        strcat(theline,page);
    }
    if (morenum) {
        strcat(theline,", ");
        strcat(theline,page);
    }
    strcpy(lastitem,item);
  }
```

```
        alldone:
            fprintf(fp_out," %s\n",theline);
            close(fp_in);
            close(fp_out);
    }
```

At first glance this appears to be a nicely structured program—until one notices that the program starts out with a **goto inhere** that branches to a label in the middle of an **if** statement in the middle of a loop! The program also uses a flag **morenum** to modify the control flow.

8.1.1 Goals

For any evolution project to be successful it is important for the project's goals to be clearly identified at the beginning. Our goals for this project are as follows.

1. To restructure the program in order to reduce complexity and make the program more maintainable;

2. To remove various restrictions on the program—specifically the hard-wired file names, field length restrictions, and the fixed-width format of the input file;

When the program was first written (in 1986) computers had much smaller memories than today's machines. More importantly, the original implementation language (DataFlex) did not have any facilities for dynamic memory allocation. Thus, it was vitally important for the original implementation to use a fixed, small amount of memory. Modern computers have much larger amounts of memory, and modern operating systems have efficient virtual memory implementations, so it is acceptable for the new implementation to load the entire file into memory. Similarly, processing time is not a major issue for the reengineered program.

8.1.2 WSL transformations

In order to translate to WSL, all the labels need to be at the top level, so that they can be converted to actions in an action system. This is easily accomplished by implementing the **for**(;;) loop as action L at the top of the loop and a **call** L at the end of the loop:

8.1 First case study: Book index generator

```
var ⟨morenum := 0, lastitem := " "⟩:
actions PROG :
PROG ≡
    morenum := 0
    !P fopen("DIDB", "r" var fp_in);
    !P fopen("DID2INX.TXT", "w" var fp_out);
    !P fscanf( var filestat, fp_in, page, item);
    call INHERE.
L ≡
    !P fscanf( var filestat, fp_in, page, item);
    if filestat = EOF then call ALLDONE fi;
    morenum := 1;
    if item ≠ lastitem
        then !P fprintf(theline var fp_out);
            theline := ""; morenum := 0; call INHERE fi;
    call MORE.
INHERE ≡
    theline := item ++ " " ++ page; call MORE.
MORE ≡
    if morenum = 1 then theline := theline ++ ", " ++ page fi;
    lastitem := item; call L.
ALLDONE ≡
    !P fprintf(theline var fp_out); call Z. endactions end
```

The first stages in reverse engineering involve restructuring and simplification transformations. These stages do not require any deep knowledge of the overall structure or purpose of the program, but only use local analysis. For example, we observe that **morenum** is set to zero in **PROG** and tested in **MORE** (via the intervening call to **INHERE**). If we unfold the call to **INHERE** in **PROG** and then the call to **MORE** we can eliminate the test and also merge some assignments:

```
PROG ≡
    morenum := 0;
    !P fopen("DIDB", "r" var fp_in);
    !P fopen("DID2INX.TXT", "w" var fp_out);
    !P fscanf( var filestat, fp_in, page, item);
    theline := item ++ " " ++ page;
    lastitem := item; call L.
```

We could continue in this way, unfolding and simplifying actions to restructure the program, but this is not necessary. The FermaT system includes a metatransformation called **Collapse_Action_System**, which implements the heuristics for restructuring action systems, selecting and calling other transformations as appropriate. The result of applying this transformation is

```
var ⟨morenum := 0, last := " "⟩:
  !P fopen("DIDB", "r" var fp_in);
  !P fopen("DID2INX.TXT", "w" var fp_out);
  !P fscanf( var filestat, fp_in, page, item);
  theline := item ++ " " ++ page;
  lastitem := item;
  do !P fscan( var filestat, fp_in, page, item);
     if filestat = EOF
        then !P fprintf(theline var fp_out);
             exit(1) fi;
     morenum := 1;
     if item≠lastitem
        then !P fprintf(theline var fp_out);
             theline := ""; morenum := 0;
             !P fscan( var filestat, fp_in, page, item);
             theline := item ++ " " ++ page fi;
     if morenum = 1
        then theline := theline ++ ", " ++ page fi;
     lastitem := item od end
```

Note that the statement **lastitem** := **item** appears at the end of the loop and also just before the loop. So loop inversion (see Chapter 4) can be applied to merge the two copies of the statement. Also, within the loop body we set **morenum** in the first **if** statement and test it in the next **if** statement. By absorbing the second **if** into the first, we can remove all the tests of **morenum** (which then becomes another redundant variable):

```
var ⟨last := " "⟩:
  !P fopen("DIDB", "r" var fp_in);
  !P fopen("DID2INX.TXT", "w" var fp_out);
  !P fscanf( var filestat, fp_in, page, item);
  theline := item ++ " " ++ page;
  do lastitem := item;
     !P fscan( var filestat, fp_in, page, item);
     if filestat=EOF
        then !P fprintf(theline var fp_out); exit(1) fi;
     if item ≠ lastitem
```

8.1 First case study: Book index generator

       then !P fprintf(theline **var** fp_out);
           !P fscan(**var** filestat, fp_in, page, item);
           theline := item ++ " " ++ page
       else theline := theline ++ ", " ++ page **fi od end**

There are two copies of the statement **theline := item ++ " " ++ page**, but the copy within the loop is not the last statement in the loop body. It can however, very easily be made to be the last statement in the loop body by converting the loop to a double loop and taking the statement out of the new inner loop. This is accomplished by the single transformation **Take_Outside_Loop**, which automatically checks for and applies loop inversion:

  var ⟨last := " "⟩:
    !P fopen("DIDB", "r" **var** fp_in);
    !P fopen("DID2INX.TXT", "w" **var** fp_out);
    !P fscanf(**var** filestat, fp_in, page, item);
    do theline := item ++ " " ++ page;
      do lastitem := item;
        !P fscan(**var** filestat, fp_in, page, item);
        if filestat = EOF
          then !P fprintf(theline **var** fp_out); **exit**(2) **fi**;
        if item ≠ lastitem
          then !P fprintf(theline **var** fp_out);
              theline := "";
              !P fscan(**var** filestat, fp_in, page, item);
              exit(1)
          else theline := item ++ ", " ++ page **fi od od end**

The two copies of the **fprintf** call can be combined by merging the two **if** statements, converting to a nested **if** statement and taking the common code out of the two branches of the outer **if**:

  do theline := item ++ " " ++ page;
    do lastitem := item;
      !P fscan(**var** filestat, fp_in, page, item);
      if filestat=EOF ∨ item ≠ lastitem
        then !P fprintf(theline **var** fp_out);
            if filestat=EOF **then** **exit**(2) **else** **exit**(1) **fi**
        else theline := item ++ ", " ++ page **fi od od**

The statement **if** filestat = EOF **then** **exit**(2) **else** **exit**(1) **fi** always causes termination of the inner loop, so we can replace it by an **exit**(1) and take it, and the preceding **fprintf**, out of the inner loop:

do theline := item ++ " " ++ page;
  do lastitem := item;
    !P fscan(**var** filestat, fp_in, page, item);
    if filestat = EOF ∨ item ≠ lastitem **then** **exit**(1) **fi**;
    theline := item ++ ", " ++ page **od**;
  !P fprintf(theline **var** fp_out);
  if filestat = EOF **then** **exit**(1) **fi**;

The transformations have revealed the "true" structure of the program, which involves a double loop; the "true" structure of a program is a structure that closely matches the function and purpose of the program. This structure was uncovered by simply following certain heuristics (in this case a technique for merging similar statements) without needing to understand the purpose of the program. When we look at the function of the program, as described in the published documentation [3], we see that this double loop does in fact precisely capture what the program is intended to do! The program scans through a sorted file consisting of items and page references. The outer loop scans through distinct items, and for each distinct item the inner loop steps through the page references for that item. Writing the program as a single loop whose body must distinguish the two cases of a new item and a repeated item obscured the simple basic structure, which has been revealed through transformations. This kind of transformation has important applications in program maintenance; the second version is far easier to understand and modify—there is only one copy of the statement that writes to the file, and the flag **morenum** that was used to direct the control flow is not needed. The transformation from first version to second used only general transformations, which have been proved to work in all cases, and so could be applied without having to understand the program first.

Translating the WSL back into C gives this reengineered program:

```
#include <stdio.h>
main()      /* DataFlex transcription */
{
  int filestat;
  char page[6], theline[51], item[31], lastitem[31];
  FILE *fopen(), *fp_in, *fp_out;
  fp_in = fopen("DIDB","r");
  fp_out = fopen("DID2INX.TXT","w");
  filestat = fscanf(fp_in," %s%s",page,item);
  for(;;) {
```

8.1 First case study: Book index generator

```
            strcpy(theline,item);
            strcat(theline," ");
            strcat(theline,page);
            for(;;) {
              strcpy(lastitem,item);
              filestat = fscanf(fp_in," %s%s",page,item);
              if ((filestat == EOF) || strcmp(item,lastitem)) break;
              strcat(theline,", ");
              strcat(theline,page);
            }
            fprintf(fp_out," %s%s",theline,"\n");
            if (filestat == EOF) break;
          }
        }
```

The program reads the file "DIDB," a sorted text file that consists of a number of lines each containing a page number followed by a word. It produces an output file "DID2INX.TXT," which lists one word per line with each word followed by a list of the page numbers on which that word appears. A sample input file is the following:

```
1    an
10   an
17   an
123  an
2    bat
3    bat
99   cow
```

while the corresponding output is

```
an 1, 10, 17, 123
bat 2, 3
cow 99
```

Note that the input is sorted alphabetically on the word field and then numerically on the page number field.

With this knowledge of the program's purpose we can see that the transformations have also revealed a bug in the program: Note that the outer loop has the test at the end (as in the usual **repeat**... **until** loop), so the body of this loop is executed at least once. Recalling that the program reads an input file and produces some output that summarizes the input, there is something rather odd about this structure! In fact, the program will not work correctly if presented with an empty file: The documentation implies that the program should produce no output for an empty input file, but this program's output consists of a single line composed from the contents of uninitialized data structures! This bug is not immediately obvious in the first version of the program. For the first version a typical fix would be to add a test for an empty file and a **goto** that jumps to a new label at the end of the program. In that case this fix is also typical in that it further obscures the program structure, increases the program length, and increases the number of identifiers used. In contrast with this, to carry out the same modification to the second version we merely change the outer loop to a **while** loop.

An alternative (and even less drastic) method of correcting the bug is to introduce the assertion **filestat** $\neq$ **EOF** after the first call to **fscanf**. This assertion states that the "empty input" case can be ignored. Using it we are able to transform the outer loop into a **while** loop. On removing the assertion we get a program that will work correctly for the empty file case and that is proven to be equivalent to the original program in all other cases. Thus, we have fixed the bug and proved that we have broken nothing else in doing so.

8.1.3 Abstracting a specification

The transformations in the previous section were basically all at the source code level. Our aim in this section is to cross the abstraction levels in order to get to an abstract specification. The first step is to change the data representation from files to a more abstract representation as lists of records. The input file is a list of records of the form of ⟨**item, page**⟩, while the output file is a list of lines. The new variable i is used to denote the "current position" in the input list (it is analogous to the file pointer in the C program). We translate the **fopen, fscanf** and **fprintf** functions into the corresponding abstract operations. The end of file test **fstat** = **EOF** becomes the test $i > \ell(\textbf{input})$:

$i := 1;$
item := input[i][1]; page := input[i][2];
output := ⟨⟩;
while $i \leq \ell(\textbf{input})$ **do**
  theline := item ++ " " ++ page;
  do lastitem := item;
    $i := i+1;$
    item := input[i][1]; page := input[i][2];
    if $i > \ell(\textbf{input}) \lor$ item $\neq$ lastitem **then** exit(1) **fi**

8.1 First case study: Book index generator

$\qquad$ theline := theline $+$ ", " $+$ page od;
output $\xleftarrow{push}$ theline od

This change in data representation allows us to remove the variable **lastitem** since the references to **lastitem** can be replaced by **input** $[i-1][1]$. We can similarly remove the variables **item** and **page**. Finally, by duplicating the statement $i := i + 1$ we can invert the inner loop to another **while** loop:

$i := 1$; output := $\langle\rangle$;
while $i \leq \ell(\text{input})$ **do**
$\quad$ theline := input$[i][1]$ $+$ " " $+$ input$[i][2]$;
$\quad i := i + 1$;
$\quad$ **while** $i \leq \ell(\text{input}) \wedge \text{input}[i][1] = \text{input}[i-1][1]$ **do**
$\quad\quad$ theline := theline $+$ ", " $+$ input$[i][2]$;
$\quad\quad i := i + 1$ **od**;
$\quad$ output $\xleftarrow{push}$ theline od

We now have a double loop that scans through the sequence **input**. Each step of the inner loop processes a single element of the sequence, so each execution of the inner loop processes a segment of the sequence. Thus, the key to the data restructuring is to split the input sequence into sections such that the outer loop processes one segment per iteration. This is easily achieved with the **split** function defined in Chapter 4—the terminating condition on the inner loop provides the predicate on which to split. Define the predicate **same_item** as

funct same_item$(x, y) \equiv$
$\quad x[1] = y[1]$.

Then the new variable q is introduced with the assignment

$q := \text{split}(\text{input, same\_item})$

We introduce q and its two index variables j and k to the program as ghost variables. j and k step through q as i steps through p; more formally we preserve the invariant

$i = +/(\ell * q[1 \ldots j-1]) + k$

which is the same as saying $i = \text{index}_q(j, k)$. From this invariant and the relation $+/q = \text{input}$ we get the invariant: **input**$[i] = q[j][k]$. Adding these ghost variables to the program we get

$i := 1$; output := $\langle\rangle$
$q := \text{split}(\text{input, same\_item})$; $j := 1$; $k := 1$;
while $i \leq \ell(\text{input})$**do**

theline := input[i][1] ++ " " ++ input[i][2];
i := i+1;
k := k+1; **if** $k > \ell(q[j])$ **then** j := j+1; k := 1 **fi**;
while $i \leq \ell(\text{input}) \wedge \text{input}[i][1] = \text{input}[i-1][1]$ **do**
  theline := theline ++ ", " ++ input[i][2]; i := i+1;
  k := k+1; **if** $k > \ell(q[j])$ **then** j := j+1; k := 1 **fi od**;
output $\xleftarrow{\text{push}}$ theline **od**

The next stage is to replace references to the concrete variables **input** and i by references to the new variables q, j and k using the invariants above. Then the concrete variables become ghost variables and can be removed from the program. Note that due to the structure of q the test **input**[i][1] = **input**[i − 1][1] is true as long as we are in the same section of **input** (i.e., as long as we have not just incremented j and reset k to 1). However, this is the case exactly when $k \neq 1$. Also, if $i > \ell(\textbf{input})$ in the inner loop we must have just incremented j (and k will be 1), so the whole test in the inner loop is equivalent to $k \neq 1$. We have

output := $\langle\rangle$;
q := split(input, same_item); j := 1; k := 1;
while $j \leq \ell(q)$ **do**
  theline := $q[j][k][1]$ ++ " " ++ $q[j][k][2]$;
  k := k+1; **if** $k > \ell(q[j])$ **then** j := j+1; k := 1 **fi**;
  while $k \neq 1$ **do**
    theline := theline ++ ", " ++ $q[j][k][2]$;
    k := k+1; **if** $k > \ell(q[j])$ **then** j := j+1; k := 1 **fi od**;
  output $\xleftarrow{\text{push}}$ theline **od**

We want to show that the inner loop processes exactly one segment of q; to do this we need to change its termination condition to $k \leq \ell(q[j])$. The easiest way to do this is to convert the inner loop to a **do**...**od** loop and absorb the **if** statement and increment of k to get

do k := k+1;
  if $k > \ell(q[j])$ **then** j := j+1; k := 1 **fi**;
  if $k \neq 1$ **then exit fi**;
  theline := theline ++ ", " ++ $q[j][k][2]$ **od**

If $k \geq \ell(q[j])$ at the beginning of this loop body then the **if** statement will be executed and the loop terminated. Conversely if $k < \ell(q[j])$, then it is certainly ≥ 1; so after k is incremented, the **if** statement has no effect and the loop is not terminated (since now $k > 1$). So, we can transform the inner loop into the following **while** loop:

8.1 First case study: Book index generator

while $k < \ell(q[j])$ **do**
  $k := k+1;$
  theline := theline $+\!\!+$ ", " $+\!\!+ q[j][k][2]$ **od**;
$j := j+1; k := 1$

The local variable k is only used in this loop (its value is always 1 outside the loop) so we can transform it into a **for** loop. Our program now looks as follows:

output := $\langle\rangle;$
$q :=$ split(input, same_item); $j := 1;$
while $j \leq \ell(q)$ **do**
  theline := $q[j][1][1] +\!\!+$ " " $+\!\!+ q[j][1][2];$
  for $k := 2$ **step** 1 **to** $\ell(q[j])$ **do**
    theline := theline $+\!\!+$ ", " $+\!\!+ q[j][k][2]$ **od**;
  $j := j+1;$
  output $\overset{\text{push}}{\longleftarrow}$ theline **od**

where we have replaced the occurrences of k outside the **for** loop by 1.

$q[j]$ is a sequence of pairs, but in the inner **for** loop we only use the second element of each pair. Thus, we can represent $q[j]$ by the sequence of second elements (i.e., the sequence $r = \pi_2 * q[j]$ where $\pi_2(\langle a,b \rangle) = b$ is a projection function) (this is another data refinement). With this abstraction the inner loop takes on the following form:

var $r := \pi_2 * q[j]$:
  theline := theline $+\!\!+ r[1];$
  for $k := 2$ **step** 1 **to** $\ell(r)$ **do**
    theline := theline $+\!\!+$ ", " $+\!\!+ r[k]$ **od end**

These statements implement a "splice" function; they are equivalent to the simple assignment: theline := theline $+\!\!+ (\text{sep}(", ")/r)$ where **sep** is defined: $\textbf{sep}(s)(a,b) = a +\!\!+ s +\!\!+ b$. Thus, we can rewrite this as follows:

var $r := \pi_2 * q[j]$:
  theline := theline $+\!\!+ (\text{sep }(", ")/r)$ **end**

The program simplifies to

output := $\langle\rangle;$
$q :=$ split(input, same_item); $j := 1;$
while $j \leq \ell(\text{q})$ **do**
  theline := $q[j][1][1] +\!\!+$ " " $+\!\!+ (\text{sep }(", ")/(\pi_2 * q[j]));$
  $j := j + 1;$
  output $\overset{\text{push}}{\longleftarrow}$ theline **od**

Finally, this program constructs output by applying a function of each element of the list q so we can implement the remaining loop as a map operation:

begin var $q :=$ split(input, same_item):
  output $:=$ process$*q$ **end**
where
funct process (seq)
  seq[1][1] $+\!\!+$ " " $+\!\!+$ (sep(", ")/(π_2*seq)).
end

To summarize this specification: We split **input** into a list of sections q starting a new section at each point where the head of one pair differs from the head of the next pair. We process each section to create a line of output that contains the head of the first pair (the item), a space and the list of second elements of the pairs (the numbers), separated by the string ",". The **output** variable is a list of the lines of output.

This is now in the form of an abstract specification that defines the precise relationship between the input and output states.

8.1.4 Reimplementation

The final stage in a reengineering process is to reimplement the specification (perhaps after some modification) in the same or a different language. For improved maintainability and flexibility we decided to reimplement the specification as a Perl script:

```
#!/usr/bin/Perl
# DataFlex transcription -- reengineered version
use strict;
use warnings;

sub same_item($$);
sub process($);
sub split_list($&);

my @input = map {[split(/\s+/, $_, 2)]} <>;
my $q = split_list(\@input, \&same_item);
print map { process($_) . "\n" } @$q;

sub same_item($$) {
  my ($x, $y) = @_;
  return($$x[1] eq $$y[1]);
}
```

8.1 First case study: Book index generator

```perl
sub process($) {
  my ($seq) = @_;
  return($$seq[0][1] . " " . join(", ", map { $$_[0] } @{$seq}));
}

sub split_list($&) {
  my ($in, $test) = @_;
  my @out = ();
  while (@$in) {
    push(@out, [shift(@$in)]);
    while (@$in && &$test($$in[0], $out[-1][-1])) {
      push(@{$out[-1]}, shift(@$in));
    }
  }
  return(\@out);
}
```

Notes

- The Perl script follows very closely the format of the specification, including separating out the **same_item** function;

- The **split_list** function (which implements the split function of Chapter 4) could be taken out into a separate Perl module containing generic list operations.

Comparing this version with the goals listed in Section 8.1.1 we can see the following:

1. All the restrictions from the C and DataFlex implementations have been removed. The Perl script takes its input either from the command line arguments or from standard input (if no arguments are given on the command line) and writes to standard output. It thus becomes a standard utility program that can appear in a pipeline. The input format is now free text rather than fixed field: each line of input contains a page number plus a word separated by spaces. The page numbers are not restricted to five digits and the words are not restricted to 30 characters. More importantly, the output lines are not restricted to 50 characters;

2. The Perl script is much easier to understand and modify; for example, to change the program to ignore case differences in

the words it is sufficient to change the **return** line in the same_item function to

return(lc($$x[1]) eq lc($$y[1]));

To enhance the program so that it will also sort the input file before processing only requires adding a line of code:

my @input = map { [split] } <>;
@input = sort { ($$a[1] cmp $$b[1]) && ($$a[0] <=> $$b[0]) } @input;

3. The Perl version is less efficient than either of the C versions (approxumately 28 times slower); however, it is able to process a 7Mb input file and generate a 4Mb output file in under 26 seconds on a 1-GHz PC. The same PC took about 50 seconds to sort the input file, and for larger files the sorting time will dominate the processing time, so even at 28 times slower, processing time is not an issue.

8.1.5 Conclusion

The Perl reimplementation of the original C program is far superior, when measured by the goals listed in Section 8.1.1. Program transformation theory gives a solid foundation to the reengineering process, enabling much greater accuracy, flexibility, and reliability.

8.2 Second case study: Topological sorting algorithm

Our second case study is a topological sorting algorithm presented by Knuth and Szwarcfiter in [1]. This algorithm is highly unstructured with complex control flow combined with complex data structures used for multiple purposes; although quite small in the number of lines of code, it is considerably more complicated than most commercial modules of this size and presents a considerable challenge to any program understanding technique. Our aim is to use program transformations to reverse-engineer a formal specification for the algorithm (and thereby also prove the correctness of the algorithm as given). If FermaT can handle programs of this complexity, then it should be able to handle lesser programs with ease!

The analysis of the algorithm breaks down into several stages, listed as follows:

8.2 Second case study: Topological sorting algorithm

1. Restructure to remove some of the control-flow complexity;

2. Recast as an iterative procedure, abstracting away the error cases so that the iteration-to-recursion transformation (in Appendix A) can be applied to generate an equivalent recursive procedure;

3. Restructure the resulting recursive procedure;

4. Add abstract variables to the program and update them in parallel with the actual (concrete) variables;

5. Replace references to concrete variables by equivalent references to abstract variables;

6. Remove the concrete variables to give an abstract program;

7. Replace the recursive call by a copy of the specification and show that the result is a refinement of the specification. Then the recursive implementation theorem shows that the recursive program (and therefore the original program) is a correct refinement of the topological sorting specification.

8.2.1 Topological sorting

Topological sorting involves ordering a set of elements in such a way as to satisfy a set of constraints on the final order. One common example is where a task is broken down into a set of subtasks: Suppose that we have a set of tasks to do but that certain tasks have to be performed before other tasks. For example, the author has to write the text of a book and the designer has to design the layout of the text on the page *before* the printer can typeset the book. But the page design and text writing tasks can be carried out in either order. Thus, there are two different "valid" orderings of the three tasks:

1. write $\longrightarrow$ design $\longrightarrow$ typeset;

2. design $\longrightarrow$ write $\longrightarrow$ typeset.

For a valid ordering to exist there must be no cycles in the set of constraints.

More formally, we are given a set P of pairs of elements taken from the set B. The pair $\langle x, y \rangle$ in P indicates that x must appear before y in the solution. The aim is to find all the ways to list the elements of B that satisfy the set P of constraints. This will be possible if and only if there are no *cycles* in the set of pairs, (i.e., if there is no sequence $\langle c_1, c_2, \ldots, c_m \rangle$ of elements of B, where $c_m = c_1$ and for each $1 \leq i < m$ the pair $\langle c_i, c_{i+1} \rangle$ is in P).

The following theorem proves the existence of a topological sort whenever there are no cycles.

Theorem 8.1 Topological sorting of a finite set P of pairs of elements in a finite base set B is possible if and only if P is cycle free.

Proof: The proof is by induction on the size of B. If B is empty, then the empty sequence $\langle\rangle$ is a solution. Otherwise, if B is cycle-free then there must be a minimum element of B (an element that does not appear as the second element of a pair in P). To find a minimal element, start with any element and "work backwards" through the pairs on P. Call this minimal element x_1. The set B' formed from B by removing x_1 is smaller than B, so by the induction hypothesis we can topologically sort B' to give the list $\langle x_2, \ldots, x_n \rangle$. Prepend x_1 to this list to get a topological sort of B.

We give the proof of this well-known result, because the proof that a solution exists also provides an algorithm for constructing the solution: Start with any minimal element, then pick a minimal element in the remainder, and so on. In addition, we note that any topological sort of P could be constructed by this algorithm. In other words, if $\langle x_1, x_2, \ldots, x_n \rangle$ is a topological sort of P, then x_1 must be a minimal element (or there will be an arrow in the wrong direction) and, by induction, $\langle x_2, \ldots, x_n \rangle$ must be a topological sort of the remainder.

So, a small modification of the algorithm will give a list of all the topological sorts of P: For each minimal element x_1 of B, prepend it to each of the topological sorts of the set $B \backslash \{x_1\}$ over the set P' of pairs formed by removing all the pairs containing x_1 from P. This will form the list of all topological sorts of P.

The algorithm in [1] prints the list of topological sorts; our algorithm will call a procedure **process** once for each topological sort of B over P. In WSL notation the specification is

process_all(P, B) $=_{\text{DF}}$ **for** $t \in$ **TOPSORTS**(P, B) **do** process(t) **od**

Here the **for** loop iterates over the set in an arbitrary (nondeterministic) order. The set **TOPSORTS**(P, B) is the set of all topologically sorted sequences, as defined above.

For efficiency reasons, we will assume that B is nonempty. Clearly, if B is a singleton, say $B = \{x\}$, then **TOPSORTS**(P, B) = $\{\langle x \rangle\}$. The proof of Theorem 8.2.1 shows that **process_all**(P, B) is equivalent to the following:

8.2 Second case study: Topological sorting algorithm

```
if #B=1
   then process(⟨B[1]⟩)
   else for q ∈ MINS(P, B) do
           for t ∈ TOPSORTS(P\{⟨x, y⟩ ∈ P | x = q}, B\{q}) do
              process(⟨q⟩ ++ t) odod
```

where $B[1]$ is the single element of B (when B has only one element) and $\text{MINS}(P, B)$ is the set of minimal elements.

These observations motivate the following definition of a generalization of **process_all**, which has an extra argument, a sequence to be prepended to each topological sort before **process** is called:

$$\text{process\_all}(s, P, B) =_{\text{DF}} \text{ for } t \in \text{TOPSORTS}(P, B) \text{ do process}(s ++ t) \text{ od}$$

By Theorem 8.1 we see that **process_all**(s, P, B) is equivalent to

```
if #B=1
   then process(s ++ ⟨B[1]⟩)
   else for q ∈ MINS(P, B) do
           for t ∈ TOPSORTS(P, B\{q}) do
              process(s ++ ⟨q⟩ ++ t) od od
```

So **process_all**(s, P, B) is equivalent to

```
if #B=1
   then process(s ++ ⟨B[1]⟩)
   else for q ∈ MINS(P, B) do
           process_all(s ++ ⟨q⟩, P, B\{q}) od
```

This shows that **process_all** is equivalent to a program containing a copy of **process_all** applied to a smaller argument (the set B is reduced in the loop). Thus we can use the recursive implementation theorem to get a recursive procedure that implements the topological sorting program: **process_all**(s, P, B) is equivalent to $T(s, P, B)$ where

```
proc T(s, P, B) ≡
   if #B=1 then process(s ++ ⟨B[1]⟩)
         else for q∈MINS(P, B) do
                T(s ++ ⟨q⟩, P, B\{q}) od
```

8.2.2 Knuth's topological sorting algorithm

The algorithm presented by Knuth and Szwarcfiter [1] is written in a pseudo PASCAL notation. Although the title claims it is a structured program, it in fact contains various features that make the program very difficult to analyze and prove correct. These include the use of comments as the labels for **goto** statements, jumping into and out of the middle of loop structures, and the use of pointers into arrays to represent linked lists.

We have translated the algorithm into WSL, with some slight changes:

- The input is taken from an array R rather than by calling the **read** procedure.

- Instead of printing the result, we call **process(s)** for each topological sorting arrangement s. This generalizes the algorithm without introducing any complications.

for $j := 1$ **to** n **step** 1 **do**
    count[j] := 0; top[j] := 0 **od**;
for $k := 1$ **to** m **step** 1 **do**
    $\langle i, j \rangle := R[k]$; suc[$k$] := j; next[k] := top[i]; top[i] := k;
    count[j] := count[j]+1 **od**;
link[0] := 0; $d := 0$;
for $j := 1$ **to** n **step** 1 **do**
    if count[j] = 0 **then** link[d] := j; $d := j$ **fi od**;
actions start:
start $\equiv$
    if $d = 0$ **then call** done **else** link[d] := link[0] **fi**;
    $k := 0$; $t := 0$; **call** alltopsorts.
alltopsorts $\equiv$
    if $k = n{-}1$ **then** $s[n] := d$; process(s)
            else base[k] := link[d]; **call** L **fi**;
call endloop.
$L \equiv$
    $q := $ link[d]; $d_1 := $ link[q];
    $p := $ top[q];
    while $p \neq 0$ **do**
        $j := $ suc[p];
        count[j] := count[j]−1;
        if count[j] = 0 **then if** $d{=}q$ **then** $d := j$ **else** link[j] := d_1 **fi**;
            $d_1 := j$ **fi**;
        $p := $ next[p] **od**;
    link[d] := d_1;
    $s[k{+}1] := q$;
    if $d_1{=}q$ **then comment** : Input contains an oriented cycle;
            call done **fi**;
    count[q] := t; $t := q$; $k := k{+}1$;

8.2 Second case study: Topological sorting algorithm

    call alltopsorts .
  return ≡
    $k := k-1$;
    $q := t$; $t := $ count$[q]$; count$[q] := 0$;
    $p := $ top$[q]$;
    while $p \ne 0$ **do**
      $j := $ suc$[p]$;
      count$[j] := $ count$[j]+1$;
      $p := $ next$[p]$ **od**;
    link$[d] := q$; $d := q$;
    if link$[d] \ne $ base$[k]$ **then call** L **fi**;
    call endloop.
  endloop ≡
    if $k > 0$
      then call return **fi**; **call** done.
  done ≡
    call Z. **endactions**

8.2.3 Restructuring

The first step in analyzing the program involves simple restructuring. We begin by looking for procedures and variables that can be "localized." In this case the variables p and j are used locally in two sections of code, which we turn into procedures. Since we have yet to determine what these procedures do, they have been called P_1 and P_2. Finding blocks of code that can be taken out into self-contained procedures with local data is a very valuable exercise in reengineering: It allows the engineer to tackle a large monolithic block of code via divide-and-conquer techniques.

The next step is to do some basic restructuring, using the techniques we have developed for removing an action system by introducing loops in appropriate places using the transformations in [4–6]:

  begin
    for $j := 1$ **to** n **step** 1 **do**
      count$[j] := 0$; top$[j] := 0$ **od**;
    for $k := 1$ **to** m **step** 1 **do**
      $\langle i, j \rangle := R[k]$; suc$[k] := j$; next$[k] := $ top$[i]$; top$[i] := k$;
      count$[j] := $ count$[j]+1$ **od**;
    link$[0] := 0$; $d := 0$;
    for $j := 1$ **to** n **step** 1 **do**
      if count$[j]=0$ **then** link$[d] := j$; $d := j$ **fi od**;

if $d \neq 0$
then link$[d] :=$ link$[0]$; $k := 0$; $t := 0$;
    do if $k = n{-}1$
        then $s[n] := d$; process(s);
            do if $k \leq 0$ **then** **exit**(2) **fi**;
                $k := k{-}1$;
                $q := t$; $t :=$ count$[q]$; count$[q] := 0$; $P_2()$;
                if link$[d] \neq$ base$[k]$ **then** **exit**(1) **fi od**
        else base$[k] :=$ link$[d]$ **fi**;
    $P_1()$; $s[k+1] := q$;
    if $d_1 = q$ **then** **comment :** Input contains an oriented cycle;
                exit(1) **fi**;
    count$[q] := t$; $t := q$; $k := k+1$ **od fi**
where
proc $P_1() \equiv$
    var p, j:
        $q :=$ link$[d]$; $d_1 :=$ link$[q]$; $p :=$ top$[q]$;
        while $p \neq 0$ **do**
          $j :=$ suc$[p]$;
          count$[j] :=$ count$[j]{-}1$;
          if count$[j] = 0$
              then if $d{=}q$ **then** $d := j$ **else** link$[j] := d_1$ **fi**; $d_1 := j$ **fi**;
          $p :=$ next$[p]$ **od**;
        link$[d] := d_1$ **end**.
proc $P_2() \equiv$
    var p, j:
        $p :=$ top$[q]$;
        while $p \neq 0$ **do**
          $j :=$ suc$[p]$; count$[j] :=$ count$[j] + 1$; $p :=$ next$[p]$ **od**;
        link$[d] := q$;
        $d := q$ **end**. **end**

Our next aim is to restructure the program in the form of a recursive procedure, by applying the iteration to recursion transformation (Appendix A). First we introduce the procedure and create an action system for its body. The **do** ...**od** loop above (which starts with **if** $k = n-1$ **then** ...) is replaced by a call to $F()$ where the new procedure F is defined as

    proc $F() \equiv$
        actions F:
        $F \equiv$
          if $k = n-1$

8.2 Second case study: Topological sorting algorithm

          then $s[n] := d$; process(s); **call** $\mathscr{F}$
          else base$[k] :=$ link$[d]$; **call** B **fi**.
$B \equiv$
    $P_1()$;
    $s[k+1] := q$;
    if $d_1 = q$ **then comment** : Input contains an oriented cycle;
                        call Z **fi**;
    count$[q] := t$;
    $t := q$;
    $k := k+1$;
    call F.
$\mathscr{F} \equiv$
    if $k \leq 0$
      then call Z
      else $k := k-1$;
          $q := t$; $t :=$ count$[q]$; count$[q] := 0$;
          $P_2()$;
          if link$[d] \neq$ base$[k]$ **then call** B
                                 else call $\mathscr{F}$ **fi fi**.

For the iteration to recursion transformation (Appendix A) to be applicable there must be a single **call** Z statement in the $\mathscr{F}$ action, and no **call** Z elsewhere. At the moment, there are two **call** Z's (one in B and one in $\mathscr{F}$). However, the comment suggests that the **call** Z in B is in fact an error case. At this stage of the analysis, we are only interested in the normal behavior of the program, ignoring its behavior for erroneous input data. We will therefore abstract the program (i.e., carry out the reverse of a refinement operation) by replacing the statement **if** $d_1 = q$ **then call** Z **fi** by a more abstract (less refined) statement: the assertion $\{d_1 \neq q\}$. For the normal case, both **if** statement and assertion are equivalent to **skip**, while for the error case, the latter statement aborts, while the former statement terminates the program. With this change, the program is now in the right form to apply the recursion removal/introduction theorem. We do so and restructure the new action system to get

    proc $F() \equiv$
      if $k = n-1$
        then $s[n] := d$; process(s)
        else base$[k] :=$ link$[d]$;
        do $P_1()$;
            $s[k+1] := q$;
            $\{d_1 \neq q\}$;

```
        count[q] := t; t := q;
        k := k+1; F(); k := k−1;
        q := t; t := count[q]; count[q] := 0;
        P₂();
        if link[d] = base[k] then exit(1) fi od fi.
```

An alternative to the abstraction step is to set a flag and call $\mathscr{F}$. If $k > 0$ but the flag is set, then the new $\mathscr{F}$ can decrement k and call itself again. As a result, there will be only one call to Z.

It is often very important to cast a program into a recursive form, as early as possible in the analysis process. This is because recursive programs are generally much easier to analyze than their iterative equivalents.

As a first step in the analysis, we can remove the array **base** since it is only used to save the value of **link**[d] across the inner recursive calls. Assuming that base is not used outside the program, we can replace the array by a local variable. It is also clear that the array elements $s[k+1 \ldots n]$ are not used, so we will replace s by a sequence of length k. The variable k is then redundant, as its value is available as the length of s:

```
proc F() ≡
    if ℓ(s) = n−1
        then s := s ++ ⟨d⟩; process(s); s := butlast(s)
        else var ⟨base := link[d]⟩:
        do P₁();
            {d₁ ≠ q};
            count[q] := t; t := q;
            s := s ++ ⟨q⟩; F(); s := butlast(s);
            q := t; t := count[q]; count[q] := 0;
            P₂();
            if link[d] = base then exit(1) fi od end fi.
```

Notice that the concept of saving and restoring a variable over a recursive call does not make sense for the original version of the program: converting to a recursive program allows us to raise the abstraction to a higher level.

8.2.4 Abstraction to a specification

In reverse-engineering a complex recursive program such as this one, it can be very valuable to have some idea of the expected specification of the main procedures. In this case, it is clear that we expect the specification of $F()$ to be something like this:

8.2 Second case study: Topological sorting algorithm

process_all(s, set(R), $\{1, 2, \ldots, n\}\backslash$set($s$))

This becomes clear when we compare the structure of $F()$ to the structure of $T(s, P, B)$ above. Most of the variables and array elements assigned in $F()$ seem to be restored before the end of $F()$ (this is a conjecture that we will have to prove). The exceptions are the variable q and the **link** array: q is saved in t and t is saved in **count**[q]. It is clear that some elements of **link** are overwritten in $P_1()$ and $P_2()$. In $P_1()$, we decrement a **count** value and, if it reaches zero, assign to the corresponding **link** value. Thus we conjecture that $F()$ preserves **link**[j] for all j such that **count**[j] = 0. Our specification for $F()$ is therefore conjectured as

$$\textbf{SPEC} =_{\text{DF}} \text{process\_all}(s, \text{set}(R), \{1, 2, \ldots, n\}\backslash\text{set}(s));$$
$$q := q'.\textbf{true};$$
$$\text{link} := \text{link}'.(\forall j, 1 \leqslant j \leqslant n.\text{count}[j] = 0 \Rightarrow (\text{link}'[j] = \text{link}[j]))$$

(In a real software maintenance task on a large system, programmers make such conjectures all the time, either base on comments or on a knowledge of how the system words, or on an analysis of the source code itself: "OK, so it looks like he is saving x here and it gets restored over there...". The problem is that they have no means of formally verifying such conjectures. Unverified assumptions about the behavior of one part of a system, when applied to another part of the system, can be a fruitful source of bugs!)

Note that the variable k is incremented before the recursive call of $F()$ and is no greater than n. So the positive expression $k - n$ is reduced before every recursive call. Consider the following nonrecursive procedure, where we have replaced the recursive call of $F()$ by **SPEC**:

proc $F'() \equiv$
    if $\ell(s) = n{-}1$
        then $s := s +\!\!+ \langle d\rangle$; process($s$); $s := $ butlast(s)
        else var $\langle$base := link[d]$\rangle$:
            do $P_1()$;
                $\{d_1 \neq \textbf{q}\}$;
                $s := s +\!\!+ \langle q\rangle$; **SPEC**; $q \xleftarrow{\text{last}} s$;
                count[q] := 0;
                $P_2()$;
                if link[d] = base **then exit**(1) **fi od end fi**.

If we can prove that $F'()$ is a refinement of **SPEC** then we can apply the recursive implementation theorem to prove that the recursive procedure $F()$ is also a refinement of **SPEC**, and we will have derived a specification for the whole program.

Procedure $F'()$ can immediately be simplified somewhat, and the result makes some progress towards the proof; for example, it is clear that k and t are preserved by F'. In order for **count**$[q]$ to be preserved, we conjecture that the assignment **count**$[q] := 0$ restores its original value (this is bourne out by Knuth's commentary on the algorithm which refers to using a spare count value to save the value of t). Thus we abstract the procedure by inserting the assertion **count**$[q] = 0$ just after $P_1()$, in the hope that this can be removed by a later transformation, thus demonstrating that the "abstraction" step was in fact an equivalence. With this addition, some further simplification becomes possible:

> **proc** $F'() \equiv$
>   **if** $\ell(s) = n-1$
>   **then** SPEC
>   **else var** $\langle$base $:=$ link$[d]\rangle$:
>   **do** $P_1()$;
> $\{\text{count}[q] = 0\}$;
> $\{d_1 \neq q\}$;
> $s := s +\!\!+ \langle q \rangle;$ SPEC; $q \xleftarrow{\text{last}} s$;
> $P_2()$;
>   **if** link$[d]$ = base **then exit**(1) **fi od fi**.

8.2.5 Changing the data representation—adding abstract variables

The program makes much use of linked lists to represent sets of integers. Our aim in this section is to replace these concrete data structures by the equivalent abstract data structures (i.e., actual sequences and sets instead of linked lists). The program represents a small set of (positive) integers by using a variable, v, and an array a. The first integer is stored in v (which is zero for if the set is empty), and for each integer i, the next integer is in $a[i]$ (which is zero if i is the last integer in the set). Thus the set is represented as an unordered list without duplicates. We define an abstraction function, list(v, a, w), which returns the list represented by v and a, where w is the special value (in this case, zero), which indicates the end of the list:

$$\text{list}(v, a, w) =_{\text{DF}} \begin{cases} \langle\rangle, & \text{if } v = w \\ \langle v \rangle +\!\!+ \text{list}(a[v], a, w) & \text{if } v \neq w \end{cases}$$

For a (possibly empty) set of positive integers, represented as a linked list terminated by 0, the list is list$(v, a, 0)$ which gives the list $\langle v, a[v], a[a[v]], \ldots \rangle$. If v is nonzero, then the effect of the assignment $v := a[v]$ is to remove the first element from the list, while the assignments $a[x] := v; v := x$ add the element x to the front of the list.

If we know that the list will be nonempty, then we can avoid the need for a terminating value by creating a circular-linked list. We do this by setting $a[l]$ to v, where l is the last element in the list: so, for example, a one element list will have $a[v] = v$. The list represented by a circular-linked list is $\text{list}(a[v], a, v) \mathbin{+\mkern-10mu+} \langle v \rangle$. Note that here, the value in v is the last element in the list. In this representation, the assignment $v := a[v]$ has the effect of rotating the list by one step, rather than removing the first element.

The first **for** loop in the program simply initializes the arrays **count** and **top** to zeros. The second loop reads each pair in the R list and updates **count**, **top**, and **suc**. We claim that **count** records for each element how many pairs in R have that element as the second component. The arrays **top** and **suc** partition the set $\{1, 2, \ldots, k\}$ of indices of elements of R into a collection of disjoint subsets, one per element, where each subset contains all the indices of pairs with the same first component. We add an abstract variable A that records the set of active indices of R (it records which pairs of R are currently included in the representations).

count$[j]$ is the number of pairs read so far that have j as the second element (this is not necessarily the number of predecessors of j in the input relation, since the same pair may appear more than once in the input).

After the second **for** loop, the statements $\text{link}[0] := 0; d := 0$ set up an empty, zero-terminated list in variable d and array **link**. The third **for** loop iterates over the set of elements that have zero **count** (i.e., they do not appear as the second component of any pair), and puts these elements into the list formed by d and the **link** array. We add another abstract variable B (the active base), which records which elements have been processed so far.

The statement $\text{link}[d] := \text{link}[0]$ turns the list into a circular list with $\text{link}[d]$ as the first element (provided $d \neq 0$). We can ignore the case $d = 0$ since this implies a cycle in R.

Note that after the third **for** loop, if $d = 0$ then the input sequence R contains a cycle, which is not allowed. Thus as above, we abstract the **if** statement to an assertion, ignoring the error case.

Having established the abstract variables and the invariants relating these to the concrete variables, the next step is to add assignments to the abstract variables to ensure that the invariants are preserved throughout the program. At this stage the abstract variables have no effect on the behavior of the program, so they are called *ghost variables*. To add the ghost variables and ensure that the invariants are preserved it is sufficient to examine each block of code in turn, without needing to understand the program as a whole. Then the invariants will be used to replace references to concrete variables by the equivalent abstract variables. Again, it is sufficient to examine each block in turn, using only local information to carry out these replacements. Eventually the concrete variables themselves become ghost variables and can be removed as all the work is now being done by the abstract variables.

This ghost variables approach is therefore able to scale up to much larger programs, because at each stage only a small part of the program needs to be examined. Only at a much later stage, when we have a more abstract and high-level version of the program, do we need to consider the program as a whole.

At this point it is sufficient to work on each small "chunk" at a time, inserting assignments to abstract variables in order to preserve the invariants that relate abstract to concrete variables.

The detailed steps whereby the abstract variables are inserted and the assertions proved correct are a little tedious, but not difficult, and so are omitted. See [7] for the details. These formal proofs are very important for safety-critical systems, but for less critical systems a more informal argument may be appropriate.

8.2.6 The abstract program

We have now built the scaffolding around the various parts of the program: This consists of adding abstract variables with assignments to them, and invariants relating the abstract and concrete variables. We were able to do this for each section of the program independently of the others, without needing to determine the big picture. We are now in a position to put all the pieces together to form a hybrid program. Having done so, we can make use of the assertions to replace references to concrete variables by equivalent references to abstract variables; for example the test **count**[j] = 0 is replaced by the equivalent test $\neg \exists x \in A.R[x][2] = j$ by appealing to an invariant. References to concrete variables appearing in assignments to other concrete variables do not need to be removed; for example the statement **count**[j] := **count**[j] + 1 can remain. Once all relevant references to concrete variables have been removed, these become ghost variables, since they have no effect on the execution of the program, and the concrete variables can be removed in their entirety. This ghost variables technique has been applied to program development in [8–11].

The result is an abstract procedure equivalent to $F'()$. We can make use of the assertions to simplify the abstract program still further, in particular by removing the two **for** loops. This is because the assertions tell us the final values of the variables modified by the loops.

8.2 Second case study: Topological sorting algorithm

proc $F''() \equiv$
  if $\ell(s) = n-1$
    then SPEC
    else $D := \text{sort}(\text{MINS}(R, B))$;
      var $\langle \text{base} := D[1] \rangle$:
        do var $\langle D_0 := D \rangle$:
          $q := D[1]$;
          $B := B \setminus \{q\}$;
          $D := \text{sort}(\text{MINS}(R, B))$;
          $s := s \mathbin{+\!\!+} \langle q \rangle$; SPEC; $q \xleftarrow{\text{pop}} s$;
          $D := D_0[2..] \mathbin{+\!\!+} \langle D_0[1] \rangle$
          $B := B \cup \{q\}$ **end**
          if $D[1] = \text{base}$ **then exit**(1) **fi od end fi**.

But D and B do not appear in SPEC, so there is no need to modify and then restore them (they were part of the scaffolding needed to relate the abstract and concrete variables):

proc $F''() \equiv$
  if $\ell(s) = n - 1$
    then SPEC
    else $D := \text{sort}(\text{MINS}(R, B))$;
      var $\langle \text{base} := D[1] \rangle$:
        do $q := D[1]$;
          $s := s \mathbin{+\!\!+} \langle q \rangle$; SPEC; $q \xleftarrow{\text{pop}} s$;
          $D := D[2..] \mathbin{+\!\!+} \langle D[1] \rangle$
          if $D[1] = \text{base}$ **then exit**(1) **fi od end fi**.

Now it is clear that the loop simply iterates over the elements of $\text{MINS}(R, B)$, so we can abstract it to a nondeterministic iteration:

proc $F''() \equiv$
  if $\ell(s) = n-1$
    then SPEC
    else for $q \in \text{MINS}(R, B))$ **do**
      $s := s \mathbin{+\!\!+} \langle q \rangle$; SPEC; $q \xleftarrow{\text{pop}} s$ **od fi**.

Finally, if we maintain the invariant $B = \{1, 2, \ldots, n\} \setminus \text{set}(s)$, then the **for** loop is equivalent to SPEC so we have:

proc $F''() \equiv$ SPEC.

Hence $F'()$ is a refinement of SPEC, and this was what we needed at the end of Section 8.2.4 to show that $F()$ is a refinement of SPEC.

The program as a whole is therefore a refinement of the abstract program

$B := \{1, 2, \ldots, n\}$; $s := \langle\rangle$;
for $t \in $ TOPSORTS(set(R), B) **do** process($s \mathbin{+\!\!+} t$) **od**

which simplifies to

for $t \in $ TOPSORTS(set(R), $\{1, 2, \ldots, n\}$) **do** process(t) **od**

8.2.7 Remarks

This case study demonstrates that the FermaT approach can be used to reverse-engineer a highly complex program (for its size) all the way to a highly abstract specification. This case study took about 2 to 3 days of work using a combination of applying transformations with the FermaT transformation engine plus manual analysis. This may seem like a lot of work for quite a small program, but in a safety-critical or mission-critical system to get a formal verification of the code for such a small effort represents a very good investment.

The next case study looks at another challenging task—that of reverse engineering from an assembler program to a specification.

8.3 Third case study: Assembler reengineering

8.3.1 IBM 370 assembler

Experiments have been undertaken on modules of assembler taken from real application programs. The majority have been between 500 and 2,000 lines but some have up to 40,000 lines. These experiments have shown that programs that have been transformed using the tool can be expressed in a form that subjectively is much easier to understand than the original. This applies particularly to real programs which have been modified over many years. A professional assembler programmer who examined the output files found the C code much easier to understand, despite having less familiarity with C than with assembler. He commented that the C code would be a useful aid to understanding the assembler prior to debugging or enhancement tasks, even in cases where migration to C was not an option.

8.3.1.1 Modeling assembler in WSL

Constructing a useful scientific model necessarily involves throwing away some information: in other words, to be useful a model must be inaccurate,

8.3 Third case study: Assembler reengineering

or at least idealized, to a certain extent. For example ideal gases, incompressible fluids, and billiard-ball molecules are all useful models that gain their utility by abstracting away some details of the real world. In the case of modeling a programming language, such as assembler, it is theoretically possible to have a perfect model of the language that correctly captures the behavior of all assembler programs. Certain features of assembler, such as branching to register addresses and self-modifying code would imply that such a model would have to record the entire state of the machine, including all registers, memory, disk space, and external devices and interpret this state as each instruction is executed. Unfortunately, such a model is useless for inverse engineering[1] purposes since such trivial changes as deleting a NOP instruction, or changing the load address of a module, can in theory change the behavior of the program.

What we need is a practical model for assembler programs that is suitable for inverse engineering and is wide enough to deal with all the programming constructs we are likely to encounter. Our approach involves three types of modeling, described as follows.

1. *Complete model:* Each assembler instruction is translated into WSL statements that capture all the effects of the instruction. The machine registers and memory are modeled as arrays, and the condition code as a variable. Thus, at the translation stage we do not attempt to recognize **if** statements as such; we translate into statements that assign to **cc** (the condition code variable), and statements that test **cc**. The automatic restructuring and simplification state can usually remove all references to **cc**, presenting the maintainer with a structured program expressed in **if** statements, loops and actions.

2. *Partial model:* Branches to register are modeled by attempting to determine all possible targets of such a branch (including all labels and jump instructions that follow labeled instructions). Each label is turned into a separate action with an associated value (the relative address). A store return address instruction stores the relative address in the register. A branch to register instruction passes the relative address to a **dispatch** action that tests the value against the set of recorded values and jumps to the appropriate label. This can deal with simple cases of address arithmetic (including jump tables)

---

1. We use the term *inverse engineering* to mean reverse engineering through formal transformations.

but may theoretically be defeated if more complex address manipulations are carried out before a branch to register instruction is executed.

3. *Self-modifying code:* This is not addressed, except for some special cases that are recognized by the translator. In many environments the code must be re-entrant, or is to be blown into a ROM, and therefore cannot be modified. In other cases, the self-modification may be recognized by the translator and may require human intervention to determine a suitable WSL equivalent.

One of the major drawbacks of automatic program restructurers [12] is that complex control structures are replaced by complex data flow structures involving additional flag and sentinel variables with meaningless names inserted by the tool. This does not occur with our tool, and users resolve the underlying structural problems because the transformations make it easy to do so. It is also straightforward to avoid dispersing code that previously was together. This method has the advantage that performance problems and errors that exist deeply buried in heavily modified code become much more easily observable.

8.3.1.2 Assembler to WSL translation

The aim of the assembler-to-WSL translator is to generate WSL code that models as accurately as possible the behavior of the original assembler module, without worrying too much about the size, efficiency, or complexity of the resulting code. Typically, the raw WSL translation of an assembler module will be three to five times bigger than the source file and have a very high McCabe cyclomatic complexity (typically in the hundreds, often in the thousands). This is, in part, because every branch to register instruction branches to the **dispatch** routine, which in turn contains branches to every possible return point. In addition, every instruction that sets the condition code flags will is translated into WSL code which assigns an appropriate value to a special variable **cc** (to emulate the condition code)—whether or not the condition code is subsequently tested. See [13] for further details of the assembler-to-WSL translation process and the various features of commercial assembler code it has to deal with.

However, the FermaT transformation engine includes some very powerful transformations for such tasks as simplifying WSL code, removing redundancies, and tracking dispatch codes. In most cases FermaT can automatically unscramble the tangle of branch and save and branch to register code to extract self-contained, single-entry single-exit procedures and so eliminate the **dispatch** procedure. In addition, FermaT can nearly always eliminate the **cc** variable by constructing appropriate conditional statements.

8.3.2 The sample program

Our sample program is from G. D. Bergland in [2], who in turn took it from a story called "Getting it Wrong" that has been related by Michael Jackson on numerous occasions:

```
proc Management_Report ≡
var ⟨SW1 := 0, SW2 := 0⟩:
  Produce_Heading;
  read(stuff);
  while NOT eof(stuff) do
      if First_Record_In_Group
      then if SW1=1
              then Process_End_Of_Previous_Group
           fi;
           SW1 := 1;
           Process_Start_Of_New_Group;
           Process_Record;
           SW2 := 1
      else
         Process_Record; SW2 := 1
      fi;
      read(stuff)
  od;
  if SW2 = 1 then Process_End_Of_Last_Group
  fi;
  Produce_Summary
end
```

The program is a simple report generator that reads a sorted transaction file; each transaction contains the name of an item and the amount received or distributed from the warehouse. The program generates a report showing the net change in inventory for each item in the transaction file.

Jackson describes in a very entertaining way how initial wrong design decisions led to a buggy program that was subsequently fixed and patched. The fixes introduced the two flag variables SW1 and SW2. The result is rather complicated and hard to understand.

Our resident assembler guru was given the above pseudocode and asked to write an assembler implementation that uses as many "features" of assembler as possible. The result is given in Section 8.3.3. (I should like to point out on his behalf that this is not his normal coding style!) The program includes self-modifying code: the first time through switch SW1 is implemented by modifying the branch labeled LAAA to a NOP in the instruction labeled LAB, and an **EX**ecute statement has been used to get a variable length move.

8.3.3 The assembler source

```
*********************************************
* TST004A0 SAMPLE PROGRAM (MCDONALDS) *
*********************************************
*

       REGEQU                              LAA   EQU  *
*                                          GET   DDIN,WREC
*      PRINT NOGEN                               CLC  WRITEM,WLAST
TST004A0 CSECT                                   BE   LAC
       STM  R14,R12,12(R13)                LAAA  B    LAB
       LR   R3,R15                               BAL  R10,ENDGROUP
       USING TST004A0,R3                   LAB   MVI  LAAA+1,0
       ST   R13,WSAVE+4                          MVC  WLAST,WRITEM
       LA   R14,WSAVE                            ZAP  WNET,=P'0'
       ST   R14,8(R13)                           BAL  R10,PROCGRP
       LA   R13,WSAVE                            MVI  XSW1,X'FF'
*                                                B    LAA
       OPEN (DDIN,(INPUT))                 LAC   BAL  R10,PROCGRP
       OPEN (RDSOUT,(OUTPUT))                    MVI  XSW1,X'FF'
*                                                B    LAA
       MVC  WPRT(17),=CL17'MANAGEMENT       *
       REPORT'                             LAD   CLI  XSW1,X'FF'
       BAL  R10,WRITE1                           BNE  LADA
       BAL  R10,WRITE1                           BAL  R10,ENDGROUP
       MVC  WPRT(20),=CL20'ITEM   NET       LADA  EQU  *
       CHANGE'                                   MVC  WPRT(17),=CL17'NUMBER
       BAL  R10,WRITE1                           CHANGED = '
       BAL  R10,WRITE1                           ED   WORKB,WCHANGE
*                                                LA   R4,WORKB
       MVI  XSW1,0                               LA   R1,9
```

8.3 Third case study: Assembler reengineering

```
        LADB    CLI   0(R4),C' '                    AP    WCHANGE,=P'1'
                BNE   LADC                          L     R10,WST10A
                LA    R4,1(R4)                      BR    R10
                BCT   R1,LADB                *
        LADC    EX    R1,WMVC1                WRITE1 EQU  *
        *WMVC1  MVC   WPRT+17(1),0(R4)              PUT   RDSOUT,WPRT
                BAL   R10,WRITE1                    MVC   WPRT,WSPACES
        *                                           BR    R10
                CLOSE DDIN                    *
                CLOSE RDSOUT                  WMVC1  MVC   WPRT+17(1),0(R4)
        *                                     *
                L     R13,WSAVE+4             WSAVE   DC   18F'0'
                LM    R14,R12,12(R13)         WST10A  DS   F
                SLR   R15,R15                 WREC    DS   0CL80
                BR    R14                     WRITEM  DS   CL4
        *                                             DS   CL1
                PROCGRP EQU  *                WRTYPE  DS   CL1
                ST    R10,WST10A                      DS   CL1
                PACK  WORKA,WRQTY             WRQTY   DS   CL3
                CLI   WRTYPE,C'R'                     DS   CL70
                BNE   LBA                     WPRT    DC   CL80' '
                AP    WNET,WORKA              WSPACES DC   CL80' '
                B     LBB                     WLAST   DC   CL4'****'
        LBA     SP    WNET,WORKA              WCHANGE DC   PL4'0'
        LBB     L     R10,WST10A              WNET    DC   PL4'0'
                BR    R10                     WORKA   DC   PL2'0'
        *                                     WORKB   DC   XL10'40206B2020206B202120'
        ENDGROUP EQU  *                       WSIGN   DC   CL1' '
                ST    R10,WST10A              XSW1    DC   X'00'
                MVC   WPRT(4),WLAST           *
                MVI   WSIGN,C'+'              LTORG
                CP    WNET,=P'0'              *
                BNL   LCA                     DDIN    DCB  DDNAME=DDIN,
                MVI   WSIGN,C'-'                           DSORG=PS,
        LCA     EQU   *                                    EODAD=LAD,
                MVC   WPRT+7(10),=                         MACRF=GM
                      X'40206B2020206B202120'  RDSOUT DCB  DDNAME=RDSOUT,
                EDMK  WPRT+7(10),WNET                      DSORG=PS,
                BCTR  R1,0                                 MACRF=PM
                MVC   0(1,R1),WSIGN           *
                BAL   R10,WRITE1              END
                BAL   R10,WRITE1
```

8.3.4 Automatic program transformation

The first stage in the transformation process is data translation. This transformation uses the restructured data file to change the data representation in the program. Initially, all data is accessed directly from memory (represented as a byte array **a**) by adding the base register to the displacement to get an address. The restructured data file gives the layout of all data in memory, so by making some reasonable assumptions about nonoverlapping DSECTS etc., FermaT is able to transform the program into an equivalent program where the data is accessed directly through variables and structures. In the case of our simple program, there is only one structure to uncover: the **wrec** print record that contains fields **writem**, **wrtype** and **wrqty** plus some unnamed fillers.

The next stage is control flow restructuring: eliminating nonessential labels and branches, introducing loops. This is carried out in a series of passes through the program; at each iteration the program is searched for points where a simplifying transformation (such as loop insertion or branch merging) can be applied. The iteration is continued until no further improvement can be achieved.

The raw WSL is written as an action system, a collection of parameterless procedures (actions) where execution of any action will always lead to either calling another action, or calling the special action Z, that terminates the whole action system. An action system itself is a simple statement, so action systems can be nested inside each other, but a subaction system cannot call actions in the main system.

The system then analyzes the remaining actions to determine which actions may form the body of a simple procedure. To do this it uses both control flow and data flow analysis. If it determines that a collection of actions form a procedure, then these actions are extracted out as a subaction system in the body of the procedure.

After control flow restructuring we have data flow analysis: In particular an extended form of constant propagation that can propagate return addresses through procedure calls. If a **dispatch** call is encountered with a known **destination** value, then it can be unfolded and simplified. The same transformation also deals with conditional assignments to the condition code (**cc**) in order to remove references to **cc** where possible.

FermaT was able to extract a collection of actions to form the **endgroup** procedure, so that the code

   r10 := 112; **call** endgroup

becomes

   r10 := 112; endgroup(); **call** dispatch

8.3 Third case study: Assembler reengineering

Table 8.1 Metrics Before and After Transformation

Metric	Raw WSL	Structured WSL
Statements	561	106
Expressions	1,589	210
McCabe	184	17
Control/data flow	520	156
Branch–loop	145	17
Structural	6,685	751

FermaT determines that the value in **r10** will be copied into **destination** by the body of **endgroup**. Within **dispatch** the value in **destination** is compared against the offsets of all the possible return points. Offset 112 is associated with the label **lab**, so this **call dispatch** can be replaced by **call lab**.

The control flow and data flow restructuring transformations are iterated until no further improvement is possible. Table 8.1 lists the metrics for the raw WSL translation and after automatic restructuring and simplifying transformations have been applied. This order of magnitude improvement in most of the metrics is typical for all sizes of assembler module. See [13] for more details of this part of the transformation process.

begin
f_laaa := 1;
!P open(ddin_ddname, input **var** os);
!P open(rdsout_ddname, output **var** os);
wprt[1..17] := "MANAGEMENT REPORT";
write1(); write1();
wprt[1..20] := "ITEM NET CHANGE";
write1(); write1();
xsw1 := 0;
do r0 := 0; r1 := 0; r15 := 0;
    !P get(ddin_ddname **var** os, r0, r1, r15, wrec);
    if !XC end_of_file(ddin_ddname)
        then exit(1) **fi**;
    if wrec.writem ≠ wlast
        then if f_laaa ≠ 1
            then endgroup() **fi**;

```
            f_laaa := 0;
            wlast := wrec.writem;
            wnet := 0 fi;
        worka := !XF pack(wrec.wrqty, 2);
        if wrec.wrtype ≠ "R"
          then wnet := wnet − worka
          else wnet := wnet + worka fi;
        xsw1 := "hex 0xFF"od;
if xsw1 = "hex 0xFF" then endgroup() fi;
wprt[1..17] := "NUMBER CHANGED = ";
!P ed(wchange[1..10] var workb);
r4 := !XF address_of(workb); r1 := 9;
do if a[r4, 1] ≠ " " then exit(1) fi;
   r4 := r4 + 1;
   r1 := r1 − 1;
   if r1 = 0 then exit(1) fi od;
a[!XF address_of(wprt) + 17, r1 + 1]
        := a[r4, r1 + 1];
write1();
!P close(ddin_ddname var os);
!P close(rdsout_ddname var os)
where
 proc endgroup()≡
    wprt[1..4] := wlast;
    wsign := " + ";
    if wnet < 0 then wsign := " − " fi;
    wprt[8..17] := "hex 0x40206B2020206B202120";
    !P edmk(wnet[1..10] var wprt[8..17], r1);
    r1 := r1 − 1; a[r1, 1] := wsign;
    write1(); write1();
    wchange := wchange + 1 end,
 proc write1() :=
    !P put(rdsout_ddname, wprt var os);
    wprt := wspaces end
end
```

8.3.5 Abstracting a specification

This is about as far as the FermaT system can get by purely automatic transformation applications with no human intervention. The next step in the abstraction process is to change the data representation so that files become lists. We unfold the **write1** procedure and abstract away from the layout of the output file by creating a list of the data elements that appear on each line of output and appending this list to the **output** array:

begin
$i := 0$; f_laaa $:= 1$;
output $:= \langle\langle$"MANAGEMENT REPORT"$\rangle$,
 $\langle$"ITEM   NET CHANGE"$\rangle\rangle$;
xsw1 $:= 0$;
do $i := i + 1$; wrec $:=$ input$[i]$;
  if $i \geqslant n$ **then** exit(1) **fi**;
  if wrec.writem $\neq$ wlast
  then if f_laaa $\neq 1$
         then endgroup() **fi**;
       f_laaa $:= 0$;
       wlast $:=$ wrec.writem;
       wnet $:= 0$ **fi**;
  if wrec.wrtype $\neq$ "R"
    then wnet $:=$ wnet $-$ wrec.wrqty
    else wnet $:=$ wnet $+$ wrec.wrqty **fi**;
  xsw1 $:=$ "hex 0xFF"**od**;
if xsw1 $=$ "hex 0xFF" **then** endgroup() **fi**;
output $:=$ output $+\!\!+ \langle\langle$"NUMBER CHANGED = ", wchange$\rangle\rangle$;
where
proc endgroup()$\equiv$
    output $:=$ output $+\!\!+ \langle\langle$wlast, wnet$\rangle\rangle$;
    wchange $:=$ wchange $+ 1$ **end**
end

We can get rid of the switches **xsw1** and **f_laaa** by unrolling the first step of the **do**...**od** loop and simplifying. We then use loop inversion to move some statements to the top of the loop:

$i := i + 1;$ wrec $:=$ input$[i];$
if $i \geq n$
  then skip
  else wlast $:=$ wrec.writem;
       wnet $:= 0;$
       do if wrec.wrtype $\neq$ "R"
         then wnet $:=$ wnet $-$ wrec.wrqty
         else wnet $:=$ wnet $+$ wrec.wrqty **fi;**
        $i := i + 1;$ wrec $:=$ input$[i];$
        if wrec.writem $\neq$ wlast $\vee$ $i \geq n$
          then endgroup();
            if $i \geq n$
              then exit(1)
              else wlast $:=$ wrec.writem;
                  wnet $:= 0$ **fi fi od fi;**

We want to roll the two statements **wlast** $:=$ **wrec.writem; wnet** $: = 0$ into the top of the loop, so convert the loop to a double-nested loop (loop doubling) and take the statements out of the inner loop (take out of loop). Then apply loop inversion. We can then take the statements starting with **endgroup**() out of the inner loop also:

$i := i + 1;$ wrec $:=$ input$[i];$
if $i \geq n$
  then skip
  else do wlast $:=$ wrec.writem;
       wnet $:= 0;$
       do if wrec.wrtype $\neq$ "R"
         then wnet $:=$ wnet $-$ wrec.wrqty
         else wnet $:=$ wnet $+$ wrec.wrqty **fi;**
        $i := i + 1;$ wrec $:=$ input$[i];$
        if wrec.writem $\neq$ wlast $\vee$ $i \geq n$
          then exit(1) **fi od;**
       endgroup();
       if $i \geq n$ **then exit**(1) **fi od fi;**

Finally, the outer **if** statement can be removed by converting the outer loop to a **while** loop (this is the **floop** to while transformation):

8.3 Third case study: Assembler reengineering

$i := i + 1;$ wrec := input$[i]$;
while $i < n$ **do**
  wlast := wrec.writem;
  wnet := 0;
  do if wrec.wrtype $\neq$ "R"
    then wnet := wnet − wrec.wrqty
    else wnet := wnet + wrec.wrqty **fi**;
  $i := i + 1;$ wrec := input$[i]$;
  if wrec.writem $\neq$ wlast $\vee$ $i \geq n$
    then **exit**(1) **fi od**;
endgroup() **od**;

Note that, after the initialization code, the invariant **wrec** = **input**$[i]$ is always true, and for $i > 1$, **wlast** = **input**$[i − 1]$.**writem** is also true, as is the invariant **wchange** = ℓ(**output**) − 2. Thus, we can remove these three variables from the program.

The program now consists of two simple nested loops; the outer **while** loop iterates over the groups of records and ends with a call to **endgroup**(), while the inner **do** ... **od** loop iterates over the records in the group.

This suggests that we restructure the data to more closely match the control structure of the program by converting the input array to a list of lists where each sublist consists of a single group of data elements, so that the outer loop processes sublists one at a time, and the inner loop processes elements of each sublist. The key to the data restructuring is to split the input sequence into sections such that the outer loop processes one segment per iteration. This is easily achieved with a function **split**(p, B), which splits p into nonempty sections with the section breaks occurring between those pairs of elements of p where B is false (see Chapter 4). In our case, the terminating condition on the inner loop provides the predicate on which to split:

funct same_item(x, y)≡
  x.writem = y.writem.

Then the new variable q is introduced as $q :=$ **split**(**input**, same_item). We index the q list with two variables k_1 and k_2 so that $q[k_1][k_2] =$ **input**$[i]$. To do this we preserve the invariant

$$i = +/(\ell * q[1..k_1 - 1]) + k$$

which, together with the invariant **input** = $+\!\!+/q$ gives the required relationship. Adding these ghost variables to the program we get

```
q := split(input, same_item);
i := 1; k₁ := 1; k₂ := 1;
while  i < ℓ (input) do
    wnet := 0;
    do if input[i].wrtype ≠ "R"
         then wnet := wnet − input[i].wrqty
         else wnet := wnet + input[i].wrqty fi;
       i := i + 1;
       k₂ := k₂ + 1;
       if k₂ > ℓ (q[k₁]) then k₁ := k₁ + 1; k₂ := 1 fi;
       if input[i].writem ≠ input[i − 1].writem ∨ i ⩾ ℓ(input)
          then  exit(1) fi od;
    endgroup() od;
```

We can now replace references to the concrete variables **input** and i by references to the new variables q, k_1 and k_2. The key point is that $i < \ell(\mathbf{input})$ if and only if $k_1 < \ell(q)$ and

input[i].writem ≠ input[$i-1$].writem

is true when we have just moved into a new section of the input—in other words, precisely when $k_2 = 1$. Therefore, we can remove the concrete variables from the program:

```
q := split(input, same_item);
k₁ := 1; k₂ := 1;
while  k₁ < ℓ(q) do
    wnet := 0;
    do if q[k₁][k₂].wrtype ≠ "R"
         then wnet := wnet − q[k₁][k₂].wrqty
         else wnet := wnet + q[k₁][k₂].wrqty fi;
       k₂ := k₂ + 1;
       if k₂ > ℓ(q[k₁]) then k₁ := k₁ + 1; k₂ := 1 fi;
       if k₂ = 1 then  exit(1) fi od;
    endgroup() od;
```

Now the inner loop reduces to a simple **for** loop

```
q := split (input, same_item);
k₁ := 1;
```

8.3 Third case study: Assembler reengineering

```
while  k₁ < ℓ(q) do
    wnet := 0;
    for k₂ := 1 to ℓ(q[k₁]) step 1 do
        if q[k₁][k₂].wrtype ≠ "R"
            then wnet := wnet − q[k₁][k₂].wrqty
            else wnet := wnet + q[k₁][k₂].wrqty fi od;
    k₁ := k₁ + 1;
    endgroup() od;
```

We can express the change to **wnet** as a function of the structure:

funct change(s) =
    if s.wrtype ≠ "R" **then** − s.wrqty **else** s.wrqty **fi**.

It is clear that the inner loop is computing the sum of the change outputs for all the structures in the sublist $q[k_1]$, so we can collapse the inner loop to a reduce of a map operation:

```
q := split(input, same_item);
k₁ := 1;
while  k₁ < ℓ(q) do
    wnet := +/change * q[k₁];
    k₁ := k₁ + 1;
    endgroup() od;
```

The **endgroup** procedure simply appends an element to the output list:

```
q := split(input, same_item);
k₁ := 1;
while  k₁ < ℓ(q) do
    wnet := +/change * q[k₁];
    output := output ++ ⟨⟨q[k₁][1], wnet⟩⟩;
    k₁ := k₁ + 1 od;
```

So, we can collapse the outer loop to a map operation to get the final WSL specification:

begin
    q := split(input, same_item);
    output := header ++ process * q
        ++ ⟨⟨"NUMBER CHANGED = ", $\ell(q)$⟩⟩

where
funct same_item$(x, y) = x$.writem $= y$.writem.
funct process$(L) = \langle L[1], +/$change $* L\rangle$.
funct change$(s) \equiv$
　　if s.wrtype $\neq$ "R" **then** $-s$.wrqty **else** s.wrqty **fi**.
end

This extracted specification looks very different to the original assembler (see Section 8.3.3), but both programs are semantically equivalent and generate identical output files (when the output from the specification is formatted to match the assembler).

8.3.6 Comments

This case study is a particularly challenging reverse engineering task: using formal program transformations to extract a high-level abstract specification from an IBM 370 assembler program. The original assembler program contains several layers of complexity including self-modifying code, a flag used to direct control flow, and a convoluted control flow structure. Fortunately the powerful automatic transformations implemented in FermaT allow us to remove the first few layers of complexity before we even have to look at the program. Moving to higher levels of abstraction requires a certain amount of human intervention, particularly to select appropriate abstract data structures. However, this intervention requires only localized analysis of the program. The higher-level control flow transformations such as loop unrolling, loop rolling, and taking code out of loops are all implemented in the FermaT system and any global analysis required by these transformations is handled automatically.

8.4 Fourth case study: A mass migration exercise

The second case study made considerable use of formal transformations to derive the specification of a very complex piece of code. Such a level of detail is entirely justified for a safety-critical system, but a less formal and more automated approach may be appropriate for a typical commercial system. The third case study illustrated the automated translation of assembler to WSL followed by automatic restructuring and simplification of the WSL program. The resulting high-level WSL may be sufficient for many users, but for more demanding requirements (such as a formal proof of correctness) the case study went on to derive an abstract specification of the program.

8.4 Fourth case study: A mass migration exercise

This case study shows what can be achieved by entirely automatic processes. It involves the migration of a large number of assembler modules to C using the FermaT transformation system with no human intervention.

8.4.1 The assembler problem

Legacy assembler systems form a significant proportion of the total software in use throughout the world (see Table 8.2). The average complexity of a COBOL program is 50 function points while the average complexity of an assembler program is 125 function points, and the maintenance cost per function point for assembler is 2.8 times higher than for COBOL (see Table 8.3).

In addition, approximately 60% of the total IT budget is spent on maintenance, and more than half of which is code comprehension (see Table 8.4). Yet there are few automated tools to assist with understanding and reengineering legacy assembler systems.

Table 8.2 Worldwide Use of Code by Function Points

Language	Number of Function Points Worldwide
COBOL	605,000,000
C	156,000,000
Assembler	93,750,000
PL/1	13,500,000

Source: Capers Jones Research.

Table 8.3 Maintenance Costs per Function Point

Language	Annual Cost/FP (£)
Assembler	48.00
PL/1	39.00
C	21.00
COBOL	17.00

Source: Capers Jones Research.

Table 8.4 Maintenance Effort

Maintenance Area	Effort (%)
Code comprehension	55
Code change	15
Testing and implementation	30

8.4.2 Decompilers

There is a long history of work in the area of decompilation—attempting to recover the source code of a compiled program. See [14] for an excellent summary. One example is the dcc decompiler for the Intel i80286 architecture running the DOS operating system [15, 16], but this is not able to determine data types, specifically arrays. The 8086 C decompiling system [17, 18] is a first attempt to recognize the types of arrays, pointers, and structures, but little detail is given in the paper.

All of these systems are limited to processing the output of a compiler. In general, they work by recognizing fragments of code produced when various high-level language (HLL) constructs are compiled, and attempting to regenerate the original constructs (**if** statements, **while** loops, for example).

Generating good-quality high-level language code from hand-written assembler is widely acknowledged to be an extremely difficult (if not impossible) undertaking. Tools such as the Autocoder to Cobol Conversion Aid Program and the Falcon Assembler to C translator by Sapiens, Ltd., simply do a one-to-one mapping of assembler instructions to HLL statements and make no attempt to analyze the program and reduce the number of instructions generated.

Tools that work with compiled C code have the advantage that function call and return points are shown by clearly recognizable instruction sequences, and return addresses are processed on a stack. In contrast, with the handwritten IBM 370 assembler a subroutine call is implemented as a **BAL** or **BAS** instruction (branch and link or branch and save), which stores the return address in a register and branches to the subroutine entry point. To return from a subroutine the programmer ensures that the right return address is available in a register and executes a **BR** (branch to register) instruction. However, there is nothing to stop the programmer from branching from the middle of one subroutine to the middle of another, or overwriting a stored return address, or having several entry points to the same subroutine. Merely determining subroutine boundaries can require a substantial and detailed analysis of the program logic. In addition, human programmers (unlike compilers) may make extensive use of programming tricks such as self-modifying code, which a migration tool must be able to cope with.

8.4.3 Our approach

The success of our approach to language migration depends on the transformability of WSL:

8.4 Fourth case study: A mass migration exercise 221

1. First the source is translated line-by-line into equivalent WSL code. No attempt is made at program analysis or efficiency of the translation; the aim at this stage is to ensure that the semantics of the original assembler is captured in equivalent WSL. Typically, each assembler instruction translates to several WSL statements.

2. Next we apply program transformations to the WSL code. Some transformations work at the local level and are applied repeatedly throughout the code. Other transformations work on the program as a whole. Some transformations use heuristics to direct the application of other transformations (so these are, in a sense, metatransformations). The transformation process is iterated until no further improvement is possible.

3. Finally, the resulting structured WSL code is translated into the target language (in this case, C code), perhaps with the aid of further transformations to remove WSL constructs that do not translate easily into C.

8.4.4 The assembler modules

A total of 1,925 assembler listings were selected for this experiment. Apart from a handful of test files, these are all live code taken from large commercial assembler systems, mostly from large financial institutions. The files came from more than 10 different organizations. Most of the listings were assembled on-site from customer-supplied source and macro files; a number of these were incomplete due to missing macro files, but these were included anyway since we wanted to test the robustness of the FermaT system in the presence of incomplete or erroneous listing data. The remaining listings were supplied by our customers and had been assembled using a number of different IBM and third-party assemblers (e.g., HLASM R1.0, HLASM R2.0, ASM H, Siemens, and Tachyon).

The 1,925 listing files contained a total of 5,884,620 lines (see Figure 8.1), of which 3,090,548 were source, copybook, or macro expansion lines (see Figure 8.2) and the remainder were page and file headers and cross reference tables. See Figure 8.1 for a distribution graph of the listing file sizes. This corresponds to approximately 1,090,000 lines of assembler source (excluding macros). The expansion of a source file into a listing varies widely, depending on the file. For example, a small source file that references one or more large copybooks or macros will generate a large listing.

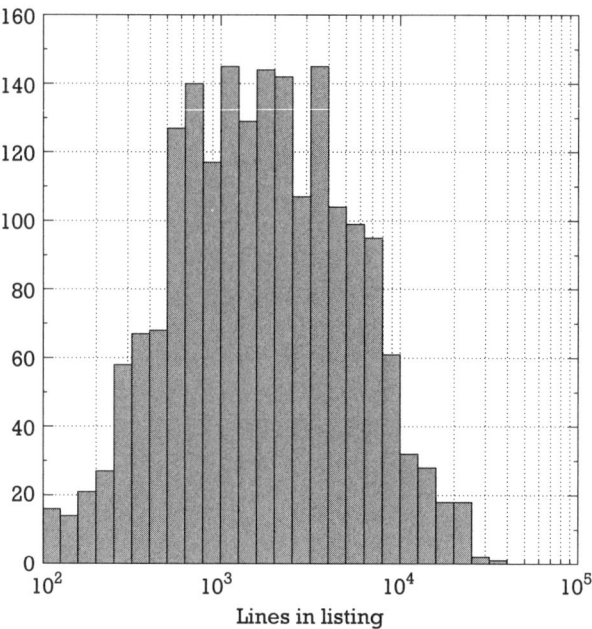

Figure 8.1 Listing files ranged from 113 to 36,897 lines in size (average 3,057).

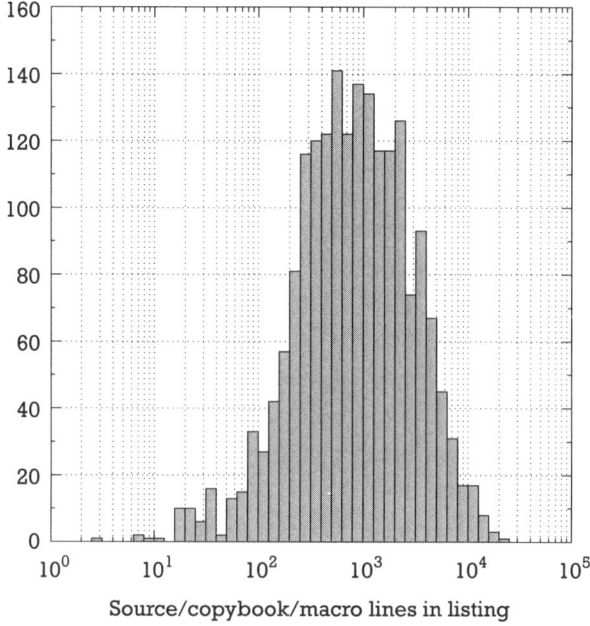

Figure 8.2 Listing files contained 3 to 23,672 lines of code (average 1,605).

8.4 Fourth case study: A mass migration exercise

The listings were organized into 127 directories, each directory containing between 1 and 41 files with an average of 15 files per directory. The directories were organized so that each contained listings from about 10,000 lines of source modules, so that they could be processed in batches a directory at a time. The **analyze** Perl script reads a directory of files and processes each file in turn: executing all the translation and transformation scripts and checking the output for validity. Figure 8.3 shows the distribution in file sizes for the raw WSL translation of each listing.

8.4.5 Experimental method

For this experiment we use two Sun UltraSparc processors, one had 128 Mb of RAM and the other had 64 Mb. We had previously determined that 64 Mb is ample for processing the largest assembler listings, so the experiment was set up to run one process on the second machine and two concurrent processes on the first machine. (Running two concurrent processes gives a small improvement in total throughput, about 20%, since one process can run while the other is accessing files.)

A Perl script was used to control the experiment, it monitored both machines and fired up a new batch process (an **analyze** script) as each one completed. Each batch process handled one directory full of files; for each

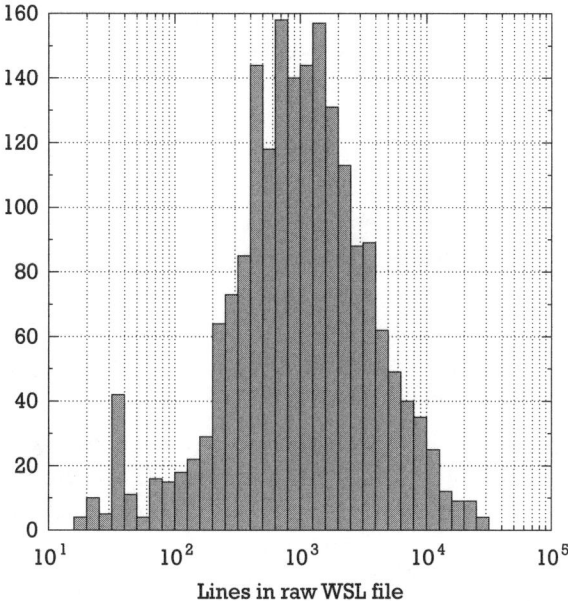

Figure 8.3 Raw WSL files ranged from 17 to 28,905 lines (average 2,049).

file in the directory, the **analyze** script translated the assembler listing to WSL, applied a standard sequence of transformations to the WSL, restructured the data layout, and generated executable C code and header files.

The experiment completed successfully after 4 days and 18 hours of elapsed time. Every module was successfully migrated to C, and every generated C file compiled with no warnings or errors. We were not able to check the semantics of each generated file against the original assembler: All the modules were components of larger systems, and we did not have access to any test harnesses or test data. However, selected modules were compared against the original source code by an experienced assembler and C programmer who could find no errors in the translation.

Since this first run of the experiment the performance of the FermaT transformation system has been improved by a factor of more than two and a half (when processing the same files on the same hardware). In addition, faster processors are now readily available; the experiment was recently repeated on a single 1-GHz PC with 256 Mb of RAM and completed in just over 12 hours elapsed time.

The generated C files would still require some work regarding such tasks as file handling, depending on whether the customer wanted to migrate to a different environment. Much of this work can be automated. In addition, the user needs to check for **FIXME** comments in the generated C code, which indicate areas where the translated code may be incorrect (for example, an **EX**ecute instruction where FermaT cannot determine at compile time which instruction will be executed).

The overall performance for the original experiment on Sun UltraSparcs was about 600 KLOC/day per CPU, or about 7 minutes CPU time per assembler module[2]. Note however that processing times vary widely, depending on the file contents. Short files and files consisting mostly of data declarations can take less than a minute each, while larger files with lots of executable code can take an hour or more. In our case, the times ranged from 2 seconds to 20,473 seconds (5 hours 41 minutes) with an average of 398 seconds (6 minutes 40 seconds). (See Figure 8.4.)

8.4.6 Results

A total of 1,132,278 lines of C code were generated (excluding the header files) of which 179,138 lines are data initialization code (generated from the data declarations in the original assembler). (See Figures 8.5 and 8.6.)

---

2. With the new version of FermaT and more modern hardware, this time is reduced to less than 23 seconds per module (over 10 MLOC/day).

8.4 Fourth case study: A mass migration exercise

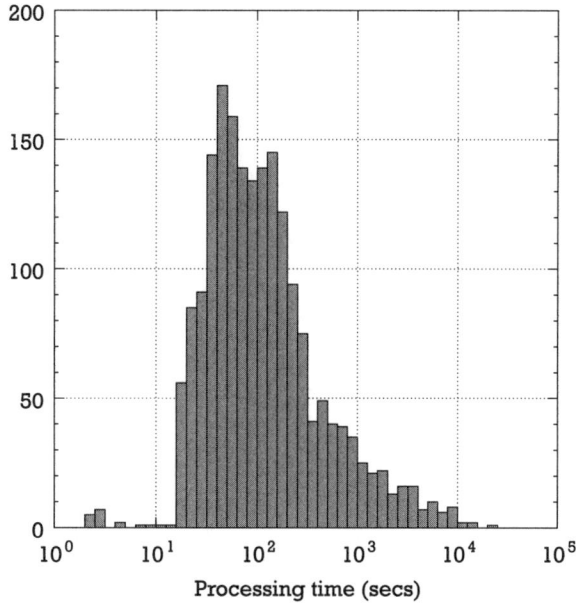

Figure 8.4 Time to process each module in seconds (average 398).

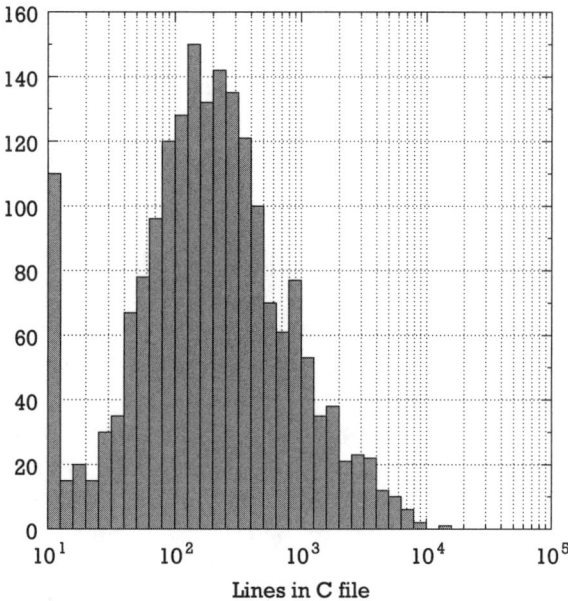

Figure 8.5 Generated C files ranged from 10 to 15,436 lines (average 495).

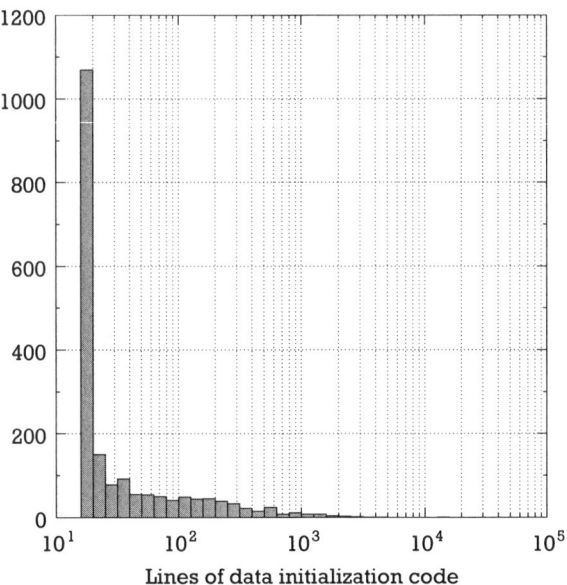

Figure 8.6 Data initialization code ranged from 16 to 12,676 lines (average 94).

Note that more than half of the files (1,069) required no extra data initialization code.

A total of 7,793 C header files were generated, totaling 1,232,156 lines. (See Figure 8.7). Each assembler module generated a header file for local data plus header files for each of the DSECTs it referenced. Note that modules in the same directory, which use the same DSECTs, will share header files since the DSECT header file is named after the DSECT. This is because the same DSECT referenced in two or more listings should generate the same header file.

In total, the 482 Mb of assembler listings were migrated into 39.5 Mb of C source files plus 46.3 Mb of C header files.

FermaT could automatically eliminate **dispatch** from 1,265 of the 1,925 files (66%) and could eliminate the cc condition code variable from 1,745 files (91%).

This experiment [13] clearly shows that assembler-to-C migration using the FermaT workbench is a practical solution to the high costs and skills shortage in assembler maintenance and to the problem of migrating legacy systems away from the mainframe environment.

The above pattern was obtained by transforming several existing programs and shows the marked reduction in complexity as a result of transformation. To provide some check on semantic equivalence a few

8.4 Fourth case study: A mass migration exercise

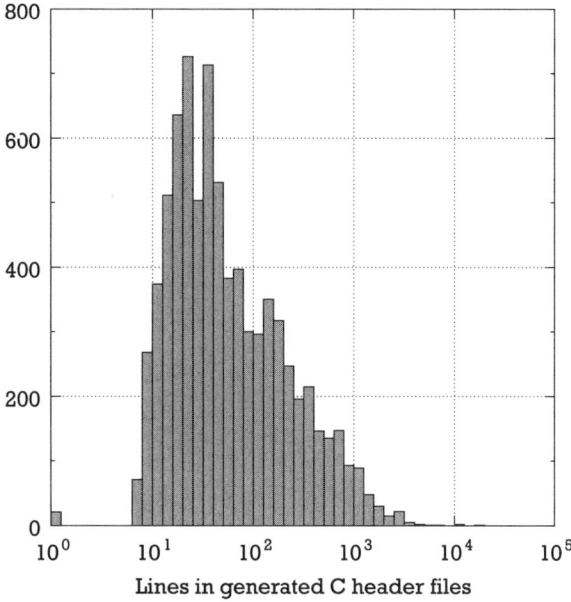

Figure 8.7 Generated C header files ranged from 1 to 17,729 lines (average 158).

modest examples have been transformed and then (in the absence of a suitable translator) hand-converted to assembler, reinstalled, and reexecuted. Apart from minor errors caused by hand translation, the examples worked first time.

A major attraction of the tool has turned out to be the transformations that convert in-line code to procedures, and global variables into parameters. This enables the user to convert a large, unstructured, monolithic piece of code into a main program that calls a set of single-entry single-exit procedures. These transformations alone can make a large difference to the understandability of the code and prepare it for the recognition of abstract data types.

8.4.7 Contributing factors

We believe that the following main features have contributed to the success of FermaT:

- Using the weakest preconditions expressed in infinitary logic;
- Starting with a small, tractable kernel language, extended via definitional transformations;

- Using an imperative kernel language, with functional constructs added via definitional transformation, rather than a functional kernel language;

- Developing the transformation theory in parallel with the language development;

- Dealing with the assembler via simple translation followed by automatic restructuring and simplification;

- Developing an interactive, semi-automatic tool, rather than attempting complete automation;

- Mechanically checking the correctness conditions at each step, with only valid transformations appearing in the menus;

- Using the prototype and manual case studies to see how the experienced user solves problem, and then implementing these methods and heuristics via knowledge elicitation;

- Using generic transformations for such processes as merging, moving, and separating, which are automatically expanded into the appropriate transformation for each situation;

- Rapidly developing a prototype, with the system organized as a collection of abstract machines with formally defined interfaces;

- Separating front-end issues into a separate program.

8.5 Fifth case study: Migrating a telecommunications system

This case study involved a fairly large embedded system consisting of about 500,000 lines of Intel 186 assembler, in 316 modules, and 250,000 lines of C code. The system controls a private automatic branch exchange (PABX) and runs on four different hardware platforms in 18 countries. The aim of the project was to use FermaT to migrate all the assembler code to efficient, structured, and maintainable C code to enable migration to a more modern processor followed by major enhancements to the functionality of the system.

8.5.1 Assembler-to-WSL translation

The first step involved developing an assembler-to-WSL translator for 186 assembler. As for IBM assembler, this worked by translating each instruction separately, capturing all the side-effects of each instruction without worrying about introducing redundancies or inefficiencies.

In this case the system consisted of relatively clean assembler; for example there was no use of self-modifying code because this is an embedded system loaded on a ROM. One complication was that the generated C code needed to be consistent with the existing C code and able to use the same header files. Because of this we developed a C header file parser that was used to determine the structure of the memory layout (the assembler code gave the layout of data but imposed no structure on this layout).

8.5.2 WSL restructuring

Once the assembler had been translated to WSL, the same general-purpose restructuring and simplifying transformations used for IBM assembler could be used to restructure the WSL code. New transformations were developed for dealing with pushing and popping registers onto the stack (not present in IBM assembler) and dealing with segmented addressing.

8.5.3 WSL-to-C translation

The WSL-to-C translator used for IBM assembler migration required only minor modifications (such as changing the lists of flag names and register names) in order to process 186 translated WSL. This shows the advantages of using language-independent WSL code for the core of the system.

8.6 Sixth case study: Mine drainage system

The last case study commonly appears in the literature and concerns the software necessary to manage a simplified pump control system for a mining environment [19]. It is a good demonstration of the real-time aspect of the proposed approach.

The system is used to pump mine water, which collects in a sump at the bottom of the shaft, to the surface. The main safety requirement is that the pump should not be operated when the level of methane gas in the mine reaches a high value due to the risk of explosion. A simple schematic diagram of the system is given in Figure 8.8.

The functional specification of the system is divided into four components: the pump operation, the environment monitoring, the operator interaction, and system monitoring.

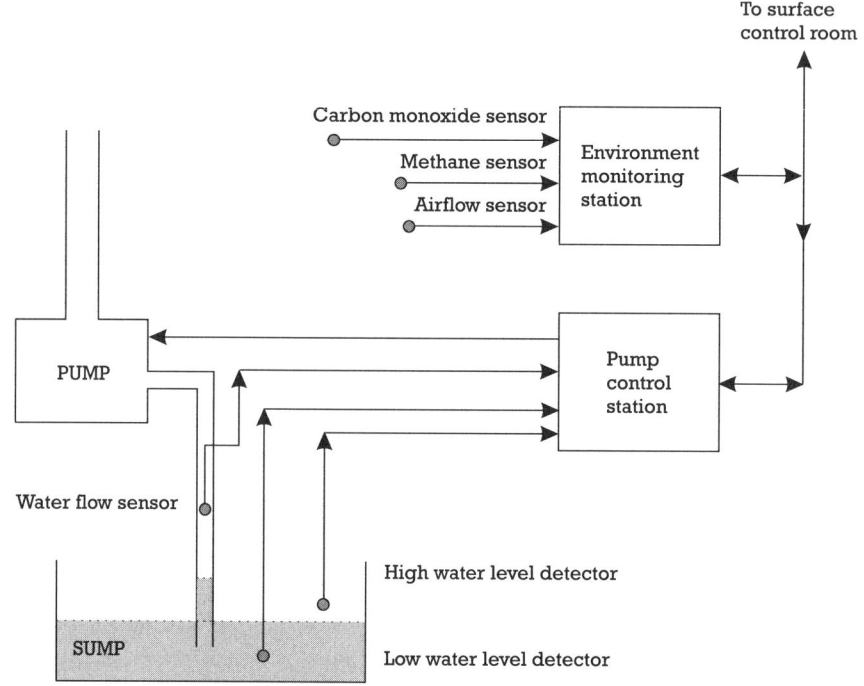

Figure 8.8 A mine drainage control system.

The required behavior of the pump is that it monitors the water levels in the sump. When the water reaches a high level, the pump is turned on and the sump is drained until the water reaches the low level. At this point, the pump is turned off. A flow of water in the pipe can be detected if required. The pump should be allowed to operate only if methane level in the mine is below a critical level.

The environment must be monitored to detect the level of methane in the air; there is a level beyond which it is not safe to cut coal or operate the pump. The monitoring also measures the level of carbon monoxide in the mine and detects whether there is an adequate flow of air. Alarms must be signaled if gas levels or air flow become critical.

The system is controlled from the surface via an operator's console. The operator is informed of all critical events. All the system events are to be stored in an archival database and may be retrieved and displayed upon request.

The nonfunctional requirements include three components: timing, dependability, and security. This case study is mainly concerned with the

8.6 Sixth case study: Mine drainage system

timing requirements, which appear as monitoring periods, the pump shutdown deadline, and the operator information deadline.

8.6.1 Extracting the specification

Translated CSL code   The mine drainage system is implemented in ADA. As preliminary process, we first translated this implementation into CSL. Here we focus on two selected modules: pump control and methane detection. For conciseness, we assume that all the global variables and constants have been defined in the main procedure.

Pump module   The CSL code is as follows:

```
proc motor_unsafe()≡
  if motor_status = On
    then sw := Off;
         motor_status := Off;
         motor_log(In "motor stopped") fi;
  motor_condition := Disabled;
  motor_log(In "motor unsafe") end;
proc motor_safe()≡
  if motor_status = Off
    then sw := On;
         motor_status := On;
         motor_log(In "motor started") fi;
  motor_condition := Enabled;
  motor_log(In "motor safe") end;
proc set_pump(In pump_status : Boolean; )≡
  if pump_status = On
    then if motor_status = Off
           then if motor_condition = Disabled
                  then err_msg(In "pump − not − safe") fi;
                if ch4_status = Motor_safe
                  then motor_status := On;
                       sw := On;
                       motor_log(In "motor started")
                  else err_msg(In "pump − not − safe") fi fi
```

else if motor_status = On

then motor_status := Off;

if motor_condition = Enabled

then sw := Off;

motor_log(In "motor stopped") **fi fi fi end**;

As the first step, we abstract the three procedures separately into the ITL specification:

motor_unsafe() $\stackrel{\wedge}{=}$ motor_status = On $\wedge$ (sw := Off;

motor_status := Off; motor_log("motor stopped"));

motor_condition := Disabled; motor_log("motor unsafe")

motor_safe() $\stackrel{\wedge}{=}$ motor_status = Off $\wedge$ (sw := On; motor_status := On;

motor_log("motor started"));

motor_condition := Enabled; motor_log("motor safe")

set_pump(pump_status) $\stackrel{\wedge}{=}$

(pump_status = On $\wedge$

(motor_status = Off $\wedge$

(motor_condition = Disabled $\wedge$ err_msg("pump not safe"));

(ch4_status = Motor_safe $\wedge$ (motor_status := On; sw := On;

motor_log("motor started"))))

$\vee$(ch4_status = Motor_unsafe $\wedge$ err_msg("pump not safe"))))

$\vee$(pump_status = Off$\wedge$

motor_status = On $\wedge$ (motor_status := Off;

motor_condition = Enabled $\wedge$ (sw := Off; motor_log("motor stopped"))))

In the above specification, there are several things that need to be simplified. First, some chop operators could be replaced by logic conjunction and therefore result in further logic composition. Second, there are quite a lot of exception test and handling details in the specification. In the high-level specification, these kinds of descriptions could be considered as implementation details and therefore be abstracted away. A more abstracted specification is given as follows:

motor_unsafe() $\stackrel{\wedge}{=}$ motor_status = On $\wedge$ (sw := Off; motor_status := Off$\wedge$

motor_log("motor stopped"));

motor_condition := Disabled $\wedge$ motor_log("motor unsafe")

motor_safe() $\stackrel{\wedge}{=}$ motor_status = Off $\wedge$ (sw := On; motor_status := On$\wedge$

8.6 Sixth case study: Mine drainage system

motor_log("motor started"));
motor_condition := Enabled ∧ motor_log("motor safe")

set_pump(pump_status) $\stackrel{\triangle}{=}$
  (pump_status = On∧
  (motor_status = Off∧
  (ch4_status = Motor_safe ∧ (motor_status := On; sw := On;
  motor_log("motor started")))))
  ∨(pump_status = Off∧
  motor_status = On ∧ (motor_status := Off;
  motor_condition = Enabled ∧ (sw := Off ∧ motor_log("motor stopped"))))

More concisely, the specification is as follows:

motor_unsafe() $\stackrel{\triangle}{=}$ motor_status = On ∧ (sw := Off; motor_status := Off∧
  motor_log("motor stopped"));
  motor_condition := Disabled ∧ motor_log("motor unsafe")

motor_safe() $\stackrel{\triangle}{=}$ motor_status = Off ∧ (sw := On; motor_status := On∧
  motor_log("motor started"));
  motor_condition := Enabled ∧ motor_log("motor safe")

set_pump(pump_status) $\stackrel{\triangle}{=}$
  (pump_status = On ∧ motor_status = Off ∧ ch4_status = Motor_safe∧
  (motor_status := On; sw := On ∧ motor_log("motor started")))
  ∨ (pump_status = Off ∧ motor_status = On∧
  (motor_status := Off; motor_condition = Enabled ∧ (sw := Off∧
  motor_log("motor stopped"))))

The log function is not directly related to system performance and therefore could be abstracted away:

motor_unsafe() $\stackrel{\triangle}{=}$ motor_status = On ∧ (sw := Off; motor_status := Off);
  motor_condition := Disabled

motor_safe() $\stackrel{\triangle}{=}$ motor_status = Off ∧ (sw := On; motor_status := On);
  motor_condition := Enabled

set_pump(pump_status) $\stackrel{\triangle}{=}$
  (pump_status = On ∧ motor_status = Off ∧ ch4_status = Motor_safe∧

(motor_status := On; sw := On))
∨ (pump_status = Off ∧ motor_status = On∧
(motor_status := Off; motor_condition = Enabled ∧ sw := Off))

Methane model The CSL code is as follows:

proc init()≡
  comment : enable device;
  ch4_sensor_status := Enabled;
  ch4_status := Motor_unsafe **end**;

proc ch4_process()≡
  read tm, ch4_level **from** ch4_sensor;
  if ch4_level ⩾ ch4_Max
    then if ch4_status = motor_safe
        then motor_unsafe();
            operator_console_alarm(In"High methane");
            ch4_status := motor_unsafe **fi**
      else if ch4_level < ch4_Max_jitterrange
        then motor_safe();
            ch4_status := motor_safe **fi fi**;
  ch4_log(In ch4_level) **end**;

proc ch4_period()≡
  init();
  while true **do**
    duration in 30 ch4_process() **end**;
    delay(80 − 30) **od end**;

As the first step, we abstract the three procedures separately into the ITL specification:

init() $\stackrel{\wedge}{=}$ ch4_sensor_status := Enabled; ch4_status := Motor_unsafe

ch4_process() $\stackrel{\wedge}{=}$ tm = $\sqrt{\text{ch4\_sensor}}$ ∧ ch4_level = read(ch4_sensor);
  (ch4_level ⩾ ch4_Max)∧
  ch4_status = motor_safe∧
  (motor_unsafe(); operator_console_alarm("High methane");

8.7 Summary

$$\text{ch4\_status} := \text{motor\_unsafe})$$
$$\vee \,(\text{ch4\_level} < \text{ch4\_Max}) \wedge$$
$$(\text{ch4\_level} < \text{ch4\_Max\_jitterrange}) \wedge (\text{motor\_safe}();$$
$$\text{ch4\_status} := \text{motor\_safe}); \text{ch4\_log}(\text{ch4\_level})$$

$$\text{ch4\_period}() \stackrel{\Delta}{=} \text{init}(); (\text{ch4\_process}() \wedge \text{len} \leq 30\text{ms}; \text{len} = 50\text{ms})^*$$

Similarly, we replace possible chop operators with logic conjunction, leaving out the unused timestamp **tm**. The final result will appear as follows:

$$\text{init}() \stackrel{\Delta}{=} \text{ch4\_sensor\_status} := \text{Enabled} \wedge \text{ch4\_status} := \text{Motor\_unsafe}$$

$$\text{ch4\_process}() \stackrel{\Delta}{=} \text{ch4\_level} =$$
$$\text{read}(\text{ch4\_sensor});$$
$$(\text{ch4\_level} \geq \text{ch4\_Max}) \wedge \text{ch4\_status} = \text{motor\_safe} \wedge$$
$$(\text{motor\_unsafe}() \wedge \text{operator\_console\_alarm}(\text{``High methane''})) \wedge$$
$$\text{ch4\_status} := \text{motor\_unsafe}) \vee (\text{ch4\_level} < \text{ch4\_Max}) \wedge$$
$$(\text{ch4\_level} < \text{ch4\_Max\_jitterrange}) \wedge (\text{motor\_safe}()) \wedge$$
$$\text{ch4\_status} := \text{motor\_safe}); \text{ch4\_log}(\text{ch4\_level})$$

$$\text{ch4\_period}() \stackrel{\Delta}{=} \text{init}(); (\text{ch4\_process}() \wedge \text{len} \leq 30\text{ms}; \text{len} = 30\text{ms})^*$$

8.6.2 Comments

The purpose of the mine drainage case study is to demonstrate that the proposed approach has the ability to tackle systems with a critical time requirement. This is achieved through the following points:

1. EWSL has the power to represent time-critical systems from specification level to the source code level.
2. The abstraction rules are specially designed to deal with time feature.
3. ITL is powerful for real-time system specification.

8.7 Summary

These case studies illustrated a reverse engineering method that is based on the following stages:

1. *Establishing the reverse engineering environment:* This will involve a CASE tool to record results and to maintain different versions of

code, specifications, and documentation and the links between them, together with a (E)WSL code browser and transformation system.

2. *Collecting the software to be reverse-engineered:* This involves finding the current versions of each subsystem and making these available to the CASE tool.

3. *Producing a high-level description of the system:* This may already be available in the documentation, since the documentation at this level rarely needs to be changed and is therefore more likely to be up-to-date. The documentation is supplemented by the results of a cross-reference analysis, which records the control flow and data dependencies among the subsystems.

4. *Translating the source code into (E)WSL:* This will usually be an automatic process involving parsing the source files and translating the language structures into equivalent (E)WSL structures.

5. *Inverse engineering, or reverse engineering through formal transformations:* This involves the automatic and manual application of various transformations to restructure the system and express it at increasingly higher levels of abstraction. This is carried out by iterating over the following four steps:

    a. *Restructuring transformations.* These include removing **goto** statements, eliminating flags, removing redundant tests, and other optimizations. The effect of this restructuring is to reveal the true structure of the program, which may be obscured by poor design or subsequent patching and enhancements. This stage is more radical than can be achieved by existing automatic restructuring systems [12, 20] since it takes note of both data flow and control flow and includes both syntactic and semantic transformations [21]. We have however had considerable success with automating the simpler restructuring transformations, by implementing heuristics elicited from experienced program transformation users.

    b. *Analyzing the resulting structures in order to determine suitable higher-level data representations and control structures.*

    c. *Redocumenting.* This involves recording the discoveries made so far and any other useful information about the code and its data structures.

d. *Implementing the higher-level data representations and control structures using suitable transformations.* A powerful technique we have developed for carrying out these data refinements is to introduce the abstract variables into the program as ghost variables (variables whose values are changed but that do not affect the operation of the program in any way), together with invariants that make explicit the relationship between abstract and concrete variables. Then, one by one, the references to concrete variables are replaced by references to the new abstract variables. Finally, the concrete variables become ghost variables and can be removed. See [5] for an example of this process; it is also used extensively in [10]. In general, if our analysis in step (5b) is correct then the result of this stage is likely to be in a form suitable for further restructuring.

6. *Acceptance testing:* We now have a high-level specification of the whole system that should go through the usual acceptance tests.

References

[1] Knuth, D. E., and J. L. Szwarcfiter, "A Structured Program To Generate All Topological Sorting Arrangements," *Inform. Process. Lett.,* Vol. 2, 1974, pp. 153–157.

[2] Bergland, G. D., "A Guided Tour of Program Design Methodologies," *Computer,* Vol. 14, No. 10, October 1981, pp. 18–37.

[3] Fenton, M., *Developing in DataFlex, Book 2, Reports and Other Outputs,* B.E.M. Microsystems, 1986.

[4] Ward, M., "Recursion Removal/Introduction by Formal Transformation: An Aid to Program Development and Program Comprehension," *Comput. J.,* Vol. 42, No. 8, 1999, pp. 650–673.

[5] Ward, M., "Abstracting a Specification from Code," *J. Software Maintenance: Research and Practice,* Vol. 5, No. 2, June 1993, pp. 101–122 (http://www.dur.ac.uk/~dcs0mpw/martin/papers/prog-spec.ps.gz).

[6] Ward, M., and K. H. Bennett, "A Practical Program Transformation System for Reverse Engineering," *Working Conference on Reverse Engineering,* Baltimore, MD, May 21–23, 1993 (http://www.dur.ac.uk/~dcs0mpw/martin/papers/icse.ps.gz).

[7] Ward, M., "Program Analysis by Formal Transformation," *Comput. J.,* Vol. 39, No. 7, 1996 (http://www.dur.ac.uk/~dcs0mpw/martin/papers/topsort-t.ps.gz).

[8] Broy, M., and P. Pepper, "Combining Algebraic and Algorithmic Reasoning: An Approach to the Schorr-Waite Algorithm," *Trans. Programming Lang. and Syst.*, Vol. 4, No. 3, July 1982, pp. 362–381.

[9] Jorring, U., and W. L. Scherlis, "Deriving and Using Destructive Data Types," in *Program Specification and Transformation: Proceedings of the IFIP TC2/WG 2.1 Working Conference Bad Tolz, FRG,* April 15–17, 1986, L. G. L. T. Meertens (ed.), Amsterdam, North Holland, April 1987.

[10] Ward, M., "Derivation of Data-Intensive Algorithms by Formal Transformation," IEEE Trans. on Software Engineering, Vol. 22, No. 9, September 1996, pp. 665–686 (http://www.dur.ac.uk/~dcs0mpw/martin/papers/sw-alg.ps.gz).

[11] Wile, D., "Type Transformations," *IEEE Trans. on Software Engineering,* Vol. 7, No. 1, January 1981.

[12] Calliss, F. W., "Problems with Automatic Restructurers," *SIGPLAN Notices,* Vol. 23, No. 3, March 1988, pp. 13–21.

[13] Ward, M., "Assembler to C Migration Using the FermaT Transformation System," *International Conference on Software Maintenance,* Oxford, England, August 30–September 3, 1999.

[14] Cifuentes, C., and F. Faase, "The Decompilation Page," 1999 at http://www.csee.uq.edu.au/csm/decompilation.

[15] Cifuentes, C., "Reverse Compilation Techniques," Queensland University of Technology, Queensland, Australia, Ph.D. thesis, July 1994.

[16] Cifuentes, C., and K. J. Gough, "Decompilation of Binary Programs," *Software-Practice and Experience,* Vol. 25, No. 7, July 1995, pp. 811–829.

[17] Fuan, C., and L. Zongtian, "C Function Recognition Technique and Its Implementation in 8086 C Decompiling system," *Mini-Micro Systems,* Vol. 12, No. 4, 1991, pp. 33–40, 47.

[18] Fuan, C., L. Zongtian, and L. Li, "Design and Implementation Techniques of the 8086 C Decompiling System," *Mini-Micro Systems,* Vol. 14, No. 4, 1993, pp. 10–18, 31.

[19] Burns, A., and A. Wellings, "HRT-HOOD: A Structured Design Method for Hard Real-Time Ada System," *Real-Time Safety Critical Systems Series,* Vol. 3, 1995.

[20] Miller, J. C., and B. M. Strauss, "Implications of Automatic Restructuring, of COBOL," *SIGPLAN Notices,* Vol. 22, No. 6, June 1987, pp. 76–82.

[21] Arsac, J., "Syntactic Source-to-Source Program Transformations and Program Manipulation," *Comm. ACM,* Vol. 22, No. 1, January 1982, pp. 43–54.

CHAPTER 9

Concluding Remarks

Contents

9.1 Is software evolution a bridge too far?

9.2 Formal or not formal?

9.3 Coping with new development paradigms

9.4 Questions answered

This book is intended for readers who face software evolution problems. Certain theoretical aspects have been analyzed to show how complicated the situation is and certain practical issues have been discussed to tackle, or at least give a starting point for tackling real applications. The book is accompanied by the FermaT tool, which readers can download and experiment with (please see the Preface for URLs).

At the beginning of the book, we mentioned that people are fighting a losing battle in evolution. Though we cannot claim that people will suddenly start fighting a winning battle as soon as they have read this book, we can definitely say that they will understand the situation more clearly and be in a much better position to take appropriate actions for the practical problems they face.

9.1 Is software evolution a bridge too far?

Computing techniques have been applied to almost every aspect of people's lives and have had a profound impact on quality of life in many areas. Computers are becoming more powerful and the number of application areas is increasing. Meanwhile, the requirements on software developers and redevelopers are increasing with increasing software complexity. In a majority of cases, when a software system has been developed and needs to change to meet people's new requirements, the cost of evolving software is lower than developing from scratch; this is likely to remain so for the foreseeable future. As a result, there will continue to be a need for evolution techniques. Will these techniques cope with constant software changes (i.e., is software evolution a bridge too far—see Figure 3.4)? Software evolution techniques can only be developed when evolution issues are met. Efforts made by evolution researchers and practitioners, including those described in this book, will undoubtedly help to close the gap.

9.2 Formal or not formal?

Formal methods or not formal methods? This is still an unsolved question for both software development and evolution. It can be fair to say that formal methods are more suitable for some tasks of software evolution than other tasks.

Currently, formal methods are both oversold and underused. However, our book presents an approach to practical evolution. In fact, formal methods have applications in the following areas:

- Safety critical systems;
- Reverse engineering and reengineering sequential legacy systems;
- Software migration as a commodity formal methods application;
- Object-oriented systems;
- Real-time and parallel systems.

Nevertheless, our view is that in all these areas we need to integrate formal methods with appropriate tools so that users do not need a deep knowledge of the foundations of the formal methods in order to benefit from them. An example of such a tool is the FermaT program transformation system, which embodies program transformation theory so that an engineer can use and apply program transformations without needing to know about correctness proofs, infinitary logic, and the rest of the theoretical foundations. Another example is the FermaT migration workbench where the formal methods are used almost as a black box technology: taking code in the source language and generating equivalent code in the target language.

9.3 Coping with new development paradigms

On one hand, software needs to be changed very rapidly. On the other hand, a good software development method takes a long time to mature and to be accepted by software engineers. The number of years that

9.3 Coping with new development paradigms

the object-oriented technology took to emerge and the number of years that unified modeling language (UML) object-oriented technology took to emerge are two examples.

At present, there are several main development paradigms that software evolution needs to cope with. The first one is the UML-based paradigm. Object-oriented development is a landmark of software engineering; it organizes data as objects in ways that "echo" how things appear, behave, and interact with each other in the real world. Object-oriented analysis and design (OOA/D) follows the concept of object oriented technology and thus has become a major trend for methods of modern software development and system modeling. A sign of the maturity of OOA/D is the convergence of object-oriented modeling notations in the form of the UML. UML is used to specify, visualize, construct, and document artifacts of software systems. UML defines diagrams, and enables users to build software models and to express important domain-related concepts, such as use case diagrams, class diagrams, collaboration diagrams, and component diagrams. UML allows the user to easily understand a system analysis or design through these diagrams as well as its widely accepted modeling notations. UML is rapidly growing to be the first choice of standards for object-oriented modeling in general. However, the lack of formality in UML limits evaluation of completeness, consistency, and content in requirements and design specifications. All the modeling techniques used in a design, including UML need more formalization to achieve system comprehension and integration in software development and reengineering.

Another development paradigm with which software evolution needs to cope is the use of design patterns. During a system design, we can observe familiar usages and constructs, known as design patterns, that are recognizable traces or blocks found in a series of observations or in a system. The objective of applying design patterns is to enable designers to reuse well-known and successful designs and architectures from expert experiences more easily. Expressing proven techniques precisely, such as design patterns do, makes them more accessible to designers of new systems. Design patterns help users choose design alternatives that make a system reusable and avoid alternatives that compromise reusability. Design patterns can even improve the documentation and maintenance of existing systems by furnishing an explicit specification of class and object interactions and their underlying intent.

A third current development paradigm with which evolution technology needs to cope is frameworks. A framework is a software technology that combines software component reuse with design reuse. Using a framework to develop a group of software systems within the same domain on an existing architecture gives high reusability and efficiency. A framework consists of a set of related abstract classes and concrete classes, as well as the interface definitions of instances of the classes. A framework consists of reusable application architectures for a specific domain. A developer can inherit useful features and functions from the instances of the classes to construct new systems. Basically, a framework provides an environment to support all the activities for software development.

It can be predicted that more advanced software development paradigms will be available in the future and therefore that evolution for software systems built with these new paradigms will also be needed. Modifying evolution techniques to keep up with the pace of emerging development paradigms is a challenge.

Ubiquitous or pervasive computing represents the concept of computing everywhere, making computing and communication essentially transparent to the users. Applications in this type of environment are context-sensitive, which means they use various contexts to adaptively communicate with each other in mobile ad hoc networks; and situation-aware, which means they can respond to both current and historical relationship of contexts and specific user actions.

It might be too early to talk about software evolution in a ubiquitous computing environment, since currently there are no well-accepted methods to facilitate the development of applications for this environment. Nevertheless, we would like to predict that evolution for this type of environment will be required very soon.

9.4 Questions answered

The readers may now be confident to face the questions posed at the end of Chapter 1. The small summary here may help the readers and the authors to finish this book together: The approach described in the book is based on a formal foundation; the framework we have developed presents a complete picture when facing a legacy software evolution situation; the evolution process suggests what to do step-by-step; the available tools help to apply rules (obtained through research and practice over many years) to the legacy system; and a metric facility is available to assess the quality of the evolution work. Because of the formal and rule-based way that evolution is conducted here, the evolved software may be regarded as having quality.

APPENDIX A

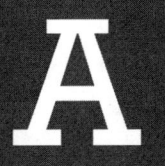

Contents

A.1 Assertions
A.2 Conditionals
A.3 Assignments
A.4 Invariants
A.5 Loops
A.6 Unbounded loops
A.7 Absorption
A.8 False loop
A.9 Loop doubling
A.10 Loop inversion
A.11 Loop unrolling
A.12 The induction rule for recursion
A.13 General recursion removal
A.14 Recursion removal examples
References

WSL Transformations

This appendix lists details of basic transformations (i.e., those for dealing with assertions, abstract data types, simplifications, assignments, if statements, while loops, for loops, reordering, and dead variable elimination and subsumption) and examples of their applications in program development; for example:

Comment: Set z to x^n where $n \geq 0$ is an integer. Slow version.

$z := 1$;
while $n \neq 0$ **do**
    $n := n - 1$; $z := z * x$ **od**;

Comment: Set z to x^n where $n \geq 0$ is an integer. Fast version.

$z := 1$;
while $n \neq 0$ **do**
    while even(n) **do**
        $n := n/2$; $z := x * x$ **od**;
    $n := n - 1$; $z := z * x$ **od**;

A.1 Assertions

Assertions give information about the context in which they occur; an assertion statement $\{P\}$ can only be inserted at a particular point in a program if the condition **P** is guaranteed to be true at that point. This section provides some basic transformations for introducing assertions and moving them around the program. These transformations allow us to migrate information from one part of the program to another. They also help in establishing global invariants—assertions that are true throughout the body of the program.

We start with some simple transformations that are trivially proved from the weakest preconditions:

Theorem A.1 *Assertion weakening*: If $\Delta \vdash P \Rightarrow P'$ then

$$\Delta \vdash \{P\} \leq \{P'\}$$

Theorem A.2 *Introducing assertions*: $\Delta \cup \{P\} \vdash S_1 \approx S_2$ if and only if

$$\Delta \vdash \{P\}; S_1 \approx \{P\}; S_2$$

A.2 Conditionals (see Table A.1)

Theorem A.3 *Prune conditional*:

(i) $\Delta \vdash \{B\};$ **if** B **then** S_1 **else** S_2 **fi** $\approx \{B\}; S_1$
(ii) $\Delta \vdash \{\neg B\};$ **if** B **then** S_1 **else** S_2 **fi** $\approx \{\neg B\}; S_2$
(iii) $\Delta \vdash$ **if** B **then** S **else** S **fi** $\approx S$
(iv) $\Delta \vdash \{B_i\};$ **if** $B_1 \to S_1 \square \ldots \square B_n \to S_n$ **fi** $\leq \{B_i\}; S_i$

Theorem A.4 *Reorder conditional*:

$$\Delta \vdash \text{if } B \text{ then } S_1 \text{ else } S_2 \text{ fi} \approx \text{if } \neg B \text{ then } S_2 \text{ else } S_1 \text{ fi}$$

A.3 Assignments

Theorem A.5 *Assignment merging*: $\Delta \vdash x := t_1; x := t_2 \approx x := t_2[t_1/x]$.

Proof:

$$\mathbf{WP}(x := t_1; x := t_2, R) \iff \mathbf{WP}(x := t_1, \mathbf{WP}(x := t_2, R))$$
$$\iff \mathbf{WP}(x := t_1, R[t_2/x])$$
$$\iff R[t_2/x][t_1/x]$$
$$\iff R[t_2[t_1/x]/x]$$

since the only free x's in $R[t_2/x]$ are those in t_2.

$$\iff \mathbf{WP}(x := t_2[t_1/x], R)$$

Table A.1 Transformations for Inserting Assertions

Condition	Before	After
$P \Rightarrow WP(S, Q)$	{P}; S	{P}; S; {Q}
	x :=t	x :=t; {x = t }
	{P}; **if** $B_1 \rightarrow S_1$ □ ... □ $B_n \rightarrow S_n$ **fi**	{P}; **if** $B_1 \rightarrow \{P \wedge B_1\}$; S_1 □ ... □ $B_n \rightarrow \{P \wedge B_n\}$; S_n **fi**
	if $B_1 \rightarrow S_1$ □ ... □ $B_n \rightarrow S_n$ **fi**; {Q}	**if** $B_1 \rightarrow S_1$; {Q} □ ... □ $B_n \rightarrow S_n$; {Q} **fi**
	while B **do** S **od**	**while** B **do** S **od**; {¬B}
	do $B_1 \rightarrow S_1$ □ ... □ $B_n \rightarrow S_n$ **od**	**do** $B_1 \rightarrow S_1$ □ ... □ $B_n \rightarrow S_n$ **od**; {¬$B_1 \wedge \ldots \wedge \neg B_n$}
For each i: $\Delta \vdash \{P \wedge B_i\}; S_i$ $\approx \{P \wedge B_i\}; S_i;$ {P}	{P}; **do** $B_1 \rightarrow S_1$ □ ... □ $B_n \rightarrow S_n$ **od**	{P}; **do** $B_1 \rightarrow \{P\}; S_1$ □ ... □ $B_n \rightarrow \{P\}; S_n$ **od**; {P}
set(x) ∩ **var**(P) = ∅	{P}; **var** x := t : S **end**; {Q}	{P}; **var** x := t : {P}; S; {Q} **end**; {Q}

Theorem A.6 *Subsumption*: If the variable m is constant in **S** and all the variables in the term t are constant in **S**, and $m \notin$ **var** (t), then

$$\Delta \vdash \textbf{var } m := t : \textbf{S end} \approx \textbf{S}[t/m]$$

The next transformation provides one way in which a complex specification statement can be analyzed into an **if** statement and two (or more) simpler specifications. This it is a kind of factoring operation on specifications.

Theorem A.7 *Exportation of independent conditions*: If no variable in **x** occurs free in the formulae **P** and **Q**, then

$$\Delta \cup \{P \wedge Q \Rightarrow (\exists x.P' \Leftrightarrow \exists x.Q')\} \vdash$$
$$x := x'.(P \wedge P' \vee Q \wedge Q') \approx \text{if } P \rightarrow x := x'.P' \;\square\; Q \rightarrow x := x'.Q' \text{ fi}$$

The transformation relies on Lemma A.1.

Lemma A.1 If $\mathbf{set}(x) \cap \mathbf{var}(B) = \emptyset$ then $\Delta \vdash \{B\}; x := x'.Q \approx x := x'.(Q \wedge B) \approx x := x'.Q; \{B\}$.

Theorem A.8 *Dead statement elimination*: If the only assignments in **T** are to variables in **x**, then:

(i) $\Delta \vdash \mathbf{var}\; x := t : S; T\; \mathbf{end} \leq \mathbf{var}\; x := t : S\; \mathbf{end}$
(ii) $\Delta\{WP(T, \mathbf{true})\} \vdash \mathbf{var}\; x := t : S; T\; \mathbf{end} \approx \mathbf{var}\; x := t : S\; \mathbf{end}$

Theorem A.9 *Dead variable elimination*: If the variables **x** in **S** only appear in assignments to themselves, then

$$\Delta \vdash \mathbf{var}\; x := t : S\; \mathbf{end} \leq S[\mathbf{skip}/x := x'.Q]$$

Here we are replacing all assignments to **x** by **skip** statements. If all the assignments are guaranteed to terminate (for example, if we can insert the assertion $\{\exists x'.Q\}$ before each assignment $x := x'.Q$), then the refinement becomes an equivalence. The equivalence provides a mechanism for introducing ghost variables into a program.

A.4 Invariants

We say that **B** is invariant over **S** if the formulae

$$B \wedge WP(S, \mathbf{true}) \Rightarrow WP(S, B)$$

and

$$\neg B \wedge WP(S, \mathbf{true}) \Rightarrow WP(S, \neg B)$$

are both true.

Lemma A.2 If **B** is invariant over **S** then $\Delta \vdash \{B\}; S \approx S; \{B\}$ and $\Delta \vdash \{\neg B\}; S \approx S; \{\neg B\}$.

Theorem A.10 *Back expansion of a conditional*: If **B** is invariant over **S**, then

$$\Delta \vdash S; \mathbf{if}\; B\; \mathbf{then}\; S_1\; \mathbf{else}\; S_2\; \mathbf{fi} \approx \mathbf{if}\; B\; \mathbf{then}\; S; S_1\; \mathbf{else}\; S; S_2\; \mathbf{fi}$$

Appendix A

Theorem A.11 *Forward expansion*: For any **B** and **S**:

$$\Delta \vdash \textbf{if B then } S_1 \textbf{ else } S_2 \textbf{ fi } ; S \approx \textbf{if B then } S_1; S \textbf{ else } S_2; S \textbf{ fi}$$

A.5 Loops

Theorem A.12 *Loop unrolling*:

$$\Delta \vdash \textbf{while B do S od} \approx \textbf{if B then S; while B do S od fi}$$

Theorem A.13 *Unroll first step*:

$$\Delta \vdash \textbf{for } i := b \textbf{ to } f \textbf{ step } s \textbf{ do S od}$$
$$\approx \textbf{if } b \leq f \textbf{ then } S[b/i]; \textbf{ for } i := b + s \textbf{ to } f \textbf{ step } s \textbf{ do S od fi}$$

Theorem A.14 *Unroll last step*:

$$\Delta \vdash \textbf{for } i := b \textbf{ to } f \textbf{ step } s \textbf{ do S od}$$
$$\approx \textbf{if } b \leq f \textbf{ then var } i := b : \textbf{ while } i \leq f - s \textbf{ do S};$$
$$i := i + s \textbf{ od}; S$$
end fi

Theorem A.15 *Unroll middle step*: If **S** does not assign to any variables in m, then

$$\Delta \vdash \{b \leq m \leq f\}; \textbf{ for } i := b \textbf{ to } f \textbf{ step } s \textbf{ do S od}$$
$$\approx \textbf{var } i := b :$$
$$\textbf{while } i < m \textbf{ do S}; i := i + s \textbf{ od};$$
$$S; i := i + s; \textbf{ while } i \leq f \textbf{ do S}; i := i + s \textbf{ od end}$$

Theorem A.16 *Loop merging*: If $\textbf{B}_1 \Rightarrow \textbf{B}_2$, then

$$\Delta \vdash \textbf{while } B_2 \textbf{ do S od} \approx \textbf{while } B_1 \textbf{ do S od} ; \textbf{ while } B_2 \textbf{ do S od}$$

Theorem A.17 *Loop elimination*: If **S** does not assign to any variables in m and there exists a natural number n such that $m = b + n.s$ and $b \leq m \leq f$, then

$$\Delta \vdash \textbf{for } i := b \textbf{ to } f \textbf{ step } s \textbf{ do if } i = m \textbf{ then S fi od} \approx S[m/i]$$

A.6 Unbounded Loops

As well as the usual **for** and **while** loops, there is a notation for unbounded loops. Statements of the form **do S od**, where **S** is a statement, are infinite or unbounded loops that can only be terminated by the execution of a statement of the form **exit**(n), which causes the program to exit the n enclosing loops. We use **exit** as an abbreviation for **exit**(1). To simplify the language we disallow **exit** which leave a block or a loop other than an unbounded loop. We also insist that n be an integer, not a variable or expression—this ensures that we can always determine the target of the **exit**.

Definition A.1 Global substitution

If $\mathbf{P}(\mathbf{S}, p)$ is a predicate on a statement $\mathbf{S}$ and position p within $\mathbf{S}$, and $\mathbf{S}'(\mathbf{S}, p)$ is a function that returns a statement for any given statement $\mathbf{S}$ and position p, then the effect of replacing or appending to the statement at position p in $\mathbf{S}$ with $\mathbf{S}'(\mathbf{S}, p)$ for every p such that $\mathbf{P}(\mathbf{S}, p)$ holds is denoted:

$$\mathbf{S}[\mathbf{S}'(\mathbf{S}, p)/p | \mathbf{P}(\mathbf{S}, p)]$$

If the statement at position p in $\mathbf{S}$ is an **exit** statement, then it is replaced by $\mathbf{S}'(\mathbf{S}, p)$. Otherwise, $\mathbf{S}'(\mathbf{S}, p)$ is appended in sequence after the statement at position p.

Within a global substitution we use $\delta(\mathbf{S}, p)$ to denote the depth of a component of a statement. This is the number of enclosing **do**...**od** loops surrounding the component. We use $\tau(\mathbf{S}, p)$ to denote the terminal value of a statement. This is the number of enclosing loops around $\mathbf{S}$ which might be terminated by execution of the statement at position p in $\mathbf{S}$. If the statement at position p in $\mathbf{S}$ does not terminate $\mathbf{S}$ then $\tau(\mathbf{S}, p) = -1$. For example, any **exit**(n) has terminal value n. If $\mathbf{S}$ contains an **exit**(n) within m nested loops (where $m \leq n$) then the terminal value of $\mathbf{S}$ itself, denoted $\tau(\mathbf{S}, \langle\rangle)$, will be at least $n - m$.

A statement $\mathbf{S}$ with terminal value zero cannot terminate any enclosing loops, so the next thing to be executed after $\mathbf{S}$ will be the next statement in the sequence containing $\mathbf{S}$ (if there is one). Such a statement is called a proper sequence. If $\mathbf{S}$ is a proper sequence, then

$$\Delta \vdash \textbf{do if B then exit fi} \ ; \textbf{S od} \approx \textbf{while } \neg\textbf{B do S od}$$

In the following transformations, the global substitutions are all applied to the simple terminal statements of $\mathbf{S}$. These are the statements that are neither a sequence, a conditional, or a **do** ... **od** loop and that will terminate **S** if they are executed; for example, in:

if B then x:= 1; y := 2 **else exit fi**

the terminal statements are $y := 2$ and **exit**. If the statement is enclosed in a **do** ... **od** loop, only the **exit** will be a terminal statement.

We usually omit the parameters from δ and τ in a global substitution when these are obvious from the context.

Definition A.2 Incrementation

The incrementation of **S** by n (where n is any nonnegative integer) is defined as the incrementation of all simple terminal statements in **S**. An **exit** is incremented by incrementing its parameter, while any other simple statement is incremented by appending an **exit**:

$$\mathbf{S} + n =_{\mathrm{DF}} \mathbf{S}[\,\mathbf{exit}\,(n+\delta)/p|\tau \geqslant 0]$$

For example:

if B then x:= 1; y := 2 **else exit fi** + 2

is

if B then x:= 1; y := 2; **exit** (2) **else exit** (3) **fi**

while

do if B then x:= 1; y := 2 **else exit fi od** + 2

is

do if B then x:= 1; y := 2 **else exit** (3) **fi od**

Definition A.3 Partial incrementation

The notation $\mathbf{S} + (n, m)$ where $m \geqslant 0$ denotes incrementation of the terminal statements in **S** with terminal value m or greater:

$$\mathbf{S} + (n, m) =_{\mathrm{DF}} \mathbf{S}[\,\mathbf{exit}\,(n+\delta)/p|\tau \geqslant m]$$

Note that **do S od** $+ (n, m) = $ **do** $\mathbf{S} + (n, m+1)$ **od**.

A.7 Absorption

For any statements $\mathbf{S}_1$ and $\mathbf{S}_2$:

$$\Delta \vdash \mathbf{S}_1; \mathbf{S}_2 \approx \mathbf{S}_1[\mathbf{S}_2 + \delta/p|\tau = 0]$$

For example:

$$\Delta \vdash \textbf{do if } B \textbf{ then } x := 1; y := 2 \textbf{ else exit fi od} ; z := 1$$
$$\approx \textbf{do if } B \textbf{ then } x := 1; y := 2 \textbf{ else } z := 1;$$
$$\textbf{exit fi od}$$

This transformation can be applied in reverse to take out code from a loop.

A.8 False loop

We can insert a loop around any statement, by incrementing it first:

$$\Delta \vdash S \approx \textbf{do } S + 1 \textbf{ od}$$

(This is a "false" loop because the body of the loop can only be executed once.)

A.9 Loop doubling

Any loop can be converted to a double loop by the last transformation, or by incrementing the body of the loop:

$$\Delta \vdash \textbf{do } S \textbf{ od} \approx \textbf{do do } S \textbf{ od} + 1 \textbf{ od}$$
$$\approx \textbf{do do } S + 1 \textbf{ od od}$$

More generally, we can arbitrarily decide whether or not to increment each terminal statement in S with terminal value zero:

$$\Delta \vdash \textbf{do } S \textbf{ od} \approx \textbf{do do } S[\textbf{ exit }(\delta+1)/p \mid \tau > 0 \lor \tau = 0 \land \Psi(S, p)]$$
$$\textbf{od od}$$

where Ψ is any condition on S and p.

This can be combined with the inverse of absorption to isolate part of a loop body; for example:

$$\Delta \vdash \textbf{do } S; \textbf{if } B \textbf{ then } S_1 \textbf{ else } S_2 \textbf{ fi od}$$
$$\approx \textbf{do do } S + (1, 1);$$
$$\textbf{if } B \textbf{ then exit else } S_2 + (1, 1) \textbf{ fi od} ;$$
$$S_1 \textbf{ od}$$

A.10 Loop inversion

If S_1 is a proper sequence, then

$$\Delta \vdash \textbf{do } S_1; S_2 \textbf{ od} \approx S_1; \textbf{do } S_2; S_1 \textbf{ od}$$

Appendix A

More generally, for any statements S_1 and S_2:

$$\Delta \vdash \textbf{do } S_1; S_2 \textbf{ od} \approx \textbf{do } S_1;\ \textbf{do } S_2; S_1 \textbf{ od} + 1 \textbf{ od}$$

A.11 Loop unrolling

If all the **exit**s of **S** with terminal value 1 are in terminal positions, then we can unroll the first step of a loop:

$$\Delta \vdash \textbf{do S od} \approx S[\textbf{do S od} + \delta/p | \tau = 0]$$
$$[\textbf{exit } (\tau + \delta - 1)/p | \tau \geqslant 1]$$

where the RHS contains two successive global substitutions on **S**.

For example, the loop

do if x=10 **then exit fi**;
$y := y * 2;\ x := x + 1$ **od**

has an **exit** that is not in a terminal position. But after applying absorption to the loop body the **exit** is moved to a terminal position:

do if x=10

   then exit

   else $y := y * 2; x := x + 1$ **fi od**

and we can unroll the first step of the loop to get

if x=10

   then skip

   else $y := y * 2; x := x + 1$;

   do if x=10

      then exit

      else $y := y * 2; x := x + 1$ **fi od fi**

A *reducible* statement in which all the terminal statements with terminal value 1 are in terminal positions. In general any statement can be made reducible by repeated applications of absorption (but in the worst case this can cause an exponential increase in the program size).

More generally, we can insert a copy of the whole loop, with certain terminal statements of the loop body incremented, after certain terminal statements in the loop body. Let **S**′ be formed from **S** by incrementing selected terminal statements with terminal value zero:

$$S' = S[\textbf{exit } (\delta+1)/p | \tau = 0 \land \Phi(S,p)]$$

where Φ is any condition (see Section A.10). Then

$$\Delta \vdash \textbf{do } S \textbf{ od}$$
$$\approx \textbf{do } S'[\textbf{do } S' \textbf{ od } + \delta + 1/p | \tau = 0 \land \Psi(S,p)]$$
$$[\textbf{exit } (\tau + \delta - 1)/p | \tau \geq 1] \textbf{ od}$$

where Ψ is any condition.

This transformation is valid for any statement S (not just reducible statements) and any conditions Φ and Ψ.

A.12 The induction rule for recursion

Our next transformation shows that to prove a refinement of a recursive or iterative program, it is sufficient to examine the set of finite truncations of the program. This result is extremely valuable in proving many transformations involving recursive and iterative statements since, in a great many cases, the proof can be carried out by induction over the set of all finite truncations. The theorem shows that the set of all finite truncations of a recursive statement tells us everything we need to know about the full recursion. Using this induction rule we have proved a powerful collection of general-purpose transformations. These enable many algorithm derivations to be carried out by appealing to general transformation rules rather than ad hoc induction proofs.

The nth truncation of a procedure **proc** $F \equiv S$. is defined recursively:

$$(\textbf{proc } F \equiv S.)^0 =_{\text{DF}} \textbf{abort}$$

and

$$(\textbf{proc } F \equiv S.)^{n+1} =_{\text{DF}} S[(\textbf{proc } F \equiv S.)^n/F]$$

Here, the notation $=_{\text{DF}}$ indicates that the left-hand side of the symbol is defined to mean the right-hand side and should be distinguished from the notation $\approx$, which means that the statement on the left-hand side is semantically equivalent to the statement on the right-hand side.

The nth truncation of any statement S^n is formed by replacing each recursive component by its nth truncation.

A statement has bounded nondeterminacy if each specification statement within it has a finite set of values it can assign to the variables to satisfy

Appendix A

the given condition. For statements with bounded nondeterminacy we have the following induction rule:

Theorem A.18 The induction rule for recursion: If **S** is any statement with bounded nondeterminacy, and **S**′ is another statement where $\Delta \vdash \mathbf{S}^n \leqslant \mathbf{S}'$ for every $n < \omega$, then $\Delta \vdash \mathbf{S} \leqslant \mathbf{S}'$.

This transformation is related to the concept of a sequence of approximations to a continuous function: a fundamental concept in denotational semantics [1, 2]. The semantics of the truncations $\mathbf{S}^n$ form a sequence of approximations to the semantics of the full statement **S**.

An example of a transformation proved by induction is the following:

Theorem A.19 Invariant maintenance:

(i) If for any statement $\mathbf{S}_1$ we can prove

$$\{\mathbf{P}\};\ \mathbf{S}[\mathbf{S}_1/X] \leqslant \mathbf{S}[\{\mathbf{P}\}\,;\mathbf{S}_1/X]$$

then

$$\{\mathbf{P}\};\ \mathbf{proc}\ X \equiv \mathbf{S} \leqslant \mathbf{proc}\ X \equiv \{\mathbf{P}\};\mathbf{S}.$$

(ii) If in addition

$$\{\mathbf{P}\};\ \mathbf{S}_1 \leqslant \mathbf{S}_1;\ \{\mathbf{P}\}$$

implies

$$\{\mathbf{P}\};\ \mathbf{S}[\mathbf{S}_1/X] \leqslant \mathbf{S}[\mathbf{S}_1/X];\ \{\mathbf{P}\}$$

then

$$\{\mathbf{P}\};\ \mathbf{proc}\ X \equiv \mathbf{S}. \leqslant \mathbf{proc}\ X \equiv \mathbf{S}.;\{\mathbf{P}\}$$

A.13 General recursion removal

Our third transformation is a general transformation from a recursive procedure into an equivalent iterative procedure, using a stack. It can also be applied in reverse: to turn an iterative program into an equivalent recursive procedure (which may well be easier to understand). The theorem was presented in [3], and the proof may be found in [4].

Suppose we have a recursive procedure whose body is a regular action system in the following form (where a **call** Z appearing in one of the action bodies in the action system will terminate the action system, and hence only the current invocation of the procedure):

proc $F(x) \equiv$
　actions A_1:
　$A_1 \equiv$
　　$\mathbf{S}_1.$
　　$\ldots$
　$A_M \equiv$
　　$\mathbf{S}_M.$
　　$\ldots$
　$B_j \equiv$
　　$\mathbf{S}_{j0}$; $F(g_{j1}(x))$; $\mathbf{S}_{j1}$; $F(g_{j2}(x))$; $\ldots$; $F(g_{jn_j}(x))$; $\mathbf{S}_{jn_j}$
　$\ldots$ **endactions**.

The actions in the action system that forms the body of the procedure are divided into two classes, the A-type actions A_i and the B-type actions B_j. The A-type action bodies may contain calls to any actions and assignments to any variables but contain no calls to F. All the calls to F are as listed explicitly in the B-type actions, which must be in the form of a sequence of statements separated by calls to F. The statements after the first call (i.e., $\mathbf{S}_{j1}, \ldots, \mathbf{S}_{jn_j}$) must preserve the value of x and all the statements but the last (i.e., $\mathbf{S}_{j0}, \mathbf{S}_{j1} \ldots, \mathbf{S}_{jn_j-1}$) must contain no action calls. Since the whole system is a regular action system, the last statement in each B-type action (i.e., $\mathbf{S}_{jn_j}$) must contain action calls. There are $M + N$ actions in total, M A-type actions $A_1, \ldots, A_M$, which contain no recursive calls, and N B-type actions $B_1, \ldots, B_N$, each of which contains one or more recursive calls. Note that the since the action system is regular, it can only be terminated by executing **call** Z, which will terminate the current invocation of the procedure. A procedure written in this way is said to be in AB-format.

At first sight the restrictions may appear stringent, but in actual fact any recursive procedure can be cast into AB-format simply by taking out each recursive call into its own B-type action. Note that there are no restrictions on the A-type actions other than not containing recursive calls. In general, there may be many different ways to restructure a recursive procedure into AB-format, and these will generally lead to different iterative versions of the procedure.

The aim of the transformation is to remove the recursion by introducing a local stack K, which records postponed operations. When a recursive call is required we postpone it by pushing the pair $\langle 0, e \rangle$ onto K (where e is the parameter required for the recursive call). Execution of the statements $\mathbf{S}_{jk}$ also has to be postponed (since they occur between recursive calls),

Appendix A

we record the postponement of $\mathbf{S}_{jk}$ by pushing $\langle\langle j,k\rangle,x\rangle$ onto K. Where the procedure body would normally terminate (by calling Z) we instead call a new action $\mathscr{F}$, which pops the top item off K and carries out the postponed operation. If we call $\mathscr{F}$ with the stack empty then all postponed operations have been completed and the procedure terminates by calling Z.

Theorem A.20 The procedure $F(x)$ above is equivalent to the following iterative procedure, which uses a new local stack K and a new local variable m:

proc $F'(x) \equiv$
  var $\langle K:=\langle\rangle,\ m:=0\rangle$:
    actions A_1:
    $A_1 \equiv$
      $\mathbf{S}_1[\mathbf{call}\ \mathscr{F}/\mathbf{call}\ Z]$
    ...
    $A_M \equiv$
      $\mathbf{S}_M[\mathbf{call}\ \mathscr{F}/\mathbf{call}\ Z]$.
    ...
    $B_j \equiv$
      $\mathbf{S}_{j0}; K := \langle\langle 0, g_{j1}(x)\rangle, \langle\langle j,1\rangle, x\rangle, \langle 0, g_{j2}(x)\rangle, \ldots,$
      $\langle 0, g_{jn_j}(x)\rangle, \langle\langle j, n_j\rangle, x\rangle\rangle + K;\ \mathbf{call}\ \mathscr{F}$.
    ...
    $\mathscr{F} \equiv$
      if $K = \langle\rangle$
        then call Z
        else $\langle m,x\rangle \xleftarrow{\text{pop}} K$;
          if $m = 0 \rightarrow \mathbf{call}\ A_1$
          $\square \ldots \square\ m = \langle j,k\rangle \rightarrow \mathbf{S}_{jk}[\mathbf{call}\ \mathscr{F}/\mathbf{call}\ Z];\ \mathbf{call}\ \mathscr{F}$
          ...**fi fi. endactions end**.

Proof: See [3, 4]

In contrast to the usual iteration plus stack method of recursion removal (discussed in [5] and elsewhere), in which only a single statement (the return point) is stacked, our method allows a whole sequence of recursive calls an intermediate statements to be stacked. As discussed above, any recursive procedure can be restructured into a suitable form for Theorem A.20 simply by putting each recursive call into its own B-type action. Many recursive procedures can be restructured differently (but still meeting the requirements of the theorem) by collecting two or more recursive calls into B-type actions. These different recursive forms will lead to very different iterative versions of the program. See [3, 4] for some examples and further applications of the theorem.

The proof of Theorem A.20 is rather involved and too long to include here. It relies on applying various transformations which have been proved using weakest preconditions, together with multiple applications of the general induction rule (Theorem A.18).

Corollary A.1 By unfolding some calls to $\mathscr{F}$ in B_j and pruning, we get a slightly more efficient version:

$B_j \equiv$
  $\mathbf{S}_{j0};$
  $K := \langle\langle\langle j, 1\rangle, x\rangle, \langle 0, g_{j2}(x)\rangle, \ldots, \langle 0, g_{jn}j(x)\rangle, \langle\langle j, n_j\rangle, x\rangle\rangle + K;$
  $x := g_{j1}(x);$ **call** $A_1.$

In the case where $n_j = 1$ for all j, this version will never push a $\langle 0, x \rangle$ pair onto the stack. This fact can be significant for a parameterless procedure with a small number of j values, since it enables us to reduce the amount of storage required by the stack. For example, if there are two j values, the stack can be represented as a binary number.

A particularly simple case is a parameterless procedure with only one B action, which contains only one recursive call. In this case, all the elements pushed on the stack will be equal; in fact they will all be $\langle 1, 1\rangle$, so we only need to record the length of the stack, ignoring its actual contents. Technically, we prove the following corollary by introducing a new local variable k, which records the length of K, and then replacing the test $K = \langle\rangle$ by $k = 0$.

Corollary A.2 The parameterless procedure:

  proc $F() \equiv$
    actions $A_1:$
  $A_1 \equiv$
    $\mathbf{S}_1.$
  $\ldots$
  $A_M \equiv$
    $\mathbf{S}_M.$
  $B_1 \equiv$
    $\mathbf{S}_{10}; F(); \mathbf{S}_{11}.$ **endactions**.

(where the only recursive call is the single call in B_1) is equivalent to the nonrecursive procedure:

```
proc F()≡
  var ⟨k := 0⟩:
    actions A₁:
    A₁≡
      S₁[call ℱ /call Z].
    ...
    Aₘ≡
      Sₘ [call ℱ /call Z].
    B₁≡
      S₁₀; k := k + 1; call A₁.
    ℱ ≡
      if k = 0 then call Z
               else k := k − 1; S₁₁; call ℱ fi.
  endactions end.
```

Proof: This is a simple application of Theorem A.20 and Corollary A.1. Since there is but a single B-type action and no parameters, the stack K consists of a list of identical elements. Such a stack can be more efficiently implemented as an integer k, where $k = \ell(K)$, and $K = \langle\langle 1, 1\rangle, \langle 1, 1\rangle, \ldots\rangle$.

A.14 Recursion removal examples

Consider the simple recursive procedure:

```
proc F(x) ≡
  if x = 0 then G(x)
           else F(x − 1); H(x); F(x − 1) fi.
```

There are two ways to convert the body of the procedure into an action system appropriate for Theorem A.20. The first method is to put both recursive calls into the same B-type action:

```
proc F(x)≡
  actions A₁:
  A₁≡
    if x=0 then G(x); call Z else call B₁ fi.
  B₁≡
    F(x − 1); H(x); F(x − 1); call Z. endactions.
```

So for Theorem A.20 S_1 is the statement

$$\text{if } x = 0 \text{ then } G(x); \textbf{ call } Z \textbf{ else call } B_1 \textbf{ fi}$$

S_{11} is the statement $H(x)$ and S_{12} is the statement **call** Z. Applying the theorem gives:

proc $F'(x) \equiv$
  var $\langle K: = \langle\rangle;\ m: = 0\rangle$:
    actions A_1:
    $A_1 \equiv$
      if $x = 0$ **then** $G(x);$ **call** $\mathscr{F}$ **else call** B_1 **fi**.
    $B_1 \equiv$
      $K := \langle\langle 0, x-1\rangle, \langle\langle 1,1\rangle, x\rangle, \langle 0, x-1\rangle,$
      $\langle\langle 1,2\rangle, x\rangle\rangle + \!\!+ K;$ **call** $\mathscr{F}$.
    $\mathscr{F} \equiv$
      if $K = \langle\rangle$
        then call Z
        else $\langle m, x\rangle \xleftarrow{\text{pop}} K;$
          if $m = 0 \rightarrow$ **call** A_1
          $\square\, m = \langle 1, 1\rangle \rightarrow H(x);$ **call** $\mathscr{F}$
          $\square\, m = \langle 1, 2\rangle \rightarrow$ **call** $\mathscr{F};$ **call** $\mathscr{F}$ **fi fi**.
  endactions.

We can represent the values $\langle 1, 1\rangle$ and $\langle 1, 2\rangle$ on the stack and in m by 1 and 2 respectively. Then, unfold everything into $\mathscr{F}$, replace the initial call to A_1 by $K := \langle\langle 0, x\rangle\rangle$, remove the recursion in $\mathscr{F}$ and then remove the action system:

proc $F'(x) \equiv$
  var $\langle K := \langle\langle 0, x\rangle\rangle\ m := 0\rangle$:
    while $K \neq \langle\rangle$ **do**
    $\langle m, x\rangle \xleftarrow{\text{pop}} K;$
    if $m = 0 \rightarrow$ **if** $x = 0$
                then $G(x)$
                else $K := \langle\langle 0, x-1\rangle, \langle 1, x\rangle,$
                        $\langle 0, x-1\rangle, \langle 2, x\rangle\rangle + \!\!+ K$ **fi**
    $\square\, m = 1 \rightarrow H(x);$ **call** $\mathscr{F}$
    $\square\, m = 2 \rightarrow$ **skip fi od end**.

The other way to restructure the recursive program is to put the two recursive calls into separate B-type actions:

proc $F(x) \equiv$
  actions A_1:
  $A_1 \equiv$
    if $x = 0$ **then** $G(x);$ **call** Z **else call** B_1 **fi**.

Appendix A   259

$B_1 \equiv$
$\quad F(x-1); H(x);$ **call** B_2.
$B_2 \equiv$
$\quad F(x-1);$ **call** Z. **endactions**.

So for Theorem A.20, S_1 is the statement
$$\text{if } x = 0 \text{ then } G(x);\text{ call } Z \text{ else call } B_1 \text{ fi}$$

S_{11} is the statement $H(x);$ **call** B_2 and S_{21} is the statement **call** Z. Applying the theorem gives

proc $F'(x) \equiv$
  var $\langle K := \langle\rangle; m := 0\rangle$:
    actions A_1:
    $A_1 \equiv$
      if $x = 0$ **then** $G(x);$ **call** $\mathscr{F}$ **else call** B_1 **fi**.
    $B_1 \equiv$
      $K := \langle\langle 0, x-1 \rangle, \langle\langle 1,1\rangle, x\rangle \rangle \;+\!\!+\; K;$ **call** $\mathscr{F}$.
    $B_2 \equiv$
      $K := \langle\langle 0, x-1 \rangle, \langle\langle 2,1\rangle, x\rangle \rangle \;+\!\!+\; K;$ **call** $\mathscr{F}$.
    $\mathscr{F} \equiv$
      if $K = \langle\rangle$
        then call Z
        else $\langle m, x\rangle \xleftarrow{\text{pop}} K;$
          if $m = 0 \rightarrow$ **call** A_1
          $\square\, m = \langle 1,1\rangle \rightarrow H(x);$ **call** B_2
          $\square\, m = \langle 2,1\rangle \rightarrow$ **call** $\mathscr{F}$ **fi fi**.
    endactions.

Note that $\langle\langle 0, x-1\rangle\rangle \;+\!\!+\; K;$ **call** $\mathscr{F}$ is equivalent to $x := x - 1;$ **call** A_1. Then we never need to push $\langle 0, x\rangle$ onto K. Also we can represent the values $\langle 1,1\rangle$ and $\langle 2,1\rangle$ on the stack and in m by 1 and 2 respectively. Then, unfold B_1 into A_1, unfold B_2 into $\mathscr{F}$, remove the recursion in $\mathscr{F}$, unfold everything into A_1, remove the recursion and the action system:

proc $F'(x) \equiv$
  var $\langle K := \langle\rangle; m := 0\rangle$:
    do do if $x = 0$
          then $G(x);$ **exit**
          else $K := \langle\langle 1, x\rangle\rangle \;+\!\!+\; K;$
              $x := x - 1$ **fi od**;
      do if $K = \langle\rangle$ **then** **exit** (2) **fi**;
          $\langle m, x\rangle \xleftarrow{\text{pop}} K;$

$$\textbf{if } m = 1 \rightarrow H(x); K := \langle\langle 2,x \rangle\rangle + K;$$
$$x := x - 1; \textbf{ exit}$$
$$\square\, m = 2 \rightarrow \textbf{skip fi od od end}.$$

Notice how the two different restructurings of the initial recursive procedure led to very different (but equivalent) interative procedures.

The power and generality of the recursion removal transformations comes from the fact that the body of the procedure is expressed as an action system, with the recursive calls collected into a number of actions. Because of this, a wide variety of recursive programs can be easily restructured into one or more forms, where the theorem can be applied.

We can also apply the theorem in reverse to produce a recursive program from an iterative one, and this is where the generality of the theorem is particularly useful since it reduces the amount of work required to reverse engineer from an iterative program to an equivalent recursive program.

References

[1] Stoy, J. E., *Denotational Semantics: The Scott-Strachy Approach to Programming Language Theory*, Cambridge, MA: MIT Press, 1977.

[2] Tennet, R. D., "The Denotational Semantics of Programming Languages," *Comm. ACM*, Vol. 19, No. 8, August 1976, pp. 437–453.

[3] Ward, M., "A Recursion Removal Theorem," *Proc. of the 5th Refinement Workshop*, London, U.K., January 8–11, 1992 (http://www.dur.ac.uk/ dcs0mpw/martin/papers/ref-ws-5/ps.gz), pp. 43–69.

[4] Ward, M., "A Recursion Removal Theorem—Proof and Applications," Durham University, Durham, U.K., Technical Report, 1991 (http://www.dur.-ac.uk/ dcs0mpw/martin/papers/rec-proof-t.ps.gz).

[5] Knuth, D. E., "Structured Programming with the GOTO Statement," *Comput. Surveys*, Vol. 6, No. 4, 1974, pp. 261–301.

APPENDIX B

Abstraction Rules

Contents

B.1 Elementary abstraction rules

B.2 Further abstraction rules

B.1 Elementary abstraction rules

B.1.1 Primitive abstraction rules

Primitive abstraction rules aim at converting the simple statements in WSL to ITL formulae. The formal definition of primitive abstraction rules is as follows:

$$St \succeq Sp$$

where St denotes a simple statement in concrete code, and Sp is the abstract specification for St—that is, the semantics of St in logical form.

Rules listed in this subsection are instances of the primitive abstraction rules and are proven sound in ITL based on the semantic weakening definition of abstraction.

Assume $\mathcal{A}, \mathcal{B}, \mathcal{A}_i, \mathcal{B}_i$ are system representations, and $\Phi, \Psi, \Phi_i, \Psi_i$ are formulae, then we have the following primitive abstraction rules:

1. *Assignment:*

    $$x := e \succeq \{x\} : \bigcirc x = e$$

    This rule extracts a logic formula of the assignment statement, which assigns the value of expression e to variable x.

2. *Input statement:*

$(x,y) \leftarrow s \succeq \{x,y\} : x = \sqrt{s} \land y = \textbf{read}(s)$

This rule extracts a logic formula of the input statement, which reads the value in shunt s to variable y and store the timestamp in x.

3. *Output statement:*

$x \rightarrow s \succeq \{s\} : \textbf{skip} \land \bigcirc s = (\sqrt{s}+1, x)$

This rule extracts a logic formula of the output statement, which writes the value of variable or expression x to shunt s, and changes the timestamp of s to the time when last write operation happened.

4. *Type definition:*

$x : T \succeq \exists x \bullet f_T(x) \land scope(x)$

The statement declares variable x of type T. This is expressed in logic as variable x has the feature of type T, which is described with function $f_T(x)$, and the valid scope of x is described with $scope(x)$, which depends on the definition context.

5. *Delay:*

$delay\ n \succeq len = n$

Delay means doing nothing during the specified period. The statement defines a delay lasting n time units, which is expressed with the formula $len = n$.

B.1.2 Compound abstraction rules

Compound abstraction rules aim at converting composite statements to ITL formulae. The formal definition of compound abstraction rules is as follows:

$$\frac{S_i \succeq \Phi_i}{\mathscr{C}(S_i) \succeq f_{\mathscr{C}}(\Phi_i)}$$

where $f_{\mathscr{C}}$ denotes logical construction corresponding to composition operator $\mathscr{C}$, and S_i denotes simple statements or composite statements.

Rules listed in this subsection are instances of the compound abstraction rules and are proven sound in ITL based on the semantic weakening definition of abstraction.

Appendix B

Assume $\mathcal{A}, \mathcal{B}, \mathcal{A}_i, \mathcal{B}_i$ are system representations, and $\Phi, \Psi, \Phi_i, \Psi_i$ are formulae, then we have the following abstraction rules:

1. *Sequential composition:*

$$\frac{\mathcal{A} \succeq \Phi \quad \mathcal{B} \succeq \Psi}{\mathcal{A}\, ;\mathcal{B} \succeq \mathit{frame}(\Phi) \cup \mathit{frame}(\Psi) : \Phi\, ;\Psi}$$

If two representation fragments have a sequential composition relation, they can be abstracted separately, and the result representations should be composed with a sequential operator. The new frame is the union of both original frames.

2. *Conditional statement:*

$$\frac{\mathcal{A}_i \succeq \Phi_i (\text{for all } i \in I)}{\mathit{if} \bigsqcup_{i \in I} g_i \text{ then } \mathcal{A}_i \text{ fi} \succeq \bigcup_{i \in I} \mathit{frame}(\mathcal{A}_i) : (\bigvee_{i \in I}(g_i \wedge \Phi_i)) \vee (\bigwedge_{i \in I} \neg g_i)}$$

This rule extracts a logic formula from a conditional statement. Each guarded branch can be abstracted separately and then composed together with disjunction. The new frame is the union of the frames of all branches.

3. *Iteration statement:*

$$\frac{\mathcal{A} \succeq \Phi}{\mathit{while}\, g\, \mathit{do}\, \mathcal{A}\, \mathit{od} \succeq \mathit{frame}(\Phi) : (g \wedge \Phi)^* \wedge \mathit{fin}(\neg g)}$$

This rule extracts a logic formula of an iteration statement. The iteration is mapped into "chopstar" formula in ITL, and the iteration body can be abstracted separately and then joined into the chopstar structure. The new frame equals the frame of the iteration body.

4. *Procedure definition:*

$$\frac{\mathcal{A}' \succeq \Phi}{\mathit{proc}\, P(\mathit{In}\, pin_i : T_i,\, \mathit{Out}\, pout_j : T_j')\{\mathcal{A}'\} \succeq \{pout_j\} \cup \mathit{frame}(\Phi) : \Phi}$$

where Observables = $\{pin_i, pout_j, \text{global variables to P}\}$

Scope = {local variables of P}

A procedure definition is abstracted into a separate specification in ITL with its input parameters stable and output parameters possibly nonstable. The procedure body can be abstracted separately and then join the parameter part with conjunction. The new frame is the union of $pout_j$ and the frame of the procedure body. Observables are defined to include parameters and global variables of the procedure, which form the interface of the procedure. Local variables should be deleted with their effects recorded in further abstraction because they are considered as implementation details.

5. *Procedure invocation:*

$$\frac{\mathcal{A}' \succeq \Phi}{P(In\ e_i,\ Out\ x_j) \succeq \{x_j\} : \Phi(pin_i/e_i, pout_j/x_j)}$$

where $proc\ P(In\ pin_i : T_i,\ Out\ pout_j : T'_j)\{\mathcal{A}'\}$

The invocation of a procedure equals the execution of the procedure's abstracted body with the input parameters' values passed in and output parameters returned.

6. *Parallel:*

$$\frac{\mathcal{A} \succeq \Phi,\ \mathcal{B} \succeq \Psi}{parbegin\ \mathcal{A}\|\mathcal{B}\ parend \succeq \mathbf{frame}(\Phi) \cup \mathbf{frame}(\Psi) : (\Phi \wedge \Psi)}$$

Two concurrency or parallel representations can be abstracted separately, and the results are composed through the conjunction operator. The new frame is the union of both original frames.

7. *Duration:*

$$\frac{\mathcal{A} \succeq \Phi}{[t].\mathcal{A} \succeq \mathbf{frame}(\Phi) : (\Delta t \wedge \Phi\ ; true) \wedge (\Phi \supset len <= t)}$$

Duration means that the execution of the specified representation should be finished within the indicated time duration. This rule extracts a logic formula from duration statement. It indicates that the execution body within a duration statement can be abstracted separately.

Appendix B

8. *Signal:*

$$\frac{\mathcal{A}_1 \succeq \Phi_1 \qquad \mathcal{A}_2 \succeq \Phi_2}{\mathcal{A}_1 \trianglerighteq^t_s \mathcal{A}_2 \succeq \textit{frame}(\Phi_1) \cup \textit{frame}(\Phi_2) \cup \{s\} : (\Delta t \wedge \textit{stable}(\sqrt{s}); \Phi_1)}$$
$$\vee (\Delta t \wedge \neg \textit{stable}(\sqrt{s}); \Phi_2)$$

The two execution bodies in a signal statement can be abstracted separately and then joined together with the formula defined above. This rule extracts a logic formula from the signal statement.

9. *Object definition:* As type specification, classes defined in COOL or ObTAM programs will disappear once they are abstracted to ITL specification. Only objects exist as formulae with frames in ITL.

   Let $T = \{x_i : T_i, m_j(\textit{In } pin_{j_k} : T_k, \textit{Out } pout_{j_l} : T'_l)[\mathcal{A}_j]\}$, then

$$\frac{\mathcal{A}_j \succeq \Psi_j}{x : T \succeq W_x : f}$$

   where $W_x = \bigcup_{i \in I} x_i$

   $f = \bigwedge_{i \in I} f_{T_i}(x_i) \wedge (\bigvee_{j \in J} \textit{frame}(\Psi_j) \cup \{pout_{j_l}\} : \Psi_j)^*$

   This rule transforms the definition of an object in source code into a logic description. W_x is the data fields of the object, it forms the object's *observables*. f is the behavior description of the object where $\textit{frame}(\Psi_j) \cup \{pout_{j_l}\} : \Psi_j$ is the description of method m_j.

10. *Object hierarchy:*

    Let $T = \{x_i : T_i, m_j(\textit{In } pin_{j_k} : T_k, \textit{Out } pout_{j_l} : T_l)[\mathcal{A}_j]\}$
    $T' = \{y_{i'} : T'_{i'}, m'_{j'}(\textit{In } pin_{j'_{k'}} : T'_{k'}, \textit{Out } pout_{j'_{l'}} : T'_{l'})[\mathcal{A}'_{j'}]\}$, then

$$\frac{\mathcal{A}_j \succeq \Psi_j, \quad \mathcal{A}'_{j'} \succeq \Psi'_{j'}}{x : T <_{sub} T' \succeq W_x : f}$$

where $W_x = \bigcup_{i \in I} x_i \cup \bigcup_{i' \in I'} y_{i'}$ iff for all x_i $i \in I, y_{i'} \neq x_i$

$$f = \bigwedge_{i \in I} f_{T_i}(x_i) \wedge \bigwedge_{i' \in I'} f_{T_{i'}}(y_{i'}) \wedge (\bigvee_{j \in J} \Phi_j \vee \bigvee_{j' \in J'} \Phi'_{j'})^*$$

iff for all x_i $i \in I, y_{i'} \neq x_i$, and iff for all Φ_j $j \in J, \Phi'_{j'} \neq \Phi_j$

$$\forall j \in J \cdot \Phi_j = \mathbf{frame}(\Psi_j) \cup \{pout_{j_l}\} : \Psi_j$$

$$\forall j' \in J' \cdot \Phi'_{j'} = \mathbf{frame}(\Psi'_{j'}) \cup \{pout_{j'_l}\} : \Psi'_{j'}$$

The subclass relation $<_{sub}$ is transitive. This rule transforms the object hierarchy definition, including inheritance, into a logic formula. Assume that T is a subclass of T', for any object x of class T, it will inherit all the data fields and methods in T' if they are not redefined in T. On the other hand, all the data fields and methods in T' will be overridden with the counterparts in T if they are redefined in T.

11. *Method invocation:*

$$\frac{\mathscr{A} \succeq \Phi}{x.m(e_i, y_j) \succeq \{y_j\} : \Phi(pin_i/e_i, \ pout_j/y_j)}$$

where $m(In \ pin_i : T_i, \ Out \ pout_j : T_j)[\mathscr{A}]$

A method invocation equals the execution of the method's abstracted agent with the input parameters passed in and the result of output parameters returned.

12. *Field reference:*

$$x.d \succeq d \in W_x$$

A data field of an object is a variable belonging to the frame of the object.

B.2 Further abstraction rules

Assume $\mathscr{A}, \mathscr{B}, \mathscr{A}_i, \mathscr{B}_i$ are representations, and $\Phi, \Psi, \Phi_i, \Psi_i$ are formulae, then we have the following abstraction rules.

1. *Transitive:*

$$\frac{\mathscr{A} \succeq \mathscr{B}}{\mathscr{B} \succeq \mathscr{C}}$$
$$\mathscr{A} \succeq \mathscr{C}$$

This rule states that a system representation can be abstracted step by step, and the final result will be an abstraction of the original representation if it is guaranteed that each step is an abstraction.

2. *Monotonic:*

$$\frac{\mathscr{A} \succeq \mathscr{B} \quad \mathscr{C}X = \wedge \vee \ ; |\ ||\ | \Rightarrow}{\mathscr{C}X(\mathscr{A}) \succeq \mathscr{C}X(\mathscr{B})}$$

For the context of conjunction, disjunction, sequential composition, parallel composition, and implication, all abstractions discussed in Chapter 7 are monotonic in the sense of weakening, temporal, hiding, and structural abstraction.

3. *Sequence folding:*

$$\frac{[[\mathscr{A} \ ; \mathscr{B}]] \Rightarrow [[\mathscr{A} \wedge \mathscr{B}]]}{\mathscr{A} \ ; \mathscr{B} \succeq \mathscr{A} \wedge \mathscr{B}}$$

If no contradiction is caused when substituting the sequential composition between two representations to conjunction composition, then the sequence can be folded through conjunction. This rule can be applied when the execution order of a sequence is not crucial. In nonparallel systems, this is true under most situations except any operation provides parts of the preconditions of its successor within the sequence. However, in parallel systems, if the sequence relates with communication or shared resources, it cannot be folded with conjunction.

4. *Specification combination:*

4.1 $(W_1 : \Phi_1) \wedge (W_2 : \Phi_2) = (W_1 \cup W_2) : \Phi_1 \wedge \Phi_2$
4.2 $(W_1 : \Phi_1) \vee (W_2 : \Phi_2) \succeq (W_1 \cup W_2) : \Phi_1 \vee \Phi_2$

This rule is used to combine specifications in ITL because there are often quite a number of specifications within one software system and some of them can be potentially combined for further abstractions. Two specifications with conjunction relation can be merged into one specification with their frames united and their description formulae conjunctively composed. Similarly, two specifications with disjunction relation can be merged into one specification with their frames united and their description formulae disjunctly composed.

5. *State test and exception handling:* State tests and exception handling are often used in programs to assure smooth execution. Although they may be important in system implementation, these details do not involve the crucial functionality of the system. Therefore, in a high-level specification, these details are unnecessary and should be abstracted away. The related abstraction pattern is called "state test and exception handling pattern," which consists of the following cases:

   - *State test and exception handling branch:* The identified state test and exception handling parts are branches in conditional structures. In this case, the branches should be abstracted away.

   - *State test and exception handling loop:* The identified state test and exception handling part is a loop structure. In this case, the loop should be abstracted away.

   - *State test and exception handling component:* The identified state test and exception handling part is a procedure or function (component). In this case, the component should be abstracted away.

   - *State test and exception handling expression:* An expression is identified as related with state test and exception handling. In this case, the expression together with the smallest representation unit (statement or ITL formula) in which the expression directly locates should be abstracted away.

   - *State test and exception handling variable:* A variable is identified as related with state test and exception handling. In this case, all the smallest representation units (statements or ITL formulae) that the variable directly locates should be abstracted away.

6. *Trivial elements:* If a part of the system's functionality is considered too trivial to be kept in high-level specification, the elements related to this part of functionality are identified as trivial elements, which should be abstracted away in further abstraction.

Appendix B

Trivial elements could be the following cases:

- *Trivial branch:* The identified trivial element is a branch in a conditional structure. In this case, the branch should be abstracted away.

- *Trivial loop:* The identified trivial element is a loop structure. In this case, the loop should be abstracted away.

- *Trivial component:* The identified trivial element is a procedure or function (component). In this case, the component should be abstracted away.

- *Trivial expression:* The identified trivial element is an expression. In this case, the expression together with the smallest representation unit (statement or ITL formula) in which the expression directly locates should be abstracted away.

- *Trivial variable:* The identified trivial element is a variable. In this case, all the smallest representation units (statements or ITL formulae) in which the variable directly locates should be abstracted away.

About the Authors

Dr. **Hongji Yang** is a reader at the Software Technology Research Laboratory, School of Computing, De Montfort University, Leicester, United Kingdom. He obtained his B.Sc. and M.Phil. from Jilin University, China, and his Ph.D. from the University of Durham, Durham, United Kingdom.

He started lecturing in the Computer Science Department at Jilin University in 1985, joined the Centre for Software Maintenance at the University of Durham, as an senior research assistant in 1989, and became a lecturer at De Montfort University in 1993.

He has been active in the research areas of distributed computing and software engineering for a number of years. He served as a program cochair for the IEEE International Conference on Software Maintenance (ICSM'99) and as a program cochair for the IEEE Workshop on Future Trend of Distributed Computing Systems (FTDCS'01), and he is serving as the program chair for the IEEE Computer Software and Application Conference (COMPSAC'02).

Dr. Martin Ward's D.Phil. research at Oxford University, Oxford, United Kingdom, involved developing the theoretical foundations for a practical program transformation system. He used the technique of expressing the weakest precondition of an imperative program in infinitary first-order logic in order to prove the correctness of program transformations.

In 1987, he moved to Durham University and worked on several research projects in which the program transformation theory was developed and applied to practical problems in reverse engineering and software maintenance.

In 1995 he joined, Software Migrations, Ltd. as principal consultant to work on the FermaT project, an industrial strength program transformation system targeted at reverse engineering, program comprehension, and migration between programming languages. The system is currently being used to translate IBM 370 assembler and Intel x86 assembler modules into equivalent readable and maintainable C or COBOL programs.

In 1999 Dr. Ward became a visiting senior research fellow with the Software Technology Research Laboratory at De Montfort University.

Index

A

Absorption, 249–50
Abstracting specifications
    assembler reengineering, 213–18
    book index generator, 184–88
    topological sorting algorithm, 198–200
    See also Case studies; Specification(s)
Abstraction rules, 131–32, 261–69
    assignment, 261
    compound, 262–66
    conditional statement, 263
    delay, 262
    duration, 264
    elementary, 261–66
    field reference, 266
    input statement, 262
    iteration statement, 23
    method invocation, 266
    monotonic, 267
    object definition, 265
    object hierarchy, 265–66
    output statement, 262
    parallel, 264
    primitive, 261–62
    procedure definition, 263–64
    procedure invocation, 264
    sequence folding, 267
    sequential composition, 263
    signal, 265
    specification combination, 267–68
    state test and exception handling, 268
    transitive, 266–67
    trivial elements, 268–69
    type definition, 262
Abstraction(s), 124–32
    data (DA), 127, 129, 130
    definitions, 127–29
    healthiness obligation, 129–30
    hiding (HA), 127, 128, 129
    identifying, 125
    level, measuring, 157
    patterns, 125–26
    problem solving for, 124–25
    process, 126
    relations between, 130–31
    structural (SA), 127, 128–29, 130
    subset relations between, 131
    temporal (TA), 127, 128, 130
    weakening (WA), 127, 128, 130
Abstractness metrics, 160–61
    ABST-DF, 161
    ABST-LOC, 161
    ABST-LOOP, 161
    ABST-MCCM, 160
    ABST-STAT, 161
    ABST-VOC, 161
    ABST-WOS, 161
    See also Software metrics
Abstract program, 202–4
Abstract variables, adding, 200–202
Acceptance testing, 237
Action systems, 75–76

defined, 76
regular, 76
Adaptive maintenance, 15
Algebraic approach, 38
    examples, 38
    general, 38
    results, 44
    See also Formal methods
Algebra of communicating processes (ACP), 39
Algorithm derivation, 70
Analysis tools, 95–100
    assembler-to-WSL translator, 95–98
    control flow analysis, 99
    data flow analysis, 99
    migration, 100
    program slicer, 100
    See also FermaT workbench
Applied technologies, 14
Assembler
    code, 88
    IBM 370, 204–7
    legacy systems, 219
    modeling, in WSL, 204–6
    modules, mass migration, 221–23
Assembler reengineering, 204–18
    automatic program transformation, 210–12
    comments, 218
    defined, 175–76
    IBM 370 assembler, 204–7
    metrics before/after transformation, 211
    sample program, 207–8
    source code, 208–9
    specification abstraction, 213–18
    See also Case studies
Assembler-to-WSL translation, 95–98
    assembler reengineering, 206–7
    telecommunications system migration, 228–29
Assertions, 243–44
    introducing, 244
    statement, 243
    transformations for inserting, 245
    weakening, 244
Assignments, 244–46
Atomic/compound names, 140–41
    match examples, 141, 142
    recovery procedure, 141

Attributes
    defined, 156
    external, 156
    internal, 156
    types of, 18
Automatic program
    restructurers, 206
    transformation, 210–12
    understanding, 132
Average module size (AMS), 167
Average parameters per method (APM), 163

B
Belief updating, 143–44
    defined, 144
    example, 144
Black box, 153
B-method, 34
Book index generator, 177–90
    code, 177–78
    conclusion, 190
    defined, 175
    goals, 178
    reimplementation, 188–90
    specification abstraction, 184–88
    specification summary, 188
    WSL transformations, 178–84
    See also Case studies
Branch-loop complexity (BL), 159
Business changes, 2–3

C
Calculus of communicating systems (CCS), 38–39
Case studies, 175–237
    assembler reengineering, 204–18
    book index generator, 177–90
    mass migration exercise, 218–28
    mine drainage system, 229–35
    overview, 175–76
    summary, 235–37
    telecommunications system migration, 228–29
    topological sorting algorithm, 190–204
Change
    business, 2–3
    software, 7

Index

Clustering transformations, 124
COBOL transformation system, 79
Common object-oriented language (COOL), 115–16
   class definition, 225
   class hierarchy, 225
   field reference, 115
   legacy source code translation into, 120
   method invocation, 115
   object declaration, 115–16
   syntax, 115
Common structural language (CSL), 114
   legacy source code translation into, 120
   statements, 114
Communicating sequential processes (CSP), 38
Complete model, 205
Complexity
   measures, 158–60
   property, 7
Complexity metrics, 159–60
   branch-loop complexity (BL), 159
   control-flow and data-flow complexity (CFDF), 159
   function points interface complexity (FPIC), 160
   lines of code (LOC), 159
   McCabe complexity (MCCM), 159
   number of node (NON), 159
   recursion and nesting complexity (RNC), 160
   structural (STRUCT), 159
Component-based development (CBD), 150–51
Components, 104–6
   abstraction, 151
   black box, 153
   defined, 104, 151–53
   elements of, 153–54
   features, 151–52
   functional effects of, 105
   functional mapping of, 106
   interface, 153
   library, 153
   mining, 152–54
   with plugs, 151
   reusing, 149–54
   static, 151
   visibility levels of, 105
   See also Legacy systems
Compound abstraction rules, 262–66
Computer science, 13
Computer systems
   elements, 5
   evolution, 5–8
Concrete semantic network, 135
   for action-action interrelationship, 137
   for action-object interrelationship, 137, 138
   See also Semantic network
Conditionals, 244
   back expansion of, 246
   prune, 244
   reorder, 244
Conformity, 7
Contribution strength (CS), 142–43
Control flow
   analysis, 99
   restructuring, 210
Control-flow and data-flow complexity (CFDF), 159
Corrective maintenance, 15
Cost ratio value in relation to lines of code (CRVL), 164
Cost ratio value in relation to SRR (CRV), 164

D

Data abstraction (DA), 127, 129
   defined, 129
   healthiness obligation, 130
   relations, 129
   See also Abstraction(s)
Data catalog, 95, 96
Data flow analysis, 89, 99, 210
Data translation, 210
Decompilers, 220
Design patterns, 241
Design recovery, 26
Development guidelines, 33
Development paradigms, 240–42
   design patterns, 241
   frameworks, 241–42
   more advanced, 242
   UML, 241
Direct measurements, 156
DKBA tool, 132–49
   architecture, 150
   nonmonotonic reasoning, 133

programming styles, 147–49
program space partitioning, 146–47
quality of conclusions, 134
requirements, 133–34
response time, 134
uncertainty, 133
Documentation level (DL), 167
Domain knowledge-based analysis tool.
    See DKBA tool
Domain knowledge slice
    candidate, 142
    matching degree calculation, 143
Duration calculus, 35
Duration for obtaining each object (TFO), 165

E

Economic metrics, 164–65
    cost ratio value in relation to lines of code
        (CRVL), 164
    cost ratio value in relation to SRR (CRV), 164
    duration for obtaining each object (TFO), 165
    effort assessment based on person-days
        (EPD), 164
    one specification per hour (SPH), 165
    productivity of reverse engineering (REP), 165
    reverse engineering duration (RED), 164
    size reduction rate (SRR), 164
    See also Measures; Software metrics
Effort assessment based on person-days (EPD),
    164
Environment independence level (EIL), 167
Error tolerance level (ETL), 167
Euro project, 100–101
Extended WSL (EWSL), 108–16
    architecture, 108–9
    COOL, 115–16
    CSL, 114
    defined, 108
    general architecture illustration, 108
    ITL, 110–12
    ObTAM, 113–14
    TGCL, 112–13
    translating into, 123
    working flow, 109–10
    working process illustration, 109
    See also WSL
External attributes, 156

F

False loop, 250
FermaT transformation system, 83, 86
    applications, 56
    assembler-to-WSL translator, 95–98
    defined, 83, 86
    projects, 90
    success factors, 227–28
    transformation engine, 95, 98, 206
FermaT workbench, 89–100
    advantages, 90
    analysis tools, 95–100
    data catalog, 95, 96
    defined, 84
    design, 89
    Euro assessment, 100–101
    function call graph, 90, 92
    function catalog, 90, 91
    program flowchart, 91–95
    results, 100–101
    text editor, 91
    tools, 89–90
First-level languages, 71–72
Flexibility, 12, 24
Flowchart, 91–95
    assembler-specific features, 94–95
    computing, 91
    nodes, 93
    partial program, 94
    whole program, 93
    See also FermaT workbench
Formalization, 13
Formal methods, 14, 46, 240
    algebraic approach, 38, 44
    application areas, 240
    application of, 33
    classification of, 33–42
    combined approaches, 45
    components, 32–33
    criteria, 42
    current state of, 31–33
    debate, 31
    defined, 32
    development guidelines, 33
    integrating, 240
    logic-based approach, 34–38, 43
    model-based approach, 33–34, 43
    net-based approach, 40–42, 44

Index   277

process algebra approach, 38–40, 44
results, 43–45
in reverse engineering, 32
semantic model, 32
specification language, 33
structural methods vs., 32
supporting tools, 33
verification system, 33
Forward engineering, 45
  defined, 26
  undertaking, 155
  See also Reverse engineering
Fourth-generation technique (4GT) model, 9, 10
Frameworks, 241–42
Function call graph, 90, 92
Function catalog, 90, 91
Function points interface complexity (FPIC), 160

G

Generic Reverse Engineering Tool (GREET), 85–86
  defined, 85
  parsers, 85
  porting exercise factors, 85–86
Ghost variables, 201, 202

H

Hiding abstraction (HA), 127, 128
  defined, 128
  healthiness obligation, 129
  See also Abstraction(s)
High-level language (HLL) constructs, 220
Hoare logic, 35
Human factors, 14
Human interaction level in relation to lines of code (HIL), 166–67

I

IBM 370 assembler, 204–7
Indirect measurements, 156
Induction rule, 67
Informal reasoning, 133
Internal attributes, 156
Interval temporal logic (ITL), 35
Invariants, 246–47
Invisibility, 7

ITL, 110–12
  choice of, 11
  defined, 110
  LISP database, 123
  specification, 112
  syntax, 111
  See also Extended WSL (EWSL)

J

JOVIAL transformation system, 78, 79

K

Kernel language
  extending, 71–73
  recursion, 61
  specification statement, 59–60
  state transformations, 60–61
  syntax, 57–58
  weakest preconditions, 61–62
Knowledge representation, 134–35

L

Language of temporal ordering specification (LOTOS), 39
Larch, 38
Legacy systems
  assembler, 219
  challenge, 103
  characteristics of, 103–6
  components, 104–6
  defined, 1
  extracting formal specification from, 107–8
  functional mapping of components, 106
  typical problems, 103–4
  visibility levels of components, 105
Lehman's five laws, 15
Logic-based approach, 34–38
  examples, 35–38
  general, 34–35
  results, 43
  See also Formal methods
Loops, 75, 247
  doubling, 250
  elimination, 247
  false, 250
  inversion, 250–51

merging, 247
unbounded, 248–49
unrolling, 247, 251–52

M

Maintainer's assistant (MA), 84–85
Maintenance, 14–19
activities, 19
adaptive, 15
corrective, 15
cost, 16
cost per function point, 219
defined, 15
effort, 219
as essential characteristic, 18
factors affecting, 17
life cycle, 16
metrics, 17
preventative, 15–16
research, 17
task model, 16
Management, 14
Mass migration exercise, 218–28
approach, 220–21
assembler modules, 221–23
assembler problem, 219
contributing factors, 227–28
data initialization code, 226
decompilers, 220
defined, 176
experimental method, 223–24
generated C files, 225
generated C header files, 227
results, 224–27
time to process each module, 225
See also Case studies
Matching degree
calculation algorithm, 143
computation example, 144
McCabe complexity (MCCM), 159, 206
Measurements
defined, 155
direct, 156
indirect, 156
Measures
abstractness, 160–61
categories of, 158–69
complexity, 158–60
defined, 155
economic/cost estimation, 163–65
object-orientedness (OO), 161–63
reusability, 165–69
Metrics. *See* Software metrics
Migration tools, 100
Mine drainage system, 229–35
comments, 235
control, 230
defined, 176, 229
functional specification, 229
illustrated, 230
nonfunctional requirements, 230–31
specification extraction, 231–35
See also Case studies
Modal logic, 36
Model-based approach, 33–34
examples, 34
general, 33
results, 42
See also Formal methods
Modeling, 13
MYCIN, 137, 139

N

Name identification, 139–41
Net-based approach, 40–42
examples, 40–42
general, 40
results, 44
See also Formal methods
Network search algorithm, 145–46
accepted domain concept (ADC), 146
candidate domain concept (CDC), 146
illustrated, 145
Nonmonotonic reasoning, 133, 146
occurrence, 146
in real world, 133
Null-free statements, 73
Number of objects (NOO), 163

O

OBJ, 38
Object-orientedness (OO) metrics, 162–63
average parameters per method (APM), 163

Index 279

coupling between object classes (CBO), 163
depth of inheritance tree (DIT), 162
number of children (NOC), 163
number of objects (NOO), 163
number of variables per class (NVC), 163
response for a class (RFC), 163
weighted methods per class (WMC), 162
Object-oriented TAM (ObTAM), 113–14
    defined, 113
    semantics, 114
    syntax, 114
    See also Extended WSL (EWSL)
Object-oriented techniques, 46
Organization, this book, xvi

P

Partial model, 205–6
Petri net, 40–41
Preventative maintenance, 15–16
Primitive abstraction rules, 261–62
Process algebra approach, 38–40
    examples, 38–40
    general, 38
    results, 44
    See also Formal methods
Process(es)
    abstraction, 126
    defined, 156
    implementing, 119–23
    outline, 119
Productivity of reverse engineering (REP), 165
Products, 156
Programming
    languages, migration between, 76
    styles, 147–49
Program slicer, 100
Program space partitioning, 146–47
Program understanding, 26–27
Projects, 90
Proof rules, 68–69
Proof-theoretic refinement, 64–65
Prune conditional, 244

Q

Quality, 11–12
    assurance, 12
    defined, 11
    factors, 11–12

R

Real-time logic (RTL), 37
Real-time temporal logic (RTTL), 37
Recoding, 27
Recursion
    defined, 61
    implementation of general statements, 69
    induction rule for, 67, 252–53
    removal, 253–57
    removal examples, 257–60
Recursion and nesting complexity (RNC), 160
Redesign, 27
Redocumenting, 26, 236
Reengineering assistant (RA), 119–20
    defined, 119–20
    metric tool in, 168, 169
    reverse engineering part, 122
    as rule-based intelligent system, 120
    software engineers interface, 122
    system structure, 121
Refinement
    characterization of, 62
    correctness, proving, 64–69
    defined, 64
    proof-theoretic, 64–65
    semantic, 64
Refutation strength (RS), 142–43
Reliability, 24
    criteria, 42
    as quality factor, 12
Reorder conditional, 244
Report generator, 207–8
Representation theorem, 66
Requirements analysis, 2
Resources, 156
Respecifying, 27
Restructuring, 45, 123–24
    control flow, 210
    defined, 27
    telecommunications system migration, 229
    topological sorting algorithm, 195–98
    transformations, 123–24, 236
Retargeting, 154–55
Reusability metrics, 166–69

average module size (AMS), 167
documentation level (DL), 167
environment independence level (EIL), 167
error tolerance level (ETL), 167
human interaction level in relation to lines of code (HIL), 166–67
self-descriptiveness (SD), 167
weight of interfaces in relation to lines of code (WOIL), 166
weight of reuse on lines of code (WOR), 169
See also Measures; Software metrics
Reusing components, 14, 149–54
defined, 149
definition and, 151–53
mining and, 152–54
Reverse engineering, 29–31, 45, 153, 154
criteria, 42
defined, 26, 29
duration (RED), 164
environment, establishing, 235–36
formal methods in, 32
general model, 28
issues, 29
objective, 29
practical system, 86
precautions, 30
program design extraction, 30–31
requirements, 86
software metrics for, 156–57
through formal transformations, 236–37
WSL and, 76
See also Reverse engineering; Software reengineering
Reverse specification, 27

S

Search
motivations, 84
targets, 83
Self-descriptiveness (SD), 167
Self-modifying code, 206
Semantic model, 32
Semantic networks, 134–35
concrete, 135, 137, 138
example, 136
nodes, 134
uncertainty reasoning in, 141–42

Shunts, 112
Size reduction rate (SRR), 164
Software
attributes, 18
change, 7
collecting, to be reverse-engineered, 236
complexity, 7
conformity, 7
enhancements, 2
everywhere, 12–14
evolutionary life of, 46
flexibility, 12, 24
invisibility, 7
maintenance, 14–19
production, 6
quality, 11–12
reliability, 12, 24
system properties, 7
visualization, 124
Software engineering, 8–11
defined, 8
definition phase, 10–11
development phase, 11
elements, 8–9
as evolving discipline, 13
generic view, 10
life cycle, 9–10
maintenance phase, 11
Software evolution, 3–4
as bridge too far?, 239–40
case studies, 175–237
measuring, 155–69
process for, 119–69
unified approach to, 106–7
Software metrics, 14, 155–69
abstractness, 160–61
adaptation and development, 157–58
complexity, 159–60
defined, 156
economic, 164–65
facility menu buttons, 168
maintainability, 17
motivation, 157
object-orientedness (OO), 162–63
property classes, 156
reusability, 166–69
for reverse engineering, 156–57
Software reengineering, 3, 14, 23–47

Index

advantages, 24
analysis and summary, 45–47
current state of formal methods, 31–33
cycle, 24–26
cycle illustration, 25
defined, 24, 27
general model, 28
introduction, 23–24
taxonomy, 26–29
See also Reverse engineering
Specification per hour (SPH), 165
Specification(s)
   abstracting, assembler reengineering, 213–18
   abstracting, book index generator, 184–88
   abstracting, topological sorting algorithm, 198–200
   extracting, mine drainage system, 231–35
   implementation of, 68–69
   language, 33
   satisfaction of, 60
   source code vs., 107, 127
   statement, 59–60, 112
   statement expression as, 66
Split function, 74
Statecharts, 41–42
Statement(s)
   equivalence, 65
   expression as specification, 66
   null-free, 73
   recursive implementation of, 69
   semantic refinement of, 64
   specification, 59–60, 112
   weakest preconditions of, 62–64
State transformations, 60–61
   defined, 60
   null-free, 73
   refinement of, 60–61
   See also Transformations
Structural abstraction (SA), 127, 128–29
   defined, 128–29
   healthiness obligation, 130
   See also Abstraction(s)
Structural methods, 32
Support, 13

T

Telecommunications system migration, 228–29
   assembler-to-WSL translation, 228–29
   defined, 176
   WSL restructuring, 229
   WSL-to-C translation, 229
   See also Case studies
Temporal abstraction (TA), 127, 128
   defined, 128
   healthiness obligation, 130
   See also Abstraction(s)
Temporal agent model (TAM), 37
Temporal logic, 36–37
Text editor, 91
Timed CSP (TCSP), 39–40
Timed guarded command language (TGCL), 112–13
   semantics, 112–13
   shunts, 112
   variables, 112
   See also Extended WSL (EWSL)
Timed Petri net, 41
Timed probabilistic calculus of communicating systems (TPCCS), 40
Timed probabilistic computation tree logic (TPCTL), 37–38
Tool support, 14
Topological sorting, 191–93
   defined, 191
   example, 191
   proof, 192–93
   theorem, 192
Topological sorting algorithm, 190–204
   abstract program, 202–4
   adding abstract variables, 200–202
   code, 194–95
   defined, 175
   Knuth's, 193–95
   remarks, 204
   restructuring, 195–98
   specification abstraction, 198–200
   stage analysis, 190–91
   See also Case studies
Transformation engine, 95, 98, 206
Transformations, 55, 157
   action systems, 75–76
   assembler reengineering metrics, 211
   assertions, 243–44
   assignments, 244–46
   automatic program, 210–12
   basic, 66–68

for book index generator, 178–84
clustering, 124
conditionals, 244
control flow, 210, 211
correctness theory, 56–69
data flow, 210, 211
example, 73–76
false loop, 250
induction rule for recursion, 252–53
invariants, 246–47
loop doubling, 250
loop inversion, 250–51
loops, 75, 247
loop unrolling, 251–52
proof, 71
recursion removal, 253–60
restructuring, 123–24, 236
state, 60–61
unbounded loops, 248–50
Turing machine, 77

U

Unbounded loops, 248–49
Uncertainty, 133
    description of evidences, 139
    description of rules, 138–39
    in name identification, 139–41
    processing descriptions, 139–42
    reasoning, 135–46
    in semantic networks, 141–42
Unified modeling language (UML), 241

V

Variables
    abstract, adding, 200–202
    concrete, 201–2
    ghost, 201, 202
Verification system, 33
Vienna development method (VDM), 34

W

Waterfall model, 1–2, 9
Weakening abstraction (WA), 127, 128
    defined, 128
    healthiness obligation, 129

See also Abstraction(s)
Weakest preconditions, 35–38, 61–64
    defined, 61–62
    for Dijkstra guarded command, 63
    importance, 62
    for Morgan's specification statement, 63
    of statements, 62–64
Weighted methods per class (WMC), 162
Weight of interfaces in relation to lines of code (WOIL), 166
Weight of reuse on lines of code (WOR), 169
Wide spectrum language. *See* WSL
WSL, 36, 53–80
    assembler modeling in, 204–6
    assembler translation, 206–7
    background, 55–56
    constructs, 77
    design, 76
    development, 76
    developmental requirements, 5–6
    extended (EWSL), 108–16
    introduction, 53–55
    reason for inventing, 76–80
    restructuring, telecommunications system migration, 229
    reverse engineering and, 76
    stages, 56
    translating source code into, 236
WSL-to-C translation, 229
WSL transformations, 243–60
    assertions, 243–44
    assignments, 244–46
    for book index generator, 178–84
    conditionals, 244
    false loop, 250
    induction rule for recursion, 252–53
    invariants, 246–47
    loop doubling, 250
    loop inversion, 250–51
    loops, 247
    loop unrolling, 251–52
    recursion removal, 253–60
    unbounded loops, 248–50

Z

Z, 34

Recent Titles in the Artech House Computing Library

Advanced ANSI SQL Data Modeling and Structure Processing, Michael M. David

Advanced Database Technology and Design, Mario Piattini and Oscar Díaz, editors

Action Focused Assessment for Software Process Improvement, Tim Kasse

Building Reliable Component-Based Software Systems, Ivica Crnkovic and Magnus Larsson, editors

Business Process Implementation for IT Professionals and Managers, Robert B. Walford

Configuration Management: The Missing Link in Web Engineering, Susan Dart

Data Modeling and Design for Today's Architectures, Angelo Bobak

Developing Secure Distributed Systems with CORBA, Ulrich Lang and Rudolf Schreiner

Future Codes: Essays in Advanced Computer Technology and the Law, Curtis E. A. Karnow

Global Distributed Applications with Windows® DNA, Enrique Madrona

A Guide to Software Configuration Management, Alexis Leon

Guide to Standards and Specifications for Designing Web Software, Stan Magee and Leonard L. Tripp

Implementing Electronic Payment Systems, Cristian Radu

Internet Commerce Development, Craig Standing

Knowledge Management Strategy and Technology, Richard F. Bellaver and John M. Lusa, editors

Managing Computer Networks: A Case-Based Reasoning Approach, Lundy Lewis

Metadata Management for Information Control and Business Success, Guy Tozer

Multimedia Database Management Systems, Guojun Lu

Practical Guide to Software Quality Management, John W. Horch

Practical Process Simulation Using Object-Oriented Techniques and C++, José Garrido

Risk-Based E-Business Testing, Paul Gerrard and Neil Thompson

Secure Messaging with PGP and S/MIME, Rolf Oppliger

Software Fault Tolerance Techniques and Implementation, Laura L. Pullum

Software Verification and Validation for Practitioners and Managers, Second Edition, Steven R. Rakitin

Strategic Software Production with Domain-Oriented Reuse, Paolo Predonzani, Giancarlo Succi, and Tullio Vernazza

Successful Evolution of Software Systems, Hongji Yang and Martin Ward

Systems Modeling for Business Process Improvement, David Bustard, Peter Kawalek, and Mark Norris, editors

User-Centered Information Design for Improved Software Usability, Pradeep Henry

Workflow Modeling: Tools for Process Improvement and Application Development, Alec Sharp and Patrick McDermott

For further information on these and other Artech House titles, including previously considered out-of-print books now available through our In-Print-Forever® (IPF®) program, contact:

Artech House
685 Canton Street
Norwood, MA 02062
Phone: 781-769-9750
Fax: 781-769-6334
e-mail: artech@artechhouse.com

Artech House
46 Gillingham Street
London SW1V 1AH UK
Phone: +44 (0)20 7596-8750
Fax: +44 (0)20 7630-0166
e-mail: artech-uk@artechhouse.com

Find us on the World Wide Web at:
www.artechhouse.com